IN THE
FULLNESS
of TIME

Other books by Paul L. Maier

First Christians
First Christmas
First Easter
The Flames of Rome
A Man Spoke, A World Listened
Pontius Pilate
A Skeleton in God's Closet
The Best of Walter A. Maier (ed.)
Josephus: The Essential Works (ed.)
Josephus: The Essential Writings (ed.)
Josephus: The Jewish War (ed., with G. Cornfeld)

IN THE FULLNESS of TIME

A HISTORIAN LOOKS AT CHRISTMAS, EASTER, AND THE EARLY CHURCH

PAUL L. MAIER

kregel
PUBLICATIONS

Grand Rapids, MI 49501

Library of Congress Cataloging-in-Publication Data
Maier, Paul L.
In the fullness of time: a historian looks at Christmas, Easter, and the early church / Paul L. Maier.
p.   cm.
Includes bibliographical references and index.
1. Jesus Christ—Nativity. 2. Jesus Christ—Biography—Passion Week. 3. Jesus Christ—Crucifixion. 4. Jesus Christ—Resurrection. 5. Pentecost. 6. Church history—Primitive and early church, ca. 30–600. 7. Bible. N.T.—History of Biblical events. 8. Bible. N.T. —History of contemporary events. I. Title.
BT315.2.M315   1997   232.9—dc21   97-49892
                                                  CIP

ISBN 0-8254-3329-0

Printed in the United States of America

1 2 3 4 5 / 01 00 99 98 97

For my brother,
Walter A. Maier, Jr.

Contents

PART III—THE FIRST CHRISTIANS

Pentecost and the Spread of Christianity

Illustrations

COLOR PLATES

(Following page 174)

Astronaut's view of Israel and Jordan
Aerial view of Bethlehem
A silver star, marking the traditional site of the birth of Jesus
Christmas Eve illumination at Bethlehem
The city of Nazareth in Galilee
Excavations at ancient Capernaum
Remains of the synagogue at Capernaum
Hull of a first-century boat
Jerusalem today, from the Mount of Olives
View over the Dome of the Rock
Mosaic map of Jerusalem discovered at Madaba in Jordan
The Jordan River at the Sea of Galilee
Tower of the Citadel in Jerusalem
Gethsemane and the Mount of Olives
Sepulcher at Abu-Gosh
Sheep and goats grazing along the Sea of Galilee
The Sea of Galilee
The Jordan River
Mars' Hill and the Acropolis at Athens
Mars' Hill and the city of Athens
Ruins of the Temple of Apollo at Corinth
The great theater at Ephesus
Facade of the library at Celsus at ancient Ephesus
Roman aqueduct at Caesarea
Ruins of the Roman Forum

Preface

I am grateful that my trilogy—*First Christmas, First Easter,* and *First Christians*—met with so generous a response among both readers and critics, here and abroad. The present volume combines all three books into a new edition, which is thoroughly revised, updated, and expanded.

Information on the life of Jesus and the birth of Christianity is *not* limited to the New Testament. Many important aspects of "the greatest story ever told" come into sharper focus when history, archaeology, geography, and other disciplines shed their light on the Gospel accounts. In offering this evidence, these chapters aim to tell the *un*familiar story of Jesus and Christianity by exploring the nooks and crannies of the past for old but overlooked evidence, new discoveries, and significant sidelights. I hope that these findings will illuminate a story that can never be embellished, but whose details can be fleshed out and clarified by little-known data and fresh insights.

I regret that space restrictions prevented more than cursory discussion of the theology of Jesus, Peter, and Paul, to which, of course, many separate commentaries have been devoted. This book is not intended as a critical analysis of the New Testament sources—we have a profusion of these—but rather as a demonstration of how well the findings of history and archaeology correlate with traditional biblical accounts. The sources used are documented in the Notes at the end of the book. To make these more useful, they are identified both by number and theme.

Western Michigan University   P.L.M.

xiii

Introduction

O F all religious beliefs in the world, past or present, none have more thoroughly based themselves on history than Judaism and Christianity. The divine-human encounter in the biblical faiths always involves claims about *real* people, living in *real* places, who acted in *real* events of the past, many of which are also cited in secular ancient history. Both testaments of the Bible use the past tense of narrative prose—history's medium—more than any other form of language.

Because Judeo-Christianity has so thoroughly influenced Western culture, we are prone to imagine that all other world religions have a similarly solid historical base. This is by no means the case. It can, in fact, be argued that *every* religious system before or since Judaism and Christianity has avoided any significant interaction with history, and instead has asked its followers to believe, by sheer faith alone, the claimed revelations of its founder(s). This is true of the mythologies of yesterday and the cults of today, the religions of the East or the "New Age" of the West.

Or, whenever links with genuine history *are* claimed—as in several modern belief systems today—these are never verified by secular history or the findings of archaeology. Typically, a single founder claims divine revelation, which is subsequently written down as a holy book for his or her following. The founder may well have been historical, of course, but one looks in vain for true correlations with secular history in the founder's holy book. Rather than any private, once-for-all-time revelation, Judeo-Christianity's Scriptures encompass a two-thousand-year-plus period—two millennia in which its holy books *constantly* interlaced themselves with history.

Instead of claiming a mythological founder, or one who materialized from the mists of the past in an appearance datable only to the nearest century or two, Christianity boldly asserts that Jesus' public ministry began (in association with that of John the Baptist) in

> . . . the fifteenth year of the reign of Tiberius Caesar, Pontius Pilate being governor of Judea, and Herod being tetrarch of Galilee, and his brother Philip tetrarch of the region of Ituraea and Trachonitis, and Lysanias tetrarch of Abilene, in the high-priesthood of Annas and Caiaphas . . . (Luke 3:1, RSV)

No mythological heroes or cardboard characters here! This sixfold documentation involves personalities and places, *all* of which are well known *and historical*. In fact, we know even more about this collection of proper names from sources *outside* the New Testament. The author of 2 *Peter* expressed Christianity's "historical advantage" splendidly: "For we did not follow cleverly devised myths . . . but we had been eyewitnesses" (1:16).

So close an intersection with history, however, could have been hazardous for Christianity. Tangencies with known facts of the past could have laid the faith open to ridicule if it had garbled those facts. But rather than seeking the shelter of unprovable traditions to avoid such risk, Christianity instead threaded its origins into the very warp and woof of the past, becoming itself part of history's fabric. For that reason, it has also been held to *much* more stringent standards of critical evaluation than any other world religious system. This, however, was the price it gladly paid for having solid historical credentials.

History, however, is not Christianity's only ally, nor the only avenue into the past. Its closest cousin is *archaeology*—the systematic excavations of sites whose buried artifacts deliver "hard evidence" from the past. Though the very term reflects a crusty patina of age, archaeology is a comparatively young discipline, since scientific archaeology is only a century old. In that hundred years, however, a bulging treasury of thousands of artifacts relating to the biblical world have been discovered, greatly enhancing our understanding of that world. Any interested person today can, if he or she wishes, know more about Jesus and the origins of Christianity than would have been possible for the greatest names in Church history, including Calvin, Luther, Thomas Aquinas, or even Augustine.

One often hears the claim, "Nothing found by archaeologists has *ever* contradicted the Bible." This is simply not true. For example, when the Hebrews fought against their enemies, foreign reports of those campaigns sometimes differed dramatically from those in the Old Testament, which is precisely what we should expect of accounts "managed" by hostile court historians. The surrounding nations never admitted their defeats and converted some, in fact, to "victories."

Nor should anyone imagine that archaeologists go off to Israel or Jordan and dig in order to "prove" something in the Bible. Scientific excavators dig only for the truth, letting the chips fall where they may. What is remarkable about the chips, however, is the vast percentage that fall in a manner highly congenial to the biblical record! Or, where archaeological evidence seems to conflict with Scripture, as in the excavations at Jericho, a new reading of the same evidence corrects previous misreadings.

Other useful tools for prying open the biblical past include such specialties within ancient history as the following:

Linguistics and *Literature:* Hebrew, Aramaic, and Greek studies sharpen our understanding of what the texts of the Old and New Testaments actually say, especially in the context of the other languages and literature of those times.

Geography: From the Old Testament patriarchs to St. Paul, biblical sorts always seem to be moving from one place to the next. Many of these places are definitely identified today and can be explored.

Meteorology and *Climatology:* Are the winds, weather conditions, and famines described in Scripture credible? These specialties provide the answers.

Politics and *Law:* How can one fully understand the trial of Jesus, for example, without invoking Roman law and politics? Or the many occasions in which St. Paul faced a judge?

Economics: The Gospels are full of references to coins, taxes, tax collectors, tribute, money changers, bills, wages, and means of livelihood. Some of the very coin issues cited in Scripture have been discovered and then dated through yet another discipline: numismatics.

Sociology, botany, zoology, medicine, and other fields also have "past tenses" in the ancient world, and thus have value for biblical research. Even astronomy can play a role in helping explain the phenomenon that was the Star of Bethlehem, for example, or the darkness on Good Friday.

In dealing with Jesus and the rise of Christianity, this book will utilize all of these avenues into the past, as well as others. The wealth of information available from ancient history should, then, enrich our quest and help bridge the gap between what is secular and what is religious in biblical antiquity.

Such an approach should yield a fourfold benefit:

1. History and its related fields give us a means by which to "check up" on the Bible, to gauge its accuracy. Those with blind faith may object that this is both faithless and unnecessary, but in view of today's critical challenges to Scripture, we have not only the right but the obligation to compare biblical evidence with secular.

2. From these different perspectives, we can see the biblical events in sharper focus and greater dimension. To use an analogy from photography, the New Testament is like the standard fifty-millimeter lens that comes with most cameras. But how gratifying it is to catch the scene from a different angle and use the telephoto or wide-angle lenses supplied by history and archaeology.

3. Problems in the biblical text can often be solved by recourse to the other ancient disciplines.

4. Gaps in the biblical record can often be filled in by correlating outside evidence from antiquity. Gaps certainly exist between the Old and New Testaments, at the close of the *Book of Acts*, and elsewhere. None of these are any impediment to faith, but because Christian origins lie so conveniently in a historical plane, history can often supply appropriate data for the rest of the story.

Christmas, Lent-Easter, and Pentecost were chosen as the primary frames in this book for several reasons. These are the three greatest Church festivals—great because they celebrate *the* most crucial foundations of Christianity in the Incarnation and Nativity, the Passion and Resurrection, and the explosive birth and growth of the Early Church. The New Testament provides progressively detailed information on each, and so does history: facts, rather than "cleverly devised myths." Christians claim that all three extraordinary episodes occurred on a divinely arranged schedule "in the fullness of time."

The First Christmas

PART I

1

A Caesar's Census

In those days a decree went out from Emperor Augustus
that all the world should be registered. . . . All went to
their own towns to be registered. Joseph also went from
the town of Nazareth in Galilee to Judea, to the city of
David called Bethlehem, because he was descended from
the house and family of David. He went to be registered
with Mary, to whom he was engaged and who was
expecting a child. LUKE 2:1–5

THE first person mentioned in Luke's familiar story of Christmas
was neither Mary, nor Joseph, nor shepherd, nor wise man. In
fact, he would seem to have had nothing at all to do with the story, for he
was the Roman emperor, Caesar Augustus. And yet it was his decision,
fifteen hundred miles away in Rome, which started the train of events
that finally led to the birth of Jesus in Bethlehem. (Luke, more than any
other New Testament author, is very careful to anchor biblical events into
the secular history of his day.)

Under normal circumstances, Jesus would have been born in Nazareth, the home of Joseph and Mary. But, as Luke explains, Augustus had
decreed a registration, or census, of his vast empire, and all subjects of
Rome had to return for enrollment at their ancestral hometowns. Since
both Joseph and Mary were distant descendants of the much-married
King David, they prepared to travel down to David's city, the sleepy little
town of Bethlehem in the sere and arid Judean hills, six miles southwest
of Jerusalem.

Was This Trip Necessary?

That Mary ever had to endure the rigors of this eighty-mile journey on the back of a jogging donkey while in a state of very advanced pregnancy has been doubted by some scholars. Rome never required her subjects to return to their original homes for such enrollments, they claim, and Luke must have garbled his facts. But this view has been disproved by the discovery of a Roman census edict from 104 A.D. in neighboring Egypt, in which taxpayers who were living elsewhere were ordered to return to their original homes for registration.[1]

The Romans required such censuses every fourteen years. The accompanying photograph of a papyrus fragment from the village of Bacchias in Egypt is a census declaration made in 119 A.D. It reads, in part, as follows:

> To Ptolemaios, village secretary . . .
> From Horos, the son of Horos, the son of Horos, his mother being Herieus, of the aforesaid village of Bacchias . . . .
> I register myself and those of my household for the house-by-house census of the past second year of Hadrian Caesar our Lord.
> I am Horos, the aforesaid, a cultivator of state land, 48 years old, with a scar on my left eyebrow, and (I register):
> my wife Tapekusis, daughter of Horos, 45 years old, and our own child, Horos, a son, . . . years old, with no identification marks, and
> Horion, another son, one year old, with no identification marks. . . .

After naming other relatives sharing their living quarters, the document is signed by the village registrar and three official witnesses.[2]

An obscure Galilean couple had to obey a distant Caesar because sixty years earlier the Roman general Pompey had conquered Palestine, and the land had orbited perforce into the Roman universe. Currently, it was under Rome's control as a "client kingdom" ruled by a local king, Herod the Great, who was directly responsible to the Roman emperor.

Augustus himself, the grandnephew and adopted heir of Julius Caesar, was Rome's first emperor. His fascinating career began in the bloody civil wars of the late Roman republic, continued beyond a victorious showdown with his archrival Mark Antony, and culminated in a lengthy era of peace and prosperity, well named the *Pax Augusta*, for Augustus created and preserved the happy concord throughout the forty-four years of his rule.

Less familiar than the vaunted glories of Augustus' reign—the conquered lands and kings, or the Rome he transformed from brick into

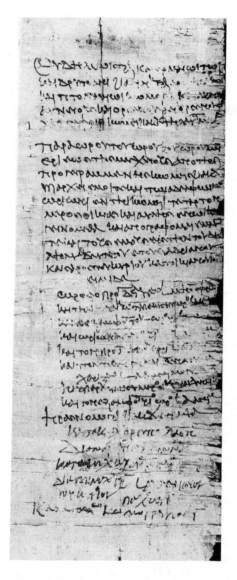

A census declaration from Bacchias, Egypt, dated 119 A.D. The Greek is written in ink on papyrus. The short line at the center of the document reads "I am," followed by "Horos," etc., on the next line.

marble—is the man's intriguing religious policy. Had he not been emperor, Caesar Augustus might well have gone down in history as a religious reformer, for he tried to revive the drooping interest in Rome's state religion. By his day, the average Roman had abandoned any belief in the gods of Greco-Roman mythology, and philosophical skepticism was growing, while the more credulous joined the foreign mystery cults that had invaded the Empire. Augustus, however, felt that this neglect of the gods was demoralizing Roman society and that only a full restoration of the old republican piety would preserve its greatness.

So he set about his religious revival with enthusiasm. He fairly rained temples and shrines down on the Empire, restoring eighty-two temples in the city of Rome alone. He became *pontifex maximus* ("highest priest") in the state cult, and tried to spark a moral renewal in society.

Too Many Bachelors

Many Roman men and women of the time were indulging in a very easy morality to escape what they called "the tedium of marriage," and soon marital and birth rates had dwindled alarmingly. One day, Augustus was disturbed enough to stalk into the Forum and devise a crude test of the situation: he told a crowd of men gathered there to separate into two groups, the bachelors on one side, the married men on the other. The handful of husbands was so much smaller that he launched into an anguished harangue against the bachelors, which began, classically,

> What shall I call you? *Men?* But you aren't fulfilling the duties of men. *Citizens?* But for all your efforts, the city is perishing. *Romans?* But you are in the process of blotting out this name altogether! . . . What humanity would be left if all the rest of mankind should do what you are doing? . . . *You are committing murder* in not fathering in the first place those who ought to be your descendants![3]

. . . and on to other such gems of imperial logic.

Augustus followed this bluster with legislation designed to reverse the tide by making promiscuity a crime, while conferring political advantages on a father of three children. Bachelors who shirked "the duty of marriage" were penalized in their right to inherit, and they could not even secure good seats at the games! The bachelors, of course, tried to circumvent such penalties by "marrying" infant girls, but Augustus quickly

This bronze head of Augustus, portraying him at the age of thirty, was discovered near the Nile River at Merowe in the Sudan.

countered by setting the minimum age for engagement at ten for girls, with a two-year upper limit for length of courtship.

Perhaps it was to gauge his success in raising the marriage and birth rates that Augustus was so concerned about the imperial census, and he took several, as in the Christmas story, during his lengthy reign. Such enrollments, of course, were also the basis for the Roman system of taxation. Later census returns showed a considerable increase in population, though this may have been due as much to the return of peace and prosperity after all the bloodshed of Rome's civil wars as to Augustus' legislation. But the emperor was pleased enough with the results that he proudly mentioned his censuses in eighth place among the thirty-five "Acts of Augustus" for which he wished to be remembered, items that were later engraved on two bronze plaques outside his mausoleum.

Unfortunately, he reported figures only for that privileged group in the Empire known as male Roman citizens:

The census of 28 B.C. showed 4,063,000 Roman citizens
    "   "   " 8 B.C.   "   4,233,000   "   "
    "   "   " 14 A.D.   "   4,937,000   "   "

At this time, however, the entire Roman Empire—like Luke, the Romans also hyperbolized it as "the whole world"—would have numbered almost 55,000,000 people.

The census mentioned in the Christmas story was a provincial enrollment possibly associated with the citizens' census of 8 B.C., but apparently the machinery necessary to take it in far-off Palestine was not prepared until about 5 B.C., since 8 B.C. is some three years too early for the birth of Christ. (For reasons that will be explained in a later chapter, we know that Jesus was *not* born in 1 A.D.)

An Unknown Subject

One might wonder how Augustus would have reacted to this Judean census in which—had he chosen to examine the returns from Bethlehem—the following group of three names would have been included:

Joseph Ben-Iacob, carpenter
Mary Bath-Ioachim, his wife
Yeshua [Jesus], first-born son[4]

When Jesus was born, the entire Mediterranean world was governed from Rome. The ruins of her ancient Forum still stand.

Did Augustus ever even see the names? The chances are virtually nil. Certainly he never learned the significance of what had happened in Bethlehem because of his decision to take the census.

At the time of Augustus' death in 14 A.D., Jesus was about nineteen years old, an apprentice carpenter in Nazareth, and the emperor still could not possibly have heard of him. He would have been astounded to know that later ages would assign his own death to the year 14 A.D. ("in the year of the Lord") rather than the Roman date, 767 A.U.C. (*ab urbe condita*, "from the founding of the city"), all because of that unknown subject, born in Bethlehem. And he would have been amazed that future generations would wish one another a "Merry Christmas" rather than "*Io Saturnalia!*"— that great end-of-the-year festival in Rome that featured pagan delights and many of the holiday trappings of our secular yuletide, including holly, mistletoe, and evergreens, the exchange of gifts, and much feasting and drinking.

But the successors of the emperor and of the baby would discover one another soon enough.

2

Palestine the Paradox

Now the Lord said to Abram, "Go from your country . . .
to the land that I will show you. I will make of you a great
nation. . . . To your offspring I will give this land."

GENESIS 12:1, 2, 7

PALESTINE is a land rippling with irony. It gave birth to two great religions and nurtured a third, yet it may be the most bitterly contested spot on earth. Jews, Christians, and Muslims all call it the Holy Land, but probably more blood has been spilled there per acre than anywhere else in the world. The ancient Hebrews claimed it as their Promised Land because of the divine pledge to Abraham, and yet they had to fight the Philistines to win it. And then they saw it crushed by invading Assyrians and Babylonians, mauled by Egyptians, torn by Syrians, and finally conquered by Romans.

But this is merely the record up to the time of the first Christmas, when the baby called "The Prince of Peace" was born. After that, the land was assaulted by the Persians, Arabs, Crusaders, Mamelukes, Turks, and British, while today it smolders with Arab-Israeli hostilities.

Why this sickening saga of bloodshed? One prime reason is because the three major faiths of Western civilization regard Palestine as their own religious cradle, and each, at one time or another, has taken up arms against the other two "strangers in the nursery." To Jews it is the land of the sacred Torah; to Christians, that of the Old and New Testaments; and to Muslims it is Abraham's country—they also claim him as patriarch through his son Ishmael—while Jerusalem marks the spot, so they teach,

11

The Dead Sea, looking eastward over the fortress-rock of
Masada. Originally a stronghold of Herod the Great, Masada
was the citadel where Jewish rebels put themselves to death
rather than submit to the might of Rome in 73 A.D.

where Mohammed's steed last touched earth before ascending into heaven
with the prophet on his back.[1]

But blame for the bloodshed must also be deposited squarely at the
doors of geography and politics. Palestine has the glory of being located
at the juncture of two continents—Africa and Asia—and so served as the
crossroads of antiquity. But this strategic location also proved a heavy
burden. The armies of the ancient world, even if they had no quarrel with
the people of Palestine, regularly used the land as a causeway en route
to attacking one another, ravaging Palestine in the process. The inhabitants
had as much safety as would a flock of sparrows that chose to build their
nests on a superhighway.

Overrun, despoiled, devastated, and small (roughly the size and
shape of a Vermont twisted upside down), Palestine still exerted probably

the most powerful influence on subsequent civilization, per capita, of any land in history. Its Hebrew inhabitants gave the world monotheism and a system of ethics that has not been superseded—Which law on any of the nations' lawbooks is not a corollary of one of the Ten Commandments?—and its Christians seeded a faith that is believed by 1.75 billion people today. As has well been said, Western civilization is like a family whose mother was Hebrew, whose father was Greek, and that moved away to live in Rome.

A Geographic Marvel

Even if it had no religious significance, Palestine would be an intriguing land. In fact, it is an earth scientist's paradise, boasting a Sea of Galilee that is almost 700 feet *below* sea level and a wriggling stream called the Jordan that channels Galilee's fresh water and empties it into an oblong, finger-shaped basin of brackish fluid known as the Dead Sea. Jordan means *descender*, an appropriate name for its own 600-foot drop, and yet it is hardly a straight gorge, for it twists and loops some 200 miles to make the 65-mile trip from Galilee to the Dead Sea as the crow flies.

The Dead Sea is 1,286 feet below sea level, and if some mad engineer were to cut a canal up to the Mediterranean, the whole Jordan valley would soon be overwhelmed with a quivering mass of water a quarter-mile high. The Dead Sea basin is quite literally the lowest place in the world, six times as far below sea level as Death Valley in California. (The lowest spot on the earth's crust is the sea bottom within the Marianas trench in the Pacific Ocean, where soundings have reached an ocean depth of more than 36,000 feet.) At least 25 percent salt and other minerals—compared with 5 percent for the ocean—the Dead Sea is so dense that a swimmer can barely submerge in it and is flipped to the surface like a cork. Fish leaving the Jordan delta waters die within minutes after swimming into the Dead Sea, and the evaporation rate is so fierce that it equals the incoming flow of the Jordan.

Even the underground regions here rumble with a separate fascination of their own. Underlying the whole depression are subterranean gases and volcanic activity that bubble up hot springs and asphalt, and periodically cause earthquakes. These phenomena may well have been responsible for the fall of those famed sin capitals in Old Testament times, Sodom and Gomorrah.[2]

More than anything else, Palestine resembles an accordion-fold of land, with four diverse bands running north and south. Bordering the Mediterranean to the west is a flat and fertile coastal plain; next to it rises a central hilly plateau on which Jerusalem and Bethlehem are located; beyond that plunges the Great Rift valley of the Jordan and the Dead Sea; and finally, the tablelands of the Transjordan rise abruptly to the east.

But political lines directly crisscrossed this geography at the time of the birth of Christ, dividing the land into three bands running east and west: rolling, verdant Galilee to the north, the picturesque home of Joseph and Mary; Samaria in the center, the bleached land of those despised half-breed cousins of the Jews called the Samaritans; and Judea to the south, the more barren and hilly religious and political center of the land. Because of their trip down to Bethlehem, the subsequent flight to Egypt, and their eventual return to Nazareth, the Holy Family would traverse the greater part of Palestine before the Christmas story reached its conclusion.

A White Christmas?

What kind of weather they would have encountered has evoked the widest range of guesses. Old sixteenth-century European woodcuts show Joseph and Mary all bundled up, braving the blizzards of a north German winter on the way to Bethlehem. But even aside from the humorous thought of a snowstorm in a subtropical climate, it is by no means certain that the Nativity even took place in the winter months.

But, assuming for the moment that it did, *could* the first Christmas have been a white one? This is highly improbable, certainly, but by no means impossible, as many insist. Snow does fall in the Jerusalem area about three or four days each winter, and sometimes in considerable quantity: in January 1950, twenty inches fell; in February 1920, twenty-nine inches. The meteorology, then, would allow a very remote possibility of snow at Bethlehem on that day that would shift history.

Palestine lies between 31° and 33° north latitude, in the same parallel as Georgia, Arizona, Nagasaki, and Shanghai. But since it is adjacent to that great climatic storage battery called the Mediterranean Sea, its weather is moderate and two-seasonal: a cool but not uncomfortable winter, when

The River Jordan, near the place where Jesus was baptized.

some rain falls; and a summer in which the sun often shines 98 percent of the daytime.

However, because of the wide variety in the forms and altitude of its tortured terrain—ranging from 9,230-foot Mt. Hermon in the north to the subthalassic Dead Sea depression, from fertile vales to blazing deserts— local climates in Palestine can vary from subarctic to torrid. Some have even suggested that one reason the Bible is intelligible nearly everywhere in the world is that Palestine offers a bit of almost all the geographic and climatic conditions on earth. At least there is reason enough for the pictorial variety offered on Christmas cards displaying backgrounds from the Holy Land that seem to clash.

3

A Galilean Couple

Now the birth of Jesus the Messiah took place in this way.
When his mother Mary had been engaged to Joseph,
but before they lived together, she was found to be
with child from the Holy Spirit.   MATTHEW 1:18

NAZARETH is usually the forgotten town in the Christmas story, but this is where it all began. The Galilean village was indeed a very forgettable place in ancient times. Astonishingly, there is no mention of Nazareth in the Old Testament or the Talmud, and later on one of Jesus' future disciples would sneer, "Can anything good come out of Nazareth?" (John 1:46).

"Indeed!" the world has since replied, not only because of the awesome figure of Jesus but also because of the very beautiful story of his origin. Nestled in one of the hills of lower Galilee overlooking the triangular Plain of Esdraelon, Nazareth was an insignificant village far smaller than the present bustling city of 30,000. Its secluded inhabitants had to travel northward over four miles of back roads to get to Sepphoris in order to purchase the many items not available in Nazareth.

This is where Joseph would buy whatever carpenter's tools and supplies he had not inherited from his father. The Gospels tell us very little about Joseph, but if he resembled the pious, hard-working class of his Jewish colleagues in Galilee, he would not think of marriage until he was at least twenty-five years old. In contrast, it was customary for girls to marry shortly after puberty, and how this young craftsman became engaged to a fifteen- or sixteen-year-old girl named Mary is not recorded. Certainly they must sometime have met at one of the harvest festivals, if

not at the village well in Nazareth—it was the sole source of water supply—
and in a hamlet the size of Nazareth, everyone knew everyone else.

Romance and courtship did not play a large role in ancient times,
and most marriages were arranged between the parents of the couple.
However, bride and groom were not simply thrown at each other in a
loveless match. Directly or indirectly, their comments and conduct often
alerted parents as to which family to contact, and love was indeed a factor
in many of the alliances.

The Engagement

What most probably happened was this. One day, Joseph asked his
parents if he could marry that village girl who was his distant relative,
Mary. They discussed it among themselves before giving him an answer,
carefully appraising Mary's parentage, ancestry, and resources. The last,
of course, was not a prime consideration, since everyone in Nazareth was
poor. And they could hardly fault Mary's background, for it was the same
as their own: although humble, both families were distant descendants
of the royal family of Israel, and they could proudly trace their family
tree back to King David and one of his many wives. They easily approved
Joseph's choice, probably with enthusiasm.

Then Joseph's father paid a call on Mary's parents, who would act
duly surprised as the purpose of the visit grew plain. But Mary's random
comments about the young carpenter Joseph had all but shouted her
interest, and so the discussion began in earnest, the two fathers doing
most of the negotiating. In biblical times, marriage was considered a
covenant between two families, not just the bridal pair, so there were
many matters to discuss besides dowry, which would have been small in
any case.

Finally, the fathers agreed to a marriage contract between their children. Joseph was then brought before Mary, and their parents uttered a
formal benediction over them as they tasted a cup of wine together. This,
the legal betrothal, was far more binding than the modern engagement.
Only divorce could break it, and even though they were not yet married,
had either Joseph or Mary been unfaithful to each other, it would have
been deemed an adultery punishable by death.[1] Had Joseph died in the
meantime, Mary would have been his legal widow.

17

The Church of the Annunciation in Nazareth, built over the presumed site where Mary was confronted by the angel.

Since betrothal was nearly tantamount to marriage, could the couple enjoy lawful sexual relations? There is some evidence that engaged Judean couples could and did exercise this privilege, even though both still lived at home with their parents. In the more conservative Galilean countryside, however, virginity was maintained until the wedding itself, which laid great stress on prior purity. In the case of Joseph and Mary, the New Testament is explicit in stating that Joseph did not know Mary sexually until after the birth of Jesus (Matt. 1:24f.).

The Annunciation

One day, during the months between her engagement and marriage, Mary's wedding preparations were momentously interrupted. Luke tells the familiar story of the angel Gabriel appearing to Mary with the words, "Greetings, favored one! The Lord is with you. . . . And now, you will conceive in your womb and bear a son, and you will name him Jesus. He will be great, and will be called the Son of the Most High . . . and of his kingdom there will be no end."

One reason many moderns doubt the story, quite apart from the angel, is that any such apparition should have frightened the poor girl out of her wits. And yet Mary was brought up immediately after Old Testament times, in which angelic visits were commonplace, her elders reported. So her immediate reaction was quite logical indeed: "How can this be, since I am a virgin?"

"The Holy Spirit will come upon you," Luke records the angel's reply, "and the power of the Most High will overshadow you; therefore the child to be born will be holy; he will be called Son of God."

Mary agreed in simple trust. "Here am I, the servant of the Lord; let it be with me according to your word" (Luke 1:26ff.).

Under the assumption that it must have taken even a divine-human baby the normal term to develop, Christendom appointed March 25 (exactly nine months before December 25) as the Feast of the Annunciation, when Jesus was also conceived. The emphasis, however, is not on any calendar precision—the exact date of the Nativity is unknown—but on the commemoration itself.

For Mary, the news that she would bear the long-awaited Messiah who had been promised her people was both joyful and staggering. It filled her with a sense of wonder to which she finally gave expression in the *Magnificat,* spoken at the home of her cousin Elizabeth, mother of John the Baptist, whom she visited shortly after the Annunciation. Her exultant words began, "My soul magnifies the Lord, and my spirit rejoices in God my Savior. . . ." and they would become part of the Christian liturgy (Luke 1:46ff.).

But Mary's pregnancy was cruel and shocking news to Joseph, for he knew that he was not the father. Probably he could not really believe Mary's story of the angelic visit, so he had to agonize over a decision based on three options: (1) marry the girl quickly, and hope the tongues in Nazareth would someday stop wagging over a six-month baby; (2) publicly divorce Mary as an adulteress, in which case she would be stoned to death; or (3) have the marriage contract set aside quietly, while Mary went off to have her baby elsewhere.

Being a good and pious sort, Joseph would not marry an adulteress, but he loved Mary too much to wish her public shame and death. So he quickly decided on the third alternative. But then, as Matthew recorded it, there was another angelic interposition in the Nativity story:

> . . . An angel of the Lord appeared to him in a dream and said, "Joseph, son of David, do not be afraid to take Mary as your wife, for the child conceived in her is from the Holy Spirit. She will bear a son, and you are to name him Jesus, for he will save his people from their sins." (Matt. 1:20)

How easily Mary's story jibed after such an experience! Now sharing his betrothed's incredible secret, Joseph could bury his suspicions and anxieties and marry his beloved as soon as possible.

The Marriage

Probably no more than a week or two afterward, the wedding was celebrated in Nazareth. From various clues scattered across Scripture, it seems that biblical nuptials were more similar to modern weddings than different from them. The two bridal parties marched in procession, accompanied by music, to the place where they would be married, the bride and groom wearing garlands and jewelry, and the bride a veil too. There were attendants on both sides, and a wedding feast followed, which could be quite elaborate. Samson's nuptial banquet lasted for seven days (Judg. 14:12), but such affairs in Nazareth were always on a smaller scale.[2]

For the next five months, Mary lived happily at Joseph's house, her pregnancy now obvious. One day came news of the Roman emperor's edict requiring all of his subjects to enroll themselves for the census at their ancestral homes. However much they must have dreaded the prospect of a four- or five-day trip down to Bethlehem when Mary was in advanced pregnancy, Joseph and Mary quickly realized that Augustus' decree very nicely solved two formidable problems for them. They could never go to Bethlehem and return again before Jesus' birth, so he would now have to be born in Judea, and any prying neighbors in Nazareth need never know that theirs was apparently a six-month baby. At this stage, it would have been useless to try to explain to them the wonderful kind of child this really was.

The other difficulty concerned the familiar prophecy that the Messiah was to be born in Bethlehem. In fact, it was the only cloud smudging Mary's happiness, for if she were intended to bear the Christ, why had God chosen a girl living in Nazareth rather than in Bethlehem? The news from Rome easily placed the last piece of the divine-human puzzle into place. Even though Joseph alone could probably have attended to the census obligations in Bethlehem, Mary had every reason to make the trip also.

Commending their few valuables to his father's keeping, Joseph and Mary gathered their necessities and set out for Bethlehem. The picture of Joseph tenderly guiding the donkey on which Mary was sitting—a little apprehensive lest the birth pangs come too early—is so enshrined in imagination, art, and literature that it needs no further comment.

What route they chose for the trip south is not so graphic or definite. It could well have been the central route via the valleys winding through the hills of Samaria, which was the shortest. However, if the pious Joseph wanted to avoid any contact with the Samaritans or wished to keep Mary warm during a chill time of the year, he could have chosen an alternate route southeast across the Plain of Esdraelon, down the Jordan River valley as far as Jericho, and then up to Jerusalem and Bethlehem.

22

In either case, Mary would suffer discomforts on this eighty- or ninety-mile journey—the legends that she was miraculously spared them are all apocryphal—but she would soon forget the pain in joy at the extraordinary thing about to happen to her. The birth of any child is a marvel of its own, but that of a divine child, as she believed hers to be, was an incalculable wonder.

4

An Undatable Date

But when the fullness of time had come, God sent his Son,
born of woman, born under the law, in order to redeem
those who were under the law, so that we might receive
adoption as children. GALATIANS 4:4–5

P AUL'S famous comment that the Nativity happened "in the
fullness of time" is usually interpreted to mean that God had a
good sense of timing, since conditions prevailing in the Mediterranean
world could not have been more favorable for the spread of Christianity.
The Old Testament had predicted the birth of a Messiah for centuries, and
the Greeks had given their world a universal language through which
Jesus' message could spread easily and quickly. The Roman Empire had
organized the whole Mediterranean basin into one vast communications
network, almost perfectly geared to foster the spread of Christianity, since
its missionaries could travel from city to city without fear of piracy at sea
or brigands by land. Rome had also spread the welcome blanket of peace
across the world, the *Pax Romana*, a time in which the new faith could
thrive.

And so the first Christmas happened "in the fullness of time" indeed.
But precisely *when* was that time? Unfortunately, there is no exact answer.
Ironically, the event that has divided our reckoning of time into years B.C.
and A.D. is itself almost undatable. "Everyone knows" Jesus must have
been born on December 25, A.D. 1, but it is not quite that simple, and
certainly this date is wrong. For Herod the Great died in the spring of
4 B.C., and the king was very much alive during the visit of the Magi in

24

the Christmas story.* Therefore, Jesus would have to have been born before this time, and his birth is usually set during the winter of 5–4 B.C. ("Before Christ," or, incredibly, "Before Himself").[1]

Why, then, is our calendar four or five years off? Why is the present decade not 1990–2000 but, literally, 1995–2005 A.D. (*anno Domini*, "in the year of the Lord")?

It was a sixth-century Roman monk-mathematician-astronomer named Dionysius Exiguus (Dionysius the Little) who unknowingly committed what became history's greatest numerical error in terms of cumulative effect. For in reforming the calendar to pivot about the birth of Christ, he dated the Nativity in the year 753 from the founding of Rome, when in fact Herod had died only 749 years after Rome's founding. The result of Dionysius' chronology, which remains current, was to give the correct traditional date for the founding of Rome, but one that is at least four or five years off for the birth of Christ.

While Jesus may have been born as early as 7 B.C., such earlier datings for the Nativity would make him a little too old for the "about thirty years" of age when he began his public ministry in 28–29 A.D. (Luke 3:23). Unfortunately, it is not possible to work back to any exact date for Jesus' birth from any later information about his adult life.[2]

The Season?

But surely the Christmas story provides other chronological clues. Luke tried to date the event with some precision in his famous prologue about Augustus' decree "that all the world should be registered. This was the first registration and was taken while Quirinius was governor of Syria" (2:1–2). The solution, then, is merely to find the date for Augustus' imperial census, as well as the dates for the Syrian governor Quirinius' term in office.

And how scholars have tried to do just that—and with what little success! The imperial citizens' census of 8 B.C., discussed in the first

---

*The English scholar W. E. Filmer has suggested that Herod may have died as late as 1 B.C., but this alternate chronology has not been generally accepted, since it is too difficult to reconcile with the regnal dates of Herod's sons and successors. It seems that Herod did indeed die in 4 B.C.—For further detail on the chronology of Christmas, see the admirable study by Professor Jack Finegan, *Handbook of Biblical Chronology* (Princeton, 1964), 215ff.

The city of Jerusalem, looking eastward over the Dome of
the Rock toward the Mount of Olives. The Dome marks the
presumed spot where Abraham bound Isaac for sacrifice, where
the Temple of Solomon was built, and where Mohammed
supposedly ascended into heaven.

chapter, reached Palestine as a broadened provincial census anytime between that year and perhaps 6 or 5 B.C., as indicated, a range too broad for much help in pinpointing the time of the first Christmas.

But the governor of Syria, Publius Sulpicius Quirinius, is known from Roman records. He had been a consul, with military and business successes to his credit, though a chronic avarice stained his memory. But when was he governor of Syria? Not until 6–7 A.D., according to ancient records, which is eleven years too late for the Nativity census, and Luke has been faulted for inaccuracy here. Elsewhere, however, Luke is extremely careful in naming Greek and Roman officials, and since a similar provincial census in Gaul required forty *years* to complete, Luke may have been referring to a preliminary enrollment in Herod's Judea, during which census data was collected and then used later for the actual assessment of taxes under Quirinius in 6 A.D. Some scholars therefore suggest an alternate reading of Luke's text: "This census was first really carried out when Quirinius was governor of Syria," i.e., a decade later. The Greek syntax here can also be translated: "This enrollment was *before* that made when Quirinius was governor of Syria." In any case, Quirinius helps very little in any dating of the Nativity.[3]

What about the great Star of Bethlehem, which attracted the Wise Men? Astral events are indeed prime props in any chronology, but astronomers have never agreed on exactly what the star may have been, so it is difficult to date it. (Nevertheless, the Star of Bethlehem is so fascinating a phenomenon in its own right that it will be discussed in a later chapter.)

Adding up all the clues, hints, and shreds of evidence from every available source, many scholars set the date for the Nativity sometime in the fall of 5 B.C. Others maintain it must have happened in spring, because the shepherds were out in the fields, "keeping watch over their flock by night" at the angelic announcement (Luke 2:8), which would suggest lambing time. Only then, presumably, did shepherds bother to guard their flocks at night. In the winter, sheep would have been in the corral.

This clue seems impressive enough, but it is by no means conclusive. In many of the rural districts of Palestine, the flocks were not fed in pens but had to forage for their food in both summer and winter. During the great winter snowfall of 1910–11 in Syria, hundreds of thousands of sheep died because snow covered the ground for weeks, interrupting their feeding. And a passage in the Jewish *Mishnah* states that some sheep pastured near Bethlehem were destined for sacrifice at the Temple in

Jerusalem, and suggests that these flocks lay out in the fields all year around.[4]

Since shepherding seems to be one of the least changed occupations in Palestine over the last two thousand years, it may be instructive to gauge the present practice. The famed Chautauqua and Lyceum lecturer, Stephen A. Haboush, the former "Shepherd Boy of Galilee," writes:

> As a boy, I kept our flock through the fall of the year and up to the first of January out among the low hills and valleys around the Sea of Galilee. But during the rainy season in January and February, I would keep the sheep in the fold back of our home in Tiberias. In Judea, however, where there is only half as much annual rainfall, the shepherds keep their flocks grazing out in the valleys for most of the months of the winter season, as I know from members of my tribe.

And Christmastime visitors to Bethlehem today tell of seeing shepherds out in the fields with their sheep, their heads muffled against the chilly weather in colorful *keffiyehs*.

The Day?

Why is Christmas celebrated on December 25? The early Christian Church seems to have observed the birth of Christ on January 6 in the East, and on December 25 in the West, but both practices began too late—the 300s A.D.—to warrant attaching any precision to these dates.

Probably it was a matter of substitution. The Romans of the time not only celebrated their Saturnalia festival at the close of December, but they also thought that December 25 marked the date of the winter solstice (instead of December 21), when they observed the pagan feast of *Sol Invictus*, the Unconquerable Sun, which was just in the act of turning about to aim northward once again. Christianity sought to replace these pagan festivals with a Christian celebration honoring the "sun of righteousness," a common epithet for Jesus as Messiah. Yet Christmas, even with its Christian name, has never been able to shake off the secular root of this end-of-the-year festival. But all this should not obscure the fact that, according to the best reckoning, Jesus may indeed have been born in the fall or winter of 5 B.C.

One could wish that an event of this importance were more precisely datable. Yet the ancients, especially in the Near East, had a less exacting

The modern city of Bethlehem.

view of time than did later ages with their accurate clocks and calendars. At a period when there was no universal system of chronology, and events were dated "in the reign of King [Such and Such]" or "in the governorship of [So and So]," when numbers were often rounded off, and even the methods of counting years differed, perhaps it is fortunate to come within months of the actual date of the first Christmas. But the final paradox, certainly, is that something as imprecisely datable as the birth of Christ later served as the technical anchor date for the calendar used almost everywhere in the world today, which we find quite precise indeed.

Time, however, had a wholly different meaning for the pair just finishing that uncomfortable journey down to Bethlehem. The question nagging at Joseph and Mary as they threaded their way through that florid symphony of noise and color that was Jerusalem was this: Would they reach Bethlehem in time for the event that now seemed imminent?

5

A Bethlehem Grotto

While they were there, the time came for her to deliver
her child. And she gave birth to her firstborn son and
wrapped him in bands of cloth, and laid him in a manger,
because there was no place for them in the inn.   LUKE 2:6–7

SOME critics doubt that Jesus was born in Bethlehem and argue instead for Nazareth or elsewhere. Such opinions, however, are based only on scholarly conjecture, and no source has been discovered to date that disproves Jesus' birth in Bethlehem.[1]

It is almost certain that Joseph and Mary reached Bethlehem in the late afternoon or early evening. Had they arrived earlier, lodging would not have been so difficult to find, although Bethlehem would have been crowded enough with the many descendants of King David returning to register at their ancestral home.

The picture of Joseph going from door to door, desperately begging shelter because Mary was in labor, has always struck a poignant chord amid the joy wreathing the rest of the Christmas story. And the nameless innkeeper who refused them refuge is usually associated with Judas Iscariot in the popular mind. But probably he—or was it his sympathetic wife?—remembered the cave behind the inn, where animals were sheltered, and he threw it open to the hapless couple. The hills around Bethlehem are perforated with such caverns, and they are still used to shelter cattle and sheep. Grateful for any refuge in the crisis of his wife's birth pangs, Joseph carefully led the donkey and its precious burden down a steep path behind the caravansary to the cave below it.

From all accounts of the Nativity, it seems that no one assisted Mary at the birth of Jesus—not even Joseph, for husbands were not to play the role of midwives. Self-delivery was by no means uncommon at the time. The women of Palestine, unlike neighboring mothers, prided themselves on delivering their babies rather easily and were quite able to take care of themselves in the absence of a midwife, though physicians and midwives were also regularly used. Luke simply relates that Mary gave birth to her firstborn son, wrapped him in bands of swaddling cloth, and laid him in a feeding trough, which must have had the sweetish, grainy smell of hay, barley, and oats.

And so the incredible paradox happened at Bethlehem: history's greatest figure was born, not in a palace or mansion, but in a cavern-stable. For Joseph and Mary, the holiest moment of all must have come before the shepherds paid their famous visit as they gazed at the extraordinary baby whose mission even they could scarcely comprehend. Small wonder that this has been the most familiar scene in all the florid history of art. Each generation, each school has attempted to portray the Nativity, with backgrounds ranging from Oriental to Italian to Flemish, and yet the tableau of the Holy Family in the Bethlehem grotto has remained an unconquered artistic challenge.

There is evidence that someone in Bethlehem relented and offered more normal accommodations to Joseph, Mary, and the newborn Jesus. For by the time the Wise Men arrived to present their gifts, the Holy Family seems to have been living in a "house" (Matt. 2:11). Or, as happens on any vacation trip today, the motel vacancies that are nonexistent on the night of arrival because the traveler failed to call ahead for reservations quickly materialize the next day.

All Bethlehem must have rustled with news about "that poor girl from Galilee" who had no sooner arrived in town than she bore a child, since the shepherds and, later, the Magi had no trouble finding the Holy Family. Clearly, they must have been directed by the townspeople.

Jesus' birth in this particular town had vast implications for the people of Palestine. Bethlehem, which means "House of Bread," was not only the setting for the story of Ruth, but it became the birthplace of David, and here the prophet Samuel anointed him King. Later it became the expected birthplace of that great "Son of David," or "Messiah," who was supposed to liberate the land from foreign control. It was no accident that over in Jerusalem, King Herod's priests came up with Bethlehem as the

The doorway of the Church of the Nativity in Bethlehem is partially walled up, permitting only children to enter without stooping. The Crusaders reduced the size of the entrance to prevent Arab horsemen from galloping into the interior.

logical place to send the Wise Men for any newborn *Christ*, the Greek translation for the Hebrew *Messiah*.[2]

The Site Today

"O little town of Bethlehem, how still we see thee lie . . . ." The lyrics fit not only the village of the first Christmas, but also the town of today. For two millennia seem to have brushed few changes into the Bethlehem scene. It remains a comparatively small town, six miles southwest of Jerusalem, and quiet enough—although the more than 30,000 who now live there have considerably increased its population from Jesus' day, and confrontations between the Arab population and Israeli authorities disturb the peace periodically.

Today, the tourist almost always approaches Bethlehem from the north—as Joseph and Mary had done—on a curvy road that twists along a bleak ridge. From a final bend, just outside the city, the so-called Shepherds' Fields are pointed out. This is the presumed place where the herdsmen were watching their flocks at the time of the angelic announcement. The rolling slopes are covered with tawny grasses and dotted with drab scrubby bushes and some pines. Individual fields are fenced off by low stone walls or rows of silver-green olive trees.

The city itself is a maze of twisting cobblestone lanes, all of which seem to lead into the past. But they find a hub in the centrally located Manger Square, where the crowning sanctuary is the ancient Church of the Nativity, erected by the Byzantine emperor Justinian. This basilica is a less-than-impressive structure of whitish stone that seems to contrast too fiercely with the deep and often cloudless blue sky hanging over the town. A low, partially walled-up doorway compels a visitor to bend down upon entering the sanctuary.

The interior of the church is cool, dark, and hardly imposing, but parts of the nave date back to the time of Constantine, making this Christendom's oldest church in continuous use. Forty-four rose-colored columns with Corinthian capitals divide the nave from its two side aisles, and a round, shiny Christmas tree ornament dangles from each of its lighting fixtures.

From the choir, stairways lead down to a thirteen-by-thirty-three-foot cavern underneath the high altar of the church, known as the Grotto of the Nativity, presumed to be the very cave in which Jesus was born. The place of birth is marked by a low, semicircular niche of white marble surrounding a polished silver star on the floor, illuminated by a collection of overornate lanterns suspended from above. Around the inner hub of the fourteen-pointed star is an inscription: "HIC DE VIRGINE MARIA JESUS CHRISTUS NATUS EST," Latin for "Here Jesus Christ was born of the Virgin Mary." Rich curtains and tapestries adorn the sacred precinct, as well as the little adjacent niche containing a stone manger where, supposedly, the infant Jesus was laid.

Visitors are often struck by conflicting impressions. There is reverence for the holy place, certainly, and some form of Christian worship is usually taking place at the shrine, led by a Coptic, Syriac, Armenian, Greek Orthodox, or Roman Catholic priest. But there is also aesthetic disappointment: the potpourri of garish votive lanterns, icons, and

The Church of the Nativity in Bethlehem, with entrance at the left center.

The Grotto of the Nativity in Bethlehem, marking the traditional site where Jesus was born.

candelabra that cluster about the shrine offend Western tastes. Yet this is a trifling and parochial objection, for the grotto is, after all, in the hands of Eastern Christendom.

But the dominant question in the mind of any thinking contemporary visitor to the shrine must be this: Did it all really happen *here*—at this spot? Though final proof is necessarily lacking, the surprising answer lurks closer to *probably* than *possibly.*

Where there is no direct archaeological evidence—and there could be none in the case of the birth of Jesus—nothing is more important in establishing the authenticity of an ancient site than antiquity: the place must have been regarded as such from earliest times. If the Church of the Nativity had been built here in 600 A.D., for example, its claims to mark the authentic site of the birth of Jesus would be almost worthless. But

Just across from the birth site in the Grotto of the Nativity stands the manger area. A stone feeding trough here is the presumed spot where Mary laid the infant Jesus.

Constantine the Great, the first Christian emperor of Rome, erected the original Church of the Nativity at this place in 326 A.D., over the very grotto that had been identified as the true site by the early church father Origen and, before him, Justin Martyr, writing in 150 A.D. Justin stated that Jesus was born in a cave that was used as a stable—not the typical stone or wooden stable so familiar in Christmas art.[3] Earlier still, in the 130s, the pagan Roman emperor Hadrian tried to desecrate the Jewish and Christian holy places in Palestine, but, ironically, thereby preserved their identity!

After he had put down an insurrection by the Jewish nationalist and would-be Messiah, Bar-Kokhba, in 135 A.D., Hadrian expelled the Jews from Jerusalem and paganized all known holy places of Jews and Christians, erecting a temple to Venus at the site of the Holy Sepulcher in

39

Stone mangers of the type used in Palestine during biblical times have been excavated at Solomon's Stables in Megiddo. Packed with straw, they provided a safe resting place for infants.

A silver star on the marble floor of the Grotto of the Nativity presumably identifies the place where Jesus was born.

Jerusalem, and a grove dedicated to Adonis over the Grotto of the Nativity in Bethlehem.

After visiting the latter in the early 200s, Origen later wrote: "In Bethlehem the grotto was shown where Jesus was born . . . . What was shown to me is familiar to everyone in the area. The heathen themselves tell anyone willing to listen that in the said grotto a certain Jesus was born whom the Christians revere" (*Contra Celsum*, i, 51).

"How still we see thee lie. . . ."

Having hosted the birth of the individual who would change history, Bethlehem seemed content to rest on its laurels, for nothing spectacular has happened there in the two thousand years since. One prominent exception, of course, was the sojourn of Jerome, who lived in the Church of the Nativity complex about 400 A.D. and translated parts of the Old Testament into Latin, which, with other translations, eventually became the famed Vulgate. The Vulgate has remained the official version of the Bible for Roman Catholicism ever since.

And in the modern era, it was a Syrian-Christian merchant in Bethlehem who first received the original Dead Sea Scrolls from the desert Bedouins who had discovered them in the early spring of 1947. The merchant brought them to the attention of religious authorities in Jerusalem, who alerted the entire scholarly world. Today, Bethlehem turns a brisk trade in religious items—candles, crucifixes, and sacred mementoes of olive wood and mother-of-pearl—for the many tourists from all parts of the world who throng the site where Christ was born. The town also bristles with churches representing all principal branches of world Christianity, while the environs of the Judean wilderness are dotted with monasteries, some quite ancient.

Each Christmas, Bethlehem decks itself in colored lights, glass lanterns, glittering stars, and illuminated crosses, while it swells in size because of the influx of Christian pilgrims. On Christmas Eve, a Protestant carol service is conducted at twilight on a hillside at the Shepherds' Fields, and again at 9 P.M. in an outer court of the Church of the Nativity. Meanwhile, the Latin patriarch of Jerusalem leads a colorful procession from the Holy City to Bethlehem in order to conduct a midnight Mass in the Church of the Nativity, a celebration transmitted by closed-circuit television to a large screen in Manger Square for the benefit of the thousands who cannot crowd inside the basilica. At the same time, the Grotto has been filled with humanity for most of Christmas Eve, as groups from all over the world read the Christmas story in a babble of foreign tongues.

Exactly at midnight, a silver bell tinkles in the Grotto, heralding Christ's birthday, and many of the pilgrims are overcome as they spirit themselves back two thousand years and try to find a place between the shepherds at the mangerside. A few move forward to try to press their lips to the metallic star marker. Then church bells peal forth throughout the city, since the people of Bethlehem are predominantly Christian.

6

Local Shepherds, Distant Magi

In that region there were shepherds living in the fields,
keeping watch over their flock by night. Then an angel of
the Lord stood before them, and the glory of the Lord
shone around them, and they were terrified. But the angel
said to them, "Do not be afraid; for see—I am bringing you
good news of great joy for all the people: to you is born
this day in the city of David a Savior, who is the Messiah,
the Lord. This will be a sign for you: you will find a child
wrapped in bands of cloth and lying in a manger."

LUKE 2:8–12

THERE was something peculiarly public about births in ancient times. There were no hospital maternity wards that only the family could visit, no looking at baby through the nursery window or donning sterile, antiseptic masks. The birth of a baby in Jewish families of the time, especially of a boy, was the signal for general rejoicing in the neighborhood and a feast for the relatives and friends, who came crowding in to see the newborn infant.

But since Joseph and Mary were in special circumstances at Bethlehem, far from their Nazareth home, festivities would be in a different key, even if they did have relatives in the Bethlehem area. Strangely, the only guests at the Nativity mentioned in the New Testament were the shepherds and the Magi.

The Herdsmen

That lowly shepherds should have been the very first to learn about what had happened in Bethlehem has struck some commentators as incongruous, and attempts have been made to "upgrade" the shepherds. So they are represented as not the ordinary kind of nomadic herdsmen who often infuriated the rabbis by their manner of life, their sometimes necessary absence from the synagogue, and their failure to fulfill the Law. Instead, these were supposed to have been special shepherds who were guarding flocks destined for sacrifice in the Jerusalem temple, and this would explain their readiness to welcome a newborn Messiah.[1]

Whether or not this is true, any special "rehabilitation" of the shepherds is hardly necessary in the Christmas story. If, resorting to symbolism, the wise men represented privilege, wealth, and intelligence, so the shepherds stood for the cross-sectional, average Judean—quite literally, too, "the man on the night shift." For shepherding was one of the oldest and most important vocations among the ancient Hebrews, who first came into their Promised Land as nomadic shepherds and herdsmen, not as farmers.

The Bible is full of references to sheep and shepherds. Such Old Testament heroes as Abraham, Isaac, Jacob, Moses, and David were all shepherds at some time in their lives, and the Twenty-third Psalm remains one of the most beautiful commentaries on shepherding ever written. In the New Testament, the familiar figure of Jesus as "The Good Shepherd" underscores the theme. In fact, the modern terms "pastor" and "bishop" both derive from the ancient words for "shepherd" and "overseer-guardian," and to this day the bishop's staff is a shepherd's crook. Perhaps it was highly appropriate, after all, that shepherds be the first guests at the first Christmas.

They may well have lived in the herdsmen's village of Beit Sahur, just below Bethlehem, and have been pasturing their flocks at night on the sloping expanse just east of Bethlehem that is still pointed out as the Shepherds' Fields. Besides keeping such long hours, herdsmen had to protect their sheep from ravaging animals and robbers by skillful use of staff and sling, or a metal-studded club about a yard long. A well-trained sheepdog was almost as effective as the shepherd in defending the flock. Herdsmen were also expected to shear the wool, aid in lambing, and see that their flocks had enough to eat and drink. While the sheep were

44

grazing, the men often passed the time by playing folk tunes on their pipes.

The names of the shepherds who witnessed the Nativity will doubtless never be known, but they win our respect. Perhaps it was fortunate that they were common laymen, for had they been scholars or theologians, they would likely first have held a debate on the hillside instead of rushing into Bethlehem after the glad announcement, the conservatives insisting they would never leave the sheep, and the liberals labeling the angelic appearance a mere hallucination. No one has bothered to inquire if anyone stayed behind to watch the sheep while they were gone, but we can safely assume that the first thing the shepherds did the morning after their night of spreading word about the newborn Christ was to take a head count of their sheep!

Today, the chief breed of sheep in Palestine is the broad-tailed variety (*Ovis laticaudata*), and there is every reason to presume that the flocks still grazing in the hills around Bethlehem today descended from the very sheep whose foraging was so extraordinarily interrupted that night of nights.

The Wise Men

In the time of King Herod, after Jesus was born in Bethlehem of Judea, wise men from the East came to Jerusalem, asking, "Where is the child who has been born king of the Jews? For we observed his star at its rising, and have come to pay him homage." (Matthew 2:1–2)

How much time elapsed between the adoration of the shepherds and the visit of the Magi is not known, but the mysterious men from the East do not seem to have arrived until after Jesus' presentation at the Temple in Jerusalem, forty days after he was born. Unfortunately, little more is known of the Magi than of the shepherds.

"We three kings of Orient are. . . ." So the beloved Christmas carol begins, but already it has made at least three errors. First, how many Wise Men made the trip to Bethlehem is not known. And they were not "kings." And they did not come from as far away as the "Orient," that is, the Far East.

Modern shepherds tend their sheep much like their ancient counterparts at the Shepherds' Fields just outside Bethlehem in the background.

Tradition, of course, has placed their number at three, probably because of the three gifts of gold, frankincense, and myrrh that they presented to the infant Jesus, the assumption being one gift, one giver. But some earlier traditions make quite a caravan of their visit, setting their number as high as twelve. Legend has also supplied names in the case of the three (Gaspar, Melchior, and Balthasar), and has even reported their ages (twenty, forty, and sixty), as well as their skin colors (white, yellow, and black). But these names arise first in the sixth century A.D., too late for any authenticity, and their ages and races are too obviously spaced.

Supposedly, Thomas, the apostle to India, found and baptized the Magi into the Christian faith, ordaining them as priests. Later, they suffered martyrdom, and their relics were presumably buried in Constantinople but then transferred to the cathedral at Cologne in Germany during the twelfth century, where they rest today. But no one takes such claims seriously.

The Greek of the New Testament calls them simply *magoi apo anatolon*, "magi from the East," and the term *magoi* is usually translated as wise men, astrologers, or magicians. "The East" has been variously identified as any country from Arabia to Media and Persia, but no farther east.

Most of the evidence points to Mesopotamian or Persian origins for the magi, who were an old and powerful priestly caste among both Medes and Persians. These priest-sages, extremely well educated for their day, were specialists in medicine, religion, astronomy, astrology, divination, and magic, and their caste eventually spread across much of the East. As in any other profession, there were both good and bad magi, depending on whether they did research in the sciences or practiced augury, necromancy, and magic. The Persian magi were credited with higher religious and intellectual attainments, while the Babylonian magi were sometimes deemed imposters.

The safest conclusion is that the Magi of Christmas were Persian, for the term originates among the Medo-Persians, and early Syriac traditions give them Persian names. Primitive Christian art in the second-century Roman catacombs dresses them in Persian garments, and a majority of Early Church fathers interpret them as Persian. Indeed, the reason invading Persians spared the Church of the Nativity in 614 was that they saw a golden mosaic over the doorway, depicting the wise men in Persian headdress.

Modes of transportation and dress often seem to have changed little in Palestine during the 2,000 years since Jesus' birth. Here a Bedouin in colorful *keffiyeh*—a versatile insulation against both heat and cold—cajoles his camel.

However, if the astronomical aspects of the Christmas story are emphasized—the great star and its role—a case could be made that the Magi were late Babylonians, since astronomy reached its highest development in Mesopotamia.[2]

Whatever the origin of the Eastern sages, their visit was of great significance for later Christianity: the Wise Men were pagans, not Hebrews, and the fact that Gentile magi performed the same adoration as Jewish shepherds symbolized the universal outreach for future Christianity. "Nations [Gentiles] shall come to your light," the prophet Isaiah had written, "and kings to the brightness of your dawn" (60:3).

The star that guided them to Bethlehem, discussed in the next chapter, had both local and international significance. The Hebrews expected a star as a sign of the birth of the Messiah (Num. 24:17)—a later pseudo-Messiah tried to capitalize on this belief by calling himself Bar-Kokhba, "Son of a Star"[3]—and Eastern sages were acquainted with Hebrew beliefs because of the large Jewish colony in Babylon and elsewhere. Even Roman authors of the time spoke of the grandiose things expected in Palestine. "There had spread all over the East an old and established belief that it was fated for men coming from Judea at that time to rule the world," wrote Suetonius.[4] Therefore when the Magi inquired of Herod, "Where is he who has been born king of the Jews?" their question was not really spoken out of a vacuum.

The scene of proud and richly costumed sages worshiping a baby in the humblest of circumstances has etched itself on the world's imagination, for it is a graphic study in contrasts. The gifts they presented are usually interpreted symbolically. Gold, a royal gift, signified Jesus' kingship. Frankincense, a fragrant gum resin burned as incense, denoted his future priesthood. This substance consisted of small whitish beads or chunks that were ground into powder and that gave off an odor like balsam when burned. The third gift, myrrh, called *smyrna* in Greek, was an aromatic orange-colored resin from the small, thorny trees of the *Commiphora* family. Myrrh was expensive and much esteemed for use in perfumes, anointing oil, medicine, and embalming. That, years later, the crucified Jesus was offered wine mixed with myrrh as a palliative (Mark 15:23) and was also buried with the substance (John 19:39) renders this gift of the Magi predictive enough.

After their adoration at the manger, the Wise Men disappear from history, leaving a multitude of questions in their wake. Almost unidentifiable, they have still become some of the most familiar figures in Western culture, for their clumsy camels have lumbered back into the Nativity scene every year since Christmas was first celebrated.

And they did achieve their purpose in the total story of Christmas, which was to expand it. Up to now, the Nativity had been highly local in nature: only a few people of the lower classes of just one nationality had been involved. But the visit of the Magi burst all that, as rich Gentiles joined poor Jews, as King Herod and the priestly establishment in Jerusalem became concerned, and even the stars looked in.

7

An Extraordinary Star

When they had heard the king, they set out; and there,
ahead of them, went the star they had seen at its rising,
until it stopped over the place where the child was.

MATTHEW 2:9

O NE of the most spectacular aspects of the Christmas story must be the great star that lured the Wise Men from their Eastern homeland to Jerusalem and on again to Bethlehem. For that star never really disappeared. In silver or gold, plastic or cardboard, it crowns the tops of Christmas trees and twinkles among the festive trappings along Main Street. In glitter or aluminum foil, it shines on as the most familiar single motif on Christmas cards.

The Star of Bethlehem has puzzled scholars for centuries. Some have skeptically dismissed the phenomenon as a myth, a mere literary device to call attention to the importance of the Nativity. Some Christians, at the other extreme, have argued that the star was miraculously placed there by God to guide the Magi and is therefore beyond all natural explanation. Most authorities, however, take a middle course that looks for some astronomical and historical explanation for the Christmas star, and several interesting theories have been offered.

First of all, there is nothing in the least improbable about a group of sages being attracted by some astral event and then trying to investigate it more closely. The ancient historians of the Near East, Greece, and Rome were fond of describing astronomical phenomena and the profound effect these had on the daily lives of the people, who were forever interpreting their future on the basis of what they saw in the sky each night. In that

The conjunction of Jupiter and Saturn in Pisces (the Fishes) in
December of 7 B.C., as extrapolated from Babylonian records.
Modern astronomical calculations place this conjunction in
approximately the same position, though a few degrees farther
west on the ecliptic. This is an actual photograph of the

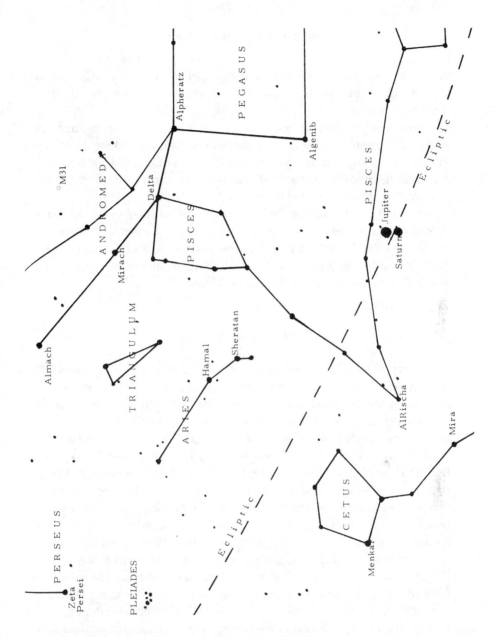

December sky over Judea, looking toward the southwest, but since a photograph is unable to reproduce the greater intensity of light from the larger planets, Jupiter and Saturn were added with enlarged diameters, as in planetariums. The constellations and stars are identified above.

region of clear air (before any industrial pollution), and in that time of poor artificial lighting, the nights were long, and the heavens extraordinarily impressive.

From reading the historical sources, one would think comets, meteors, and other celestial wonders were almost constantly streaking across the ancient skies, and it is no accident that the present mania for astrology is traceable historically to exactly this area of the world. Indeed, the Babylonians first set up the signs of the zodiac.

There is another reason for taking the celestial event in the skies over Palestine quite seriously. If the phenomenon could be identified, astronomy could then also hope to date it, and the mystery of an exact date for the birth of Jesus would be largely solved. Here are the most logical astronomical explanations for the Star of Bethlehem.

Planetary Conjunction

Every 805 years, the planets Jupiter and Saturn come into extraordinary repeated conjunction, with Mars joining the configuration a year later. Since the great Kepler first alerted them to it in the early seventeenth century, astronomers have computed that for ten months in 7 B.C., Jupiter and Saturn traveled very close to each other in the night sky, and in May, September, and December of that year, they were conjoined. Mars joined this configuration in February of 6 B.C.—a massing of planets that must have been quite spectacular indeed. But more. The astrological interpretations of such a conjunction would have told the Magi much, if, as seems probable, they shared the astrological lore of the area. For Jupiter and Saturn met each other in that sign of the zodiac called *Pisces*, the Fishes.

In ancient astrology, the giant plant Jupiter was known as the "King's Planet," for it represented the highest god and ruler of the universe: Marduk to the Babylonians, Zeus to the Greeks, Jupiter to the Romans. And the ringed plant Saturn was deemed the shield or defender of Palestine, while the constellation of the Fishes, which was also associated with Syria and Palestine, represented epochal events and crises[1]. So Jupiter encountering Saturn in the Sign of the Fishes would have meant that a cosmic ruler or king was to appear in Palestine at a culmination of history. This, at least, may help to explain why the Magi were well enough informed to look for some "King of the Jews" in Palestine. And the time of this rare conjunction in 7 B.C. fits part of the Nativity chronology very well indeed, even if Jesus were born in 5 B.C. King Herod would later order the slaughter of all male infants in Bethlehem "who were two years old or under, according to the time that he had learned from the wise men" (Matt. 2:16). Seven minus two is five.

But there is a significant objection to this theory: the two or three planets would not have come together closely enough to represent one superstar, for they would always have been separated from each other by at least one or two moon diameters. Rather, they would have appeared as a close pair of very bright stars or as a tight triangle, as in the accompanying illustrations. And the triangle would have been so close to the setting sun in February of 6 B.C. that some astronomers doubt if all three planets could have been seen.[2]

Comet

The Greek term for "star" in the Gospel account, *aster,* can mean any luminous heavenly body, including a comet, meteor, nova, or planet. Meteors, brief and brilliant slashes across the skies that they are, would seem too transitory for consideration. But nothing impressed the ancient eye so much as a comet, for comets were thought to herald important changes in the state, particularly by the Romans. Historians of the time reported that a blood-red comet, so bright that it could be seen in the daytime, dominated the skies in the year that Caesar was assassinated, 44 B.C.. A comet also preceded the battle of Philippi, where Caesar was avenged. The death of Augustus was signaled by a comet too, as were other political crises.

Was the Christmas star really a comet? With its brilliant pointing head and long luminous tail, a comet makes a far more startling impression in the night sky than any planetary conjunction. When Halley's comet passed over Palestine in 1910, Jerusalemites reported that it seemed to pass quickly from east to west, growing somewhat diffused but nearly reappearing in all its grandeur in the west, much as the phenomenon in the Nativity story. But Halley's comet passed over the skies too early (12 B.C.) in its visit at that time to be the Star of Bethlehem, although it undoubtedly aroused the interest of people in the Near East to astral events.

The massing of Jupiter, Mars, and Saturn over the western
horizon in February of 6 B.C., shortly after sunset.

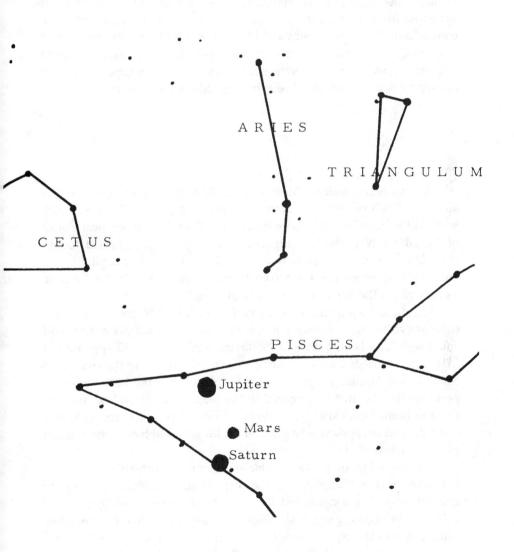

It happens that the Chinese have more exact and more complete astronomical records than the Near East, particularly in their tabulations of comets and novas. In 1871, John Williams published his authoritative list of comets derived from Chinese annals.[3] Now, Comet No. 52 on the Williams list may have special significance for the first Christmas. It appeared for some seventy days in March and April of 5 B.C., near the constellation Capricorn, and would have been visible in both the Far and Near East. As each night wore on, of course, the comet would seem to have moved westward across the southern sky. Since the time is also very appropriate, this *could* have been the Wise Men's astral marker.

Nova

A nova is not really a "new" star, as its name implies, but one that suddenly has a tremendous increase in brilliance, due to internal explosion, and no astral event is more spectacular than this. In our local galaxy of the Milky Way, the last supernova (as it is usually termed today) exploded in 1604, so brightly that it could also be seen in daylight. The ancients sometimes confused comets and novas, though the Chinese usually called the latter "comets without a tail."

It is quite fascinating to note that Comet No. 53 on the Williams list (next after the one previously mentioned) is such a tailless comet, and could well have been a nova, as Williams admitted. No. 53 appeared in March and April of 4 B.C.—a year after its predecessor—in the area of the constellation Aquila, which also was visible all over the East. Was this, perhaps, the star that reappeared to the Magi once Herod had directed them to Bethlehem (Matt. 2:9)? Probably not. Herod died about April 1 of 4 B.C., and the audience he granted the Magi would have to have taken place months earlier.

The following, then, is a possible astronomical reconstruction of what happened that first Christmas. The remarkable conjunctions of Jupiter and Saturn in 7–6 B.C. alerted the Magi to important developments in Palestine, for the astrological significance closely paralleled what they had learned from Hebrew lore about a star heralding the expected Messiah. The comet of 5 B.C. (Williams No. 52) dramatically underscored this interpretation and sent them on their way.

Comet Arend-Roland, named for the Belgians who discovered
it, as photographed by the Schmidt telescope at Mount Palomar
Observatory on May 1, 1957.

That the star went before them "until it stopped over the place where
the child was" need not imply any sudden visible movements on the part
of the astral phenomenon. Because of the rotation of the earth, anything
in the night sky appears to move westward as the night progresses, except
Polaris and the relatively few stars north of it. And, as people travel, the
stars do seem to move with them or before them, stopping when they

The white arrow indicates a supernova in Galaxy NGC 4725 in the constellation Coma Berenices. Note its absence in an earlier photograph (opposite) of the same sector. This supernova appeared in late 1940.

stop. So when it reached a zenith in the skies over Bethlehem, the gleaming blue-white star of Christmas would indeed have seemed to stop for the Magi as they reached their destination.

Even the artistic conceptions of the star shedding its rays down on Bethlehem might not be quite so fanciful as one would think. In subtropical latitudes on very clear nights, a faint luminous band similar to the Milky Way is visible on the southwest horizon. This band, called *zodiacal light*, is the reflection of sunlight on meteoric particles concentrated in the plane of the ecliptic, and it appears as a luminous cone shining from the planetary path down to earth at the point where the sun has set. *If* it appeared to the Magi leaving Jerusalem, zodiacal light might have seemed to beam down from the Christmas star to intersect Bethlehem at the southwest. But this is an embellishment to the Christmas story, on which the New Testament is silent.

Perhaps this reconstruction of the astral events seems too pat to be true, and additional astronomical evidence may one day disprove it. But at least it is not so fanciful as some of the current theories. Perhaps the most grotesque is that offered by the Russian V. Zaitsev, who claims that the Star of Bethlehem was really a spaceship from a higher civilization carrying cosmonaut Jesus into this world! But beyond any (more serious) debate, astronomy does play an important role in the history of the Nativity.

8

Herod the King

When Herod saw that he had been tricked by the wise
men, he was infuriated, and he sent and killed all the
[male] children in and around Bethlehem who were two
years old or under, according to the time that he had
learned from the wise men.   MATTHEW 2:16

I T was only natural for the Magi to assume that a newborn king of
the Jews would have entered this world in the royal palace at
Jerusalem. But wise as they were, their inquiry before King Herod showed
no great tact and even less diplomacy. "Where is the child who has been
born king of the Jews?" might have sounded more courteous to the king
had it been worded: "Where is the new prince who will one day succeed
you?" For Herod's suspicious mind immediately warped the Magi's query
into: "Where is the *real* king, you imposter?" At the time, Herod mistrusted
everyone and thought himself surrounded by young aspirants all plotting
to seize his throne.

Probably his first impulse was to clap the mysterious visitors into
irons for asking such a question, but his native shrewdness checked it.
He would have to pose interest and ferret out whatever information he
could from them in order to kill off a possible rival. Instead, then, he
assembled his priests and demanded to know where the Messiah-king
was expected to be born. On the basis of an Old Testament prophecy, the
scholars were able to pinpoint Bethlehem. "And you, Bethlehem, in the
land of Judah, are by no means least among the rulers of Judah; for from
you shall come a ruler who is to shepherd my people Israel" (Mic. 5:2;
Matt. 2:6).

Bronze

Obv. Helmet with crest and cheek piece; inscription: ΒΑΣΙΛΕΩΣ ΗΡΩΔΟΥ (King Herod); date and monogram as below.
Rev. Circular shield, surrounded by a wavy line.

Bronze

Obv. Tripod with bowl; in field right, monogram ₽ ; left, date: Γ (year 3); inscription: ΒΑΣΙ-ΛΕΩΣ ΗΡΩΔΟΥ (King Herod).
Rev. Thymiaterium (incense burner) between two palm branches.

Bronze

Obv. Anchor; inscription: ΒΑCΙ ΗΡWΔ (King Herod).
Rev. Double cornucopia with caduceus between horns.

Bronze coinage of Herod the Great.

His eyes crinkling with suspicion even as his face wore a mask of affability, Herod directed his guests to David's city: "Go and search diligently for the child; and when you have found him, bring me word so that I may also go and pay him homage . . . "

" . . . in mockery and then kill him!" Herod's mind completed the thought.

And the Wise Men would have done just that but for the sudden change of plans recorded by Matthew: "Having been warned in a dream not to return to Herod, they left for their own country by another road" (2:12). Probably they headed due east into the Judean badlands, brushing just north of the Qumran wilderness community that would one day give the world the Dead Sea Scrolls. Then they crossed the Jordan River ford just above the head of the Dead Sea and returned to their Eastern homeland.

Herod took that snub with all the rage of the deluded and suspicious old paranoid he had become. Ordering the ruthless massacre of all male babies two years old and under in Bethlehem and vicinity, he hoped that the infant "king" must certainly have been among the victims. Estimating a town of some 2,000 inhabitants at the time, about twenty male babies would have fallen into this category and been slain, for some doubtless escaped detection. The scene of mothers madly trying to hush their crying infants so as not to be discovered, only to see them snatched out of their arms by Herod's soldiers, thrown to the floor, and run through with swords sends a bristle of shock into the Christmas story so utterly discordant with the rest of it. To anyone with even the slightest knowledge of the Nativity, Herod emerges quite clearly as "the monster of the Christmas story."

So incredibly brutal was this slaughter of the innocents that many scholars have superimposed a great question mark over this part of the Nativity record, suggesting that nothing of the kind ever happened. But such a crime was very much in character for Herod in his last years, when illness and court intrigue had nearly deranged the man. He married ten wives, who spawned a wriggling, ambitious brood of sons that turned the palace into a human can of worms in their scheming to succeed him.

Herod was so jealous of his favorite wife, Mariamme, that on two occasions he ordered that she be killed if he failed to return from a critical mission. And then he finally killed her anyway, as well as her grandfather, her mother, his brother-in-law, and three of his sons, not to mention numerous subjects. During a swimming party at Jericho, he also drowned

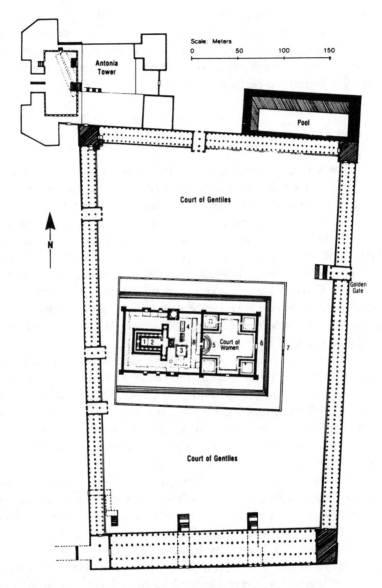

Plan of the Temple at Jerusalem constructed by Herod the Great.
1. Holy of Holies   2. Temple sanctuary   3. Altar   4. Court
of the Priests   5. Nicanor Gate   6. The Beautiful Gate
7. Balustrade warning Gentiles not to enter the sacred precincts
8. Court of the Israelites.

the high priest, who happened to be another of his brothers-in-law. The real villain behind many of these murders was his sister Salome, who was so jealous of Herod's wives that she sowed the seeds of suspicion for years in the Jerusalem palace, concocting monstrous lies about everyone—lies that Herod too easily believed.

Herod the Great

The young Herod, however, had been an exceptionally able ruler, governing Palestine as client-king in behalf of the Roman emperor Augustus. And the House of Herod had the uncanny knack of being able to sniff the airs of Mediterranean politics and make the right decisions. Herod's father had given crucial help to Julius Caesar when he was down in Egypt, cut off from his supplies, and Caesar rewarded him handsomely for that. Herod himself shrewdly advised his friend Mark Antony to drop Cleopatra and make peace with Rome. (Antony should have followed that advice.) And once Augustus emerged victorious from the civil wars, he was so impressed with young Herod that he allowed him to become one of his most intimate friends.

The face of Palestine was groomed and beautified during Herod's thirty-three-year reign. Across the land he erected palaces, fortresses, temples, aqueducts, cities, and—his crowning achievement—the great new Temple in Jerusalem. He created the magnificent port of Caesarea and stimulated trade and commerce. He also patronized culture in Greek cities far from Palestine and easily became the talk of the eastern Mediterranean.

In fallow years or seasons of famine, Herod remitted taxes, and during one crisis he even sold his dinnerware to buy food for the populace. He also served as protector of overseas Jews in the Dispersion by conciliating their Gentile rulers. He was so highly respected by Rome that he would actually go down in history as "Herod the Great."[1]

But he had little support in his own kingdom. Herod was only a half-Jew and seemed far too romanizing for his subjects, whom he also taxed heavily. Soon he was hated as a tyrant, even by members of his own family. A maddening maze of intrigues infested the palace, and Herod began suspecting everyone, tormented, as he was, by fears of assassination. In his advancing paranoia, he was continually writing to Rome for

The Herodium, one of the fortresses constructed by Herod the Great, also marked his place of burial. Today the ruins of the Herodium tower over Bethlehem's southeastern horizon.

permission to execute one or two of his sons for treason. Finally, even his patron and friend Augustus had to admit, "I'd rather be Herod's pig than his son."[2] It was not only a play on the similar-sounding Greek words for *son* and *pig,* but a wry reference to the fact that pork, at least, was not consumed by Jews.

Old and very ill from arteriosclerosis, Herod worried that no one would mourn his death—a justified concern. So he issued orders from his deathbed that leaders from all parts of Judea were to be locked inside the great hippodrome at Jericho. When he died, archers were to massacre these thousands in cold blood, so that there would indeed be universal mourning associated with his death.

This was the Herod at the time of the Christmas story. Would he, then, have scrupled at the lives of a few babies in little Bethlehem? Hardly!

As it was, Bethlehem lay just northwest of his favorite fortress-palace, the great breast-shaped mountain called the Herodium, where he was arranging his own tomb. Here, least of all, would he tolerate sedition in the name of any newborn "king of the Jews."

After changing his will three times and attempting suicide, Herod finally contracted a very loathsome disease in the spring of 4 B.C. that ulcerated his digestive system, inflamed his abdomen, rotted his privates, and blocked his breathing. After a last, fevered convulsion, he died.

But alas, Herod's final plans—both of them—miscarried. The Jewish leaders who were jammed inside the hippodrome were not slaughtered but released, on orders of Herod's sister, Salome. And the baby who was supposed to die in the Bethlehem massacre was instead in the arms of his mother as she sat astride a donkey en route to refuge in Egypt. That infant, however, was getting used to travel: this was his third trip.

9

Up to Jerusalem, Down to Egypt

After eight days had passed, it was time to circumcise the
child; and he was called Jesus, the name given by the angel
before he was conceived in the womb. When the time came
for their purification according to the law of Moses, they
brought him up to Jerusalem to present him to the Lord.

LUKE 2:21–22

TRAVEL is as typical of the modern yuletide as the blazing Christmas
tree itself. In our mobile society, highways, railroads, and airlines
are crowded each December as younger members of the family come
home for Christmas and relatives get together for the holidays. What
other society has nearly made a carol out of "I'll be Home for Christmas"?

Travel also characterized the first Christmas. Besides Joseph and
Mary's tedious journey from Galilee to Bethlehem, there was the immense
westward trek of the Wise Men across hundreds of miles of desert to
Judea and back again. Then, too, soon after the Nativity, the Holy Family
took three important trips—two in order to fulfill Jewish religious law
and the third to save the very life of the newborn child.

The Circumcision

On the eighth day after he was born, every Hebrew boy baby was
circumcised, a token of the special covenant between God and his chosen
people dating back to Abraham (Gen. 17:10ff.). At this ceremony, the child

was also formally given his name. The rite became one of the most important hallmarks of Judaism, and some of its savants even claimed that the higher angels were created in a circumcised condition!

Under normal circumstances, the nearest rabbi would have come to the home of Joseph and Mary to perform the ceremony, but since they may still have been living in the grotto, or more likely in a rented dwelling at Bethlehem, they probably took the infant to a nearby synagogue for the all-important rite. Presumably, Joseph asked the rabbi to let him help officiate, a common request in these happy circumstances, and the rabbi easily agreed.

However it happened, the circumcision-naming ceremony was an occasion for great joy among parents, relatives, and friends, with many overtones of the later Christian baptism. In Jesus' case, probably only Joseph, Mary, and the nameless rabbi shared the gladness that another son of Israel had been included in the great covenant with God. And the baby was given a proper scriptural name, that of Moses' successor as leader of the Hebrews: *Joshua* or *Yeshua*. It meant "God saves" or "God is salvation." Later ages would prefer the Greek form of the name, Jesus.

For some days after circumcision, the baby would be uncomfortable, the first token pain and bloodshed in a career that would see considerably more of both.

The Presentation at the Temple

After forty days it was time for Jesus' first longer journey. Moses' law required that women had to purify themselves after childbirth by offerings at the Tabernacle (or, later, the Temple) forty days after the birth of a boy and eighty after that of a girl. It was a simple, six-mile trip north to Jerusalem, doubtless on the same patient little jackass that had carried Mary down to Bethlehem, and it should not have taken more than two hours.

The magnificent Temple in Jerusalem was approaching completion at the time, a gleaming white jewel wedged into the northeastern corner of the city. The sprawling enclave was rimmed with a labyrinth of colonnaded porticoes and gates, and to all pious Jews this was the very center of the world. What Joseph and Mary offered for her purification showed how poor they were, for in lieu of sacrificing an unblemished yearling

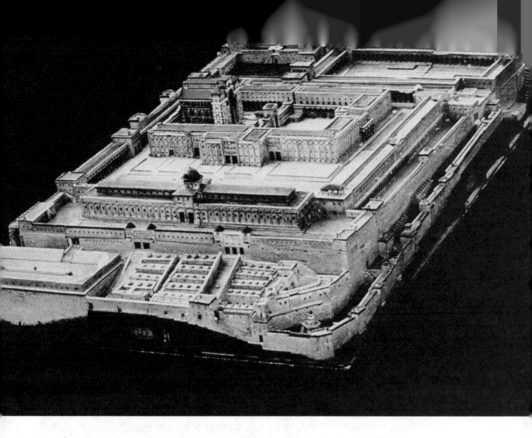

Reconstruction of the great Temple in Jerusalem, built by Herod the Great, where the infant Jesus was presented. In the upper left center is the Holy of Holies. (This model was designed by scholar-engineer Dr. Conrad Schick.)

lamb, they offered a pair of turtledoves or pigeons (Lev. 12), the minimum requirement of religious law.

At the same time they also formally presented the infant Jesus back to God in fulfillment of Exodus 13:2 ("Consecrate to me all the firstborn . . . "), redeeming, or buying him back again, through an offering of five silver shekels (Num. 18:16). This shows, incidentally, that Jesus was free of any bodily blemish, or this ceremony would not have been necessary.

Everything had happened normally enough up to that moment. But then, as Joseph and Mary were standing with their bundled infant in the Court of the Women at the great Temple, a righteous and devout old man named Simeon walked purposefully over to them with a strange glint in his eyes. For years he had been waiting for the fulfillment of messianic expectations, he explained to the awestruck couple, and God had assured him that he would indeed live to see the infant Christ. That very morning he had been inspired to come into the Temple and view the culmination of his hopes. Exuberantly taking the baby in his arms, old Simeon exulted:

> Master, now you are dismissing your servant in peace,
> according to your word;
> for my eyes have seen your salvation,
> which you have prepared in the presence of all peoples,
> a light for revelation to the Gentiles,
> and for glory to your people Israel. (Luke 2:29–32)

The words would ring down in Christian history as one of the most beloved prayers of the church, and artists would never tire of trying to catch on canvas the sacred fire in Simeon's eyes.

Then Simeon turned to Joseph and Mary and blessed them, adding some prophetic words: "This child is destined for the falling and the rising of many in Israel, and to be a sign that will be opposed. . . . " And so Simeon had played out his role as a transition figure, the man, more than any other, who stands between the Old and New Testaments, rooted in the ancient scriptural promises and prophecies, yet gazing at their fulfillment.

Old as Simeon looked, his face almost took on the bloom of youth compared with the decrepit figure that now hobbled over to them, her leathery skin mottled with bleached or browned patches and deeply latticed with wrinkles. Her name was Anna, her role was that of prophetess, and she had been a human fixture at the Temple for most of her incredible life span. She was either eighty-four or about one hundred and six years old, since Luke's language is not explicit. Anna came from the tribe of Asher—clearly, the so-called "Ten Lost Tribes" of Israel had not lost all their members—and she formed the perfect female counterpart to Simeon, thanking God and immediately telling others of the wonder that had happened in the form of the six-week-old Jesus.

The Flight to Egypt

> Now after they [the wise men] had left, an angel of the Lord appeared to Joseph in a dream and said, "Get up, take the child and his mother, and flee to Egypt, and remain there until I tell you; for Herod is about to search for the child, to destroy him." (Matthew 2:13)

Shortly after Joseph and Mary returned to Bethlehem at the close of their astonishing day at the Temple, their sense of wonder was only compounded by the visit of the Magi. But the brimming happiness of the first Christmas was abruptly cut short by what was more properly Joseph's nightmare than his dream, alerting him to Herod's designs on Jesus. Without even waiting for the morning light, Joseph roused his sleeping family, packed the drowsy, dumbfounded donkey, and they all set out on the highway south toward Hebron. The journey down to Egypt would be far more ambitious than that which led from Nazareth to Bethlehem—well over twice as long.

The New Testament tells us nothing about the route they took, but the regular caravan trail from Bethlehem led south on the Hebron road, then sharply west to Gaza and the coastal highway down to Pelusium, the portal to Egypt. An alternate route lay in the desert interior, but it would have been extremely dangerous for a lone couple and baby to try to brave the howling sands of the northern Sinai. With an average twenty miles per day of fairly level travel along the coastal route, the Holy Family would reach Egypt in about ten days.

Wherever the Bible is silent, legend is highly vocal. And so the apocryphal *Arabic Gospel of the Infancy* tries to fill in the details of the Flight to Egypt. One of its "charming" stories tells how Joseph and Mary were waylaid by robbers on the Sinai road, but they found nothing to steal from the poor couple. Taking pity on them instead, the bandits gave them provisions and sent them on their way. One of these likeable brigands, of course, would cross Jesus' path thirty years later at the Crucifixion. Who but the penitent thief on his right?[1]

Another apocryphal story has a very hungry Mary looking longingly at a date palm tree and wishing that, somehow, she could feast on its fruit. The infant Jesus smiled, and the palm bent down so that Mary could pick its dates![2]

Many kindred Jews were living in Egypt at the time with whom Joseph and Mary could have sought refuge. In fact, more Jews lived in Alexandria than in Jerusalem, forming 40 percent of the population there. But it seems unlikely that the Holy Family would have traveled that far west in the Nile delta. Their place of sojourn in Egypt is unknown, although two late traditions have tried to identify it.

Near the ruins of Heliopolis, outside Cairo, pilgrims as early as the fifth century visited the "Tree of Mary," a spreading sycamore under which

Panorama of Egypt, the Red Sea, the Sinai peninsula, Palestine
(upper center), and across the Arabian desert to the Euphrates
River valley (extreme upper right), taken by the *Gemini II*
mission with astronauts Conrad and Gordon in September 1966.
The dotted line indicates the most likely route taken by the
Holy Family on the Flight to Egypt. The arrow at center points
to the Sinai massif.

74

The great pyramids and sphinx at Gizeh, near Cairo, which had already been standing some 2,500 years by the time the Holy Family reached Egypt.

Mary is supposed to have shaded herself. And in the Coptic quarter of Old Cairo stands the church of St. Sergius, below which is a crypt venerated from the sixth century as the place where the Holy Family stayed for three months while in Egypt. The crypt was originally a cave or grotto, and visitors are still shown a niche in the wall where the baby Jesus is supposed to have slept. Elsewhere in Egypt, more Coptic churches are dedicated to the Virgin or to events surrounding the Nativity than to any other theme.

Wherever they stayed, it could not have been for long, since King Herod died soon after Joseph and Mary had fled from Bethlehem. Matthew finishes his version of the Christmas story by telling of another angelic dream, in which Joseph is alerted to Herod's demise and is told to return to Palestine, fulfilling the prophecy "Out of Egypt I called my son" (Hos. 11:1).

When Joseph and Mary returned to their homeland, an unhappy surprise awaited them. Herod was indeed dead, but his son Archelaus ruled Judea as his successor, and he had begun his reign with a massacre of three thousand Jews who had rebelled against him in the Temple at Jerusalem.[3] Better to return home to Galilee, they decided, where a milder son of Herod, named Antipas, had been appointed tetrarch, with the kind permission of the Roman emperor Augustus.

10

Joseph the Carpenter

"Is not this the carpenter's son?
Is not his mother called Mary?"

MATTHEW 13:55

THE focal point of any Nativity scene or of any crèche under the
Christmas tree lies just over the heads of the adoring shepherds
and Wise Men. It is a husband and wife flanking a manger, looking down
on the Child with a magnificent mixture of joy and wonder.

Joseph and Mary would become history's most famous couple because
of the all-but-incredible circumstances. Mary was the baby's mother, but
Joseph served only as its foster father, according to Christian theology,
with God himself the true father. (Liberal theologians, however, and non-
Christians generally deny the Virgin Birth.) If Joseph himself harbored
any human misgivings about the extraordinary role his wife had been
called upon to play, they are not recorded in the New Testament. Nor is
there any hint that he chafed at not being able to assert his marital rights
before the birth of Jesus, which would have been easy grounds for divorce
in the courts today.

There are very few glimpses of Joseph in the Bible, and most of these
are tied in with the Christmas story. Here the attractive figure of a consid-
erate, protective, mature individual—a truly good man—playing his difficult role obediently and well is unmistakable. He did not resent the
intrusion of shepherds and Magi but rejoiced with them in the birth of a
son whom they all believed to be the long-awaited Messiah-king. A pious
Jew, he saw to it that the circumcision and presentation of the infant Jesus

went according to Old Testament schedule. A good provider and defender, he managed the lengthy trips to and from Egypt with no recorded diffi-culty—hardly a mean accomplishment for desert travel. By any measure, the noble Joseph is the unsung hero of the Christmas story.

The Craftsman

Up in Nazareth he was known as Joseph the Carpenter. And like the famous patriarch Joseph for whom he was named, he too seems to have had a father named Jacob, of whom nothing is known save that he was the son of Matthan, and so on up the famous genealogy given at the beginning of Matthew's Gospel.[1]

Joseph may also have been born in Bethlehem, since his ancestors lived there, and this is where he came to register for the Roman census. But why, in that case, had he moved up to Nazareth? Perhaps it was economic competition from Bethlehem's too plentiful supply of craftsmen, or it may have been some construction project in Galilee that drew him north. It seems he was not planning to live there permanently, for after the Flight to Egypt, Joseph was thinking of returning to Bethlehem. It was only when he learned that Herod's son Archelaus ruled in Judea that he was frightened away from the land and turned back to Nazareth. The Galilean village would take on fresh importance now, since Sepphoris, which had overshadowed it, had just been destroyed because it had served as headquarters for Judas, a Galilean rebel.[2] Then, too, with most of her family in Galilee, Mary was doubtless just as happy.

After that, the obedient Joseph almost drops out of recorded history. Twelve years later comes a final glance at him in the role of a puzzled parent, wondering what had become of his prodigy-son during a trip to Jerusalem for the Passover festival. At the time, the almost-teenage Jesus was holding theological discussions with savants in the Temple, but he quickly returned with his parents to Nazareth and was obedient to them.

After giving Jesus a normal upbringing, Joseph started training him to be an apprentice carpenter, for later Jesus could even be called a "carpenter" as such. In a revealing passage in Mark's record, the Gali-leans, amazed at Jesus' teachings, asked, "Where did this man get all this? . . . Is not this the carpenter, the son of Mary?" (6:2–3). The apoc-ryphal *Gospel of Thomas* tells several charming stories of Jesus at work in the carpenter shop, miraculously extending the length of several beams that Joseph had not cut to the proper size.[3]

But after this, nothing more is heard of Joseph. At no time does he appear again during the three-year public ministry of Jesus, and the safest assumption is that he had died in the meantime. His wife, Mary, however, emerges at several important incidents in Jesus' career, including the Crucifixion, for which Joseph would certainly have been present had he been alive.

Another important, but overlooked, clue that Joseph did not live to see the culmination of Jesus' career comes from the Christmas record itself. When Joseph and Mary were presenting the infant Christ at the Temple, the aged Simeon turned only to Mary when he prophesied, "And a sword will pierce your own soul too," indicating that the sorrows of Calvary would affect Mary but not Joseph. Luke, who certainly wrote his Gospel after the death of Joseph, saw no reason to adjust that prediction but simply related it (2:35).

Again, however, tradition and legend have exuberantly sketched in the areas left blank by the New Testament. The *Protevangelium of James* and the *History of Joseph the Carpenter*, both apocryphal works of the second and fourth century respectively, portray Joseph as a widower with children when he became engaged to Mary, who was presumably only twelve years old at the time. Joseph himself worked in the timber yards of Galilee, according to these sources, and also made tabernacles along the Sea of Galilee. Supposedly, he died at the ripe old age of 111.[4] Needless to say, these traditions have little value.

Other Children?

But this does raise the question of whether or not Joseph and Mary had children after the birth of Jesus and were an otherwise normal family. The evidence is much disputed. Several passages in the New Testament seem to provide an obvious answer, for they do indeed mention brothers and sisters of Jesus. For example, here is the full reaction of the Galileans at the start of Jesus' public ministry: "Is not this the carpenter, the son of Mary and brother of James and Joses and Judas and Simon, and are not his sisters here with us?" (Mark 6:3). The identical listing is repeated in Matthew 13:55, with the exception of "Joseph" for "Joses." The names of

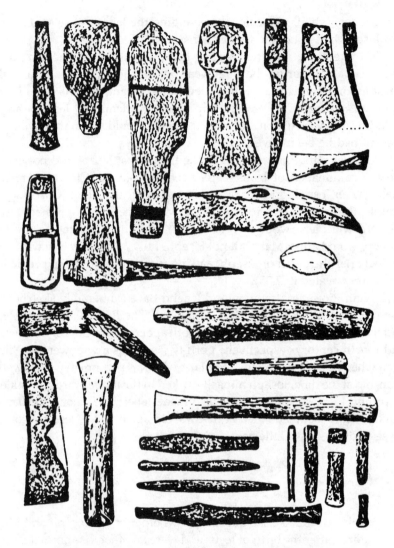

Israelite carpenter's tools, discovered in archaeological excavations at Gezer.

the sisters are not given anywhere in the New Testament, though the apocryphal *History of Joseph* calls them Anna and Lydia.[5]

The Protestant interpretation, generally, is to take the passages at face value and reply: Yes, Jesus did indeed have half-brothers and half-sisters, and these are their names, at least in the case of the men. Matthew's statement that Joseph engaged in no marital privileges with Mary "until she had borne a son" (1:25) is often cited to support this interpretation, as is Luke's assertion that she gave birth to "her *first*born son" (2:7).

At first these brothers were indifferent to, or critical of, Jesus (John 7:5), but after the Crucifixion, they became active Christians and leaders of the early church (*Acts* 1:14). James became the patriarch of the Christian church in Jerusalem, and Judas presumably wrote the *Letter of Jude* in the New Testament.

Nevertheless, Roman Catholicism, Eastern Orthodoxy, and some Protestants affirm the perpetual viriginity of Mary and identify the brothers and sisters either as children of Joseph by a prior marriage, or as Jesus' cousins, the children of Mary, wife of Alphaeus, who was the sister of the Virgin Mary. The term "brother" is usually used in the New Testament in the literal sense, but sometimes may indicate cousins, close relatives, and friends.

Christendom has lived very comfortably with either interpretation, even while theologians continue to debate the issue. The New Testament has the happy habit of being a little less than explicit in areas that do not pertain to the core of the faith.

11

Mary the Virgin

And Mary said, "My soul magnifies the Lord, and my
spirit rejoices in God my Savior, for he has looked with
favor on the lowliness of his servant." LUKE 1:46–48

WHETHER or not she had other children after Jesus, Mary
occupies a wholly unique place in the history of religion.
All three major branches of Christianity—Roman Catholicism, Protestantism, and Eastern Orthodoxy—agree with Mary's own prediction in
The Magnificat. Because of her extraordinary role in bearing Jesus, she
said, "from now on all generations will call me blessed" (Luke 1:48). And
they have done just that, in painting, carving, sculpture, hymnody, verse,
prose, prayer, and whatever other media can communicate human feeling.

It was a simple Galilean girl who made so apparently extravagant a
prediction. Critics may claim that the author of the Third Gospel put the
words into her mouth, but even if that were true the statement continues
to amaze, since these words were first written down in about 70 A.D., at
a time when the tiny Christian Church was undergoing what seemed a
bloody and terminal persecution. And yet Mary is recorded as saying
that all future generations would know of her role in the Christmas event,
which is exactly what happened in fact!

The little fifteen- or sixteen-year-old Jewess was called by an alternate
form of the name of Moses' sister Miriam. *Mary* meant, approximately,
"the Lord's beloved," and it was as common in Palestine at the time as it
is today. She was undoubtedly of Davidic descent, while a very early
tradition identifies her parents as Joachim and Anna.

This source, the *Protevangelium of James*, is an apocryphal work of the second century A.D. that was the first to sketch in so many of the details missing in the pre-Christmas story about Mary. It tells of the pious Joachim and Anna, who had been married for many years, but without any offspring—a humiliating sorrow for them both. The wealthy old couple prayed so ferverntly for a child that an angel finally announced to each separately that they would have a daughter.[1]

After Mary was born, so the *Protevangelium* continues, Joachim and Anna gratefully dedicated her when she was only three years old to a life of service at the Temple. Little Mary eagerly skipped up the fifteen steps at the gate of the Temple and, without so much as a backward glance at her parents, she remained there until she was twelve years old "like a dove that dwelt there, and she received food from the hand of an angel."[2]

Later, she and six other virgins were given the task of weaving a new scarlet and purple curtain for the Temple, and it was while she was engaged in this work that the angelic Annunciation took place. But when her pregnancy was discovered, Mary and her elderly protector-betrothed Joseph were brought before the high priest, protesting their innocence. Both were forced to undergo the water test for adultery, which would have caused a miscarriage according to Old Testament law (Num. 5:16ff.). But they passed the ordeal successfully.

Finally, the apocryphon has its own version of the events in Bethlehem. It tells of Joseph searching for a midwife while Mary took shelter in a cave. As the midwife approached the cavern with Joseph, a great cloud obscured it and then an intense light appeared. The clouds broke to reveal the newborn infant, nursing at Mary's breast.

These may be charming additions to the Christmas story, but are they reliable or historical? While so early a source as the second-century *Protevangelium* must command a good deal of respect, the document was proscribed as heretical by the very earliest papal *Index*, and its embellishments, however picturesque, are not accepted as authentic today.

The Sites in Nazareth

Sometimes archaeology can supply hard evidence in place of the flimsies of literary fantasy, and efforts have been made to locate Mary's childhood home in Nazareth, as well as the house she later shared with Joseph and Jesus. But the results are much disputed.

Mary's Well in Nazareth, a natural spring that has flowed for centuries and may well have been the place where Mary drew water for her household. Today it is sheltered inside the apse of the Greek Orthodox Church of St. Gabriel in Nazareth.

Today, to be sure, visitors are shown the Church of the Annunciation, the largest Christian sanctuary in the Near East, constructed over the rockhewn Grotto of the Annunciation, where Mary presumably lived and was greeted by the angel. Eloquent Latin words still identify the mystery of the Incarnation in metal lettering over the base of the altar erected there: "VERBUM CARO HIC FACTUM EST"—"Here the Word was Made Flesh."

Some distance north of the Church of the Annunciation stands the Church of St. Joseph, so named because it is commonly believed to shelter in its crypt Mary and Joseph's house and workshop, the place where Jesus spent his boyhood. And west of the church is a chapel supposedly built over the synagogue where Jesus gave his first public address in his home town (Luke 4:16ff.). Even the fountain or well where Mary drew her water

"Here the Word was made flesh"—the Latin lettering reads—in a crypt below the altar in the Church of the Annunciation in Nazareth.

has been marked by an adjacent chapel, the Church of St. Gabriel, where Eastern Orthodoxy believes the Annunciation took place. The *Protevangelium of James* has Mary accosted for the first time by the angel as she drew water here.[3]

But are these sites authentic? Unfortunately, the identifications are rather precarious because the task of locating the true sites has been severely complicated by the fact that Christian shrines were not erected here until well into the fourth century A.D., and they were later devastated by Muslim attacks. Since there is only one natural spring in Nazareth, however, the "Well of Mary" may be authentic, and water seems to have been drawn from it for two millennia and more. Today, Nazareth is the largest Christian city in Israel and also contains its largest Arab population.

Mary's Later Life

Unlike Joseph, Mary appears at several important episodes in her son's public ministry, and her various vignettes in the New Testament show a woman of much spiritual sensitivity, loyalty, and concern, even at times when she, like the disciples, did not seem to understand the fathomless depths of Jesus' mission. Yet even at the tragedy of Calvary she stood as the grieving but submissive model of all that was finest in Jewish motherhood, as Jesus commended her into the care of his disciple John.

After the New Testament accounts of Christ's death and resurrection, a new fulfillment brightened Mary's life as she finally plumbed the whole dimension of Jesus' renewed existence, and she was closely associated with the disciples in the founding of the Jerusalem church. From this point on, history breaks off, and various early traditions have Mary accompanying John to Asia Minor, or remaining in Judea. One record tells of her spending the rest of her days in Ephesus and finally dying there, while another legend has her death and assumption in Jerusalem, as witnessed by the apostles, who had been miraculously reassembled.[4]

Because of her absolutely unique role in bearing the man whom Christians call the Son of God, two thousand years of theology would further explore Mary's role, culminating in 1854, when Roman Catholicism officially defined her as both sinless and immaculately conceived, and in 1950, when it declared her bodily assumption into heaven. Protestants, however, deny these dogmas because of the lack of New Testament evidence.

The most familiar view of Mary, however, is the Mary of Christmas, rejoicing not only in the natural experience of motherhood but in reverent awe at the extraordinary son she had brought into the world. There would be sorrow ahead—not just the rigorous journey into Egypt but the future fact of Calvary. Yet, for the present, Mary would rejoice.

And she also had enough presence of mind to serve as historian for the exceptional event in the absence of any historians: "But Mary treasured all these words and pondered them in her heart" (Luke 2:19). This reflective attitude also characterizes Mary after the episode of the twelve-year-old Jesus in the Temple (Luke 2:51). According to earliest church tradition, it was Mary herself who told Matthew and Luke all about the Nativity, and it was they who wrote it down. And that is how we got the story of the first Christmas.

12

Jesus of Nazareth

*. . . They returned to Galilee, to their own town of
Nazareth. The child grew and became strong, filled with
wisdom; and the favor of God was upon him.* LUKE 2:39–40

T HE baby is what it was all about. If he had not grown up to
become the Jesus Christ of the New Testament, we would never
even have heard of the story of Christmas, despite its beauty, simplicity,
and wonder. But something began at the Nativity that has never ended.
The infant would change history, wrench the world's chronology so that
its years would pivot about his birth, and touch countries, cultures,
civilizations, and untold millions of lives.

Whenever those strange public-opinion polls are taken, asking "Who
is the most admired man in history?" Jesus of Nazareth has no trouble
vastly outdistancing Winston Churchill or Mohammed, the current favorite
runners-up. However the child of Christmas is regarded—Son of God or
merely a mortal man—there is no question that his life affected the future
more than that of any other human being who ever lived. For the Christianity that he founded has become the most successful single phenomenon in the history of the world: no other religion, philosophy, way of
life, nation, or cause has commanded the loyalties of over 1.75 billion
people—in the present generation alone—and none is so widespread.

The supreme paradox must be this: the person behind this achievement taught publicly for only three and one-half years. He wrote no book.
He had no powerful religious or political machine behind him—indeed,
the ranking spiritual and governmental authorities opposed him—and
yet he became the central figure in human history.

The Book about him now has several billion copies in print in a thousand languages, and yet no one even wrote his biography in our sense of the term, since the four accounts of him given in the Gospels offer detail only on the two extremities of his life: his birth and his last three years. Two of the Gospels are silent on his birth, and of the some thirty intervening years, we know next to nothing. The only reported episode happened when Joseph and Mary took the twelve-year-old Jesus along with them to Jerusalem for their annual Passover festival visit, but then lost him in the Holy City. Their astonishment at finding the lad sitting among the scholars in the Temple, amazing them by his intellectual expertise, is as familiar as the Nativity story itself.[1]

The Hidden Years

The Gospels were never intended as full biographies in the modern sense, but rather as records of Jesus' public ministry. They focus, then, not on the thirty "hidden years," as they are called, when he grew to manhood and prepared his mission, but on the all-important forty-two months after he came out of obscurity. Only then was he finally old enough to be listened to by his countrymen, who never really trusted anyone *under* thirty in matters religious.

But Jesus was also a human being—and humans love childhood stories—so, once again, the apocryphal gospels were only too happy to supply them. Several of the anecdotes are pleasant enough. When he was a three-year-old toddler, Jesus took a dried fish, put it in a basin of water, and ordered it to shed its salt and come back to life. The fish, of course, did just that, swimming happily about.[2] Several years later, Jesus was out playing with some neighborhood boys, and he made twelve model sparrows out of clay. When he clapped his hands, the birds came to life, and they flew away chirping.[3] Then there was the time two great snakes slithered out of a cave, sending his playmates running off screaming. But Jesus calmly ordered the creatures to prostrate themselves at Mary's feet, which they promptly did.

He had no trouble getting down from precarious perches. Once while he was playing on a roof in Nazareth—obviously Mary was not around at the time—Jesus simply grabbed onto a shaft of sunlight and slid down on it to the ground. Other stories tell of his healing people long before his teens, and even raising one of his chums, named Zeno, from the dead.

But the other apocryphal childhood tales are not so charming. In one of them, Jesus was acting like a precocious "brat" in school, not only rattling off the alphabet far in advance of his classmates, but proceeding to explain the architecture behind each letter. When the schoolmaster tried to slap him, he found his own hand withering instead.[4] In some of the stories, Jesus appears as an almighty urchin—a dangerous enough combination—with no control over his cruel and childish caprice. So one of his playmates, who accidentally hit Jesus in the shoulder, fell over dead when Jesus cursed him, and the parents of the stricken child begged Joseph to take Jesus away "or at least teach him to bless and not to curse." When Joseph reprimanded Jesus and twisted his ear, the lad warned, "I am not thine. Vex me not."[5]

Another playmate, who offended Jesus less, was merely changed into a ram. And vice versa: once, when Jesus rode a mule, the animal was released from some magical curse and turned back into a fine young man.

Needless to say, each of these puerile stories has as much validity as a fairy tale and as much substance as a fantasy. One wonders why medieval artists were so impressed with them as themes for their canvas and stained glass. The Fourth Gospel is clear in suggesting that Jesus' first miracle did not take place until he was an adult, at the Galilean marriage in Cana (John 2:11).

An Apprentice Carpenter

These may have become years of silence for subsequent ages, but they were normal enough for the child Jesus. Some missing pieces of the picture-puzzle of his youth can easily be carved to fit. His schooling, for example, was probably no different from that of the other village children in Nazareth. His first lessons, inevitably, came from Mary. But when he was about five, Jesus, like other Jewish children of the time, received much of his primary education at the synagogue, where he and the other pupils sat on the floor about the *hassan*, or teacher, repeating verses from the Torah until they knew them by heart. Jesus could read and write both Aramaic and Hebrew, and he undoubtedly knew common Greek as well, for he seems to have had no trouble conversing with the Syrophoenician woman or with Pontius Pilate. A few Latin words are sprinkled in his vocabulary as well.[6]

He also had to learn a trade of some kind, for it was a rule among the Jews that every man had to work with his hands, even those destined for a religious profession. "Whoever fails to teach his son a craft teaches him to steal" was a rabbinical maxim. The great Rabbi Hillel was a wood-cutter, the later apostle Paul of Tarsus a tentmaker, and Jesus of Nazareth a carpenter, like his foster father. In Jesus' case there was probably the added necessity of learning a craft to supplement the family's meager income.

The early church father Justin Martyr, born in Samaria around 100 A.D., wrote that Joseph and Jesus specialized in plows and yokes in their carpenter shop. They were of excellent durable quality, Justin claimed, and some of them were still in use in the mid-second century.[7]

Carpenters of the time also constructed beds, boxes, coffins, benches, stools, troughs, and threshing boards, as well as more elaborate projects like boats and houses. Though the first floors of nearly all homes in Nazareth would be cut out of the soft limestone of the hill in which the town is situated, or built of stone blocks, the upper stories of larger houses were made of wood. The bronze and iron tools the carpenters used have been found in excavations at Galilee and elsewhere, and some of them have a familiar, almost modern, design. Only the power tools, it seems, are missing. And wooden joints were mitered, mortised, or dovetailed in the same configurations learned in any high school shop classes today.

There were also specialist carpenters who did inlay work and even carved artificial teeth. Skilled carpentry was late in arriving in Palestine, for David had to import Tyrian carpenters to build his palace, and Solomon his temple, while Ezra had to bring in Phoenician craftsmen even to repair it.

Images at Maturity

One old tradition, the *History of Joseph the Carpenter*, has Jesus a nineteen-year-old when Joseph died. This is very possible. In that case, if Joseph had married between the ages of twenty-five and thirty, he would have died when he was nearly fifty, which was about the average life expectancy for the time, though many lived longer.

Jesus was now a man—a man who has been the subject of more books than any other person in history. But, apart from the many familiar accounts of his extraordinary ministry, what was he really like?

His physical appearance is not certain. Because of the famous Hebrew restriction against idolatry—"You shall not make for yourself a graven image, or any likeness of anything . . . " (Exod. 20:4, RSV)—art suffered among the Jews, and the earliest representations of Jesus are not Jewish but Roman. In the Christian catacombs, he is pictured as a beardless Roman youth tending sheep, though in fact he probably wore a trimmed beard in the style of his fellow Galileans.

The earliest bronze statue of Jesus could well have been authentic, for the church historian Eusebius himself saw it in the Gentile city of Caesarea Philippi near the base of Mt. Hermon. It was said to have been erected by the woman whom Jesus had healed of a chronic hemorrhage (Mark 5:25ff.), and it showed her resting on one knee in the position of a suppliant before the figure of Christ, who wore "a double cloak neatly draped over his shoulders with his hand stretched out to the woman." But this statue was destroyed by the emperor Julian "the Apostate."[8] Luke, a Gentile Greek, is supposed to have painted likenesses of Jesus, Peter, and Paul, but no trace of these has been found.

Jesus' physical appearance must have seemed very normal indeed— no towering figure, no nimbus, no halo. His enemies required the services of a Judas to point him out in the dusk of Jerusalem, Mary Magdalene mistook him for a gardener at the Easter tomb, and to the Emmaus disciples he looked like nothing more than a fellow traveler.

Yet he must have been an arresting figure of great intellect and much oratorical ability—persuasive, attractive, impressive. Crowds could listen to him for hours, since he spoke with authority. To his enemies, however, he appeared as a deceiver, a blasphemer, a false prophet. The response to Jesus, then, was hardly ever neutral. He captured the people or antagonized them.

He was no ascetic: he enjoyed a good time, provided party supplies on one famous occasion, and loved good friendships and people at every level, especially children. He was no legalist: if someone needed healing on the Sabbath, he simply healed. He was not intolerant: he ate with hated publicans and obvious sinners. Nor was Jesus the namby-pamby, soft-

Each Christmas, these bells in the tower of the Church of the Nativity at Bethlehem peal forth at midnight to announce the festival.

and-sweet sort of person conjured up in so much art: he had an athletic vigor that could enable him to stay up all night in prayer or singlehandedly drive the money changers out of the Temple with a whip. He was a man totally committed to his mission of announcing the kingdom of God and then dying to make it all possible.

Even though future ages would enthrone him as the greatest individual who ever lived and Christians accalim him as the God-man, Jesus always had a sensitivity for the past, and he was continually quoting the Old Testament. One very luminous part of that past he could never forget, since Mary must have told him the story again and again, as mothers will. And even Jesus must have marveled at it, because he was so human: the story of angels over Bethlehem . . . the story of adoring shepherds and humbled wise men . . . the story of the first Christmas.

The First Easter

PART II

13

Teaching and Healing

Jesus went throughout Galilee, teaching in their
synagogues and proclaiming the good news of the
kingdom and curing every disease and every sickness
among the people. So his fame spread . . . and
great crowds followed him.   MATTHEW 4:23–25

And they were filled with great awe and said to one
another, "Who then is this, that even the wind
and the sea obey him?"   MARK 4:41

"IF Jesus is so important, how come his very *name* doesn't show
up in any sources outside the New Testament in the century after
his death?"

Quite probably, this is the commonest taunt that Christianity encoun-
ters from those whose little knowledge is indeed "a dangerous thing."
The faithful often try to answer this challenge with a lame, "Well, the
Bible is enough. You've got to believe it"—a pathetic response to an inane
question.

In fact, Jesus' name *does* appear outside the New Testament in such
a time frame. The Roman authors Tacitus, Suetonius, and Pliny all refer
to Jesus in a manner that correlates with the biblical record, as do the
Jewish historian Josephus and the rabbinical traditions. The ultra-critical
claim in the last century that Jesus was an "invention" of the Church and
never lived even as a human being is rejected by all scholars today, except
for several isolated curiosities who can be counted on the fingers of one
hand.

This is not to say that we have enough data on Jesus to write his full biography in the modern sense. Aside from the "silent years," there are other source problems introduced by variations in the four Gospels. In the Nativity account, for example, Luke tells of the shepherds and a return to Nazareth after Christmas, while Matthew reports on the Magi and the Flight to Egypt. While these two versions can be harmonized, Jesus' famous cleansing of the Temple in Jerusalem is not so easily adjusted. John places this event early in Jesus' ministry (2:13ff.), whereas the other Gospels assign it to the end. Superimposing a chronological grid on Jesus' ministry, then, can be quite complicated.

In fact, many of the critical problems in discovering "the historical Jesus" would more easily be solved if we had but one Gospel consistent in itself rather than four. An early heretic, Marcion, seized on *Luke* alone for just this purpose. Wisely, however, the Church carefully preserved all four records. Not only was this the honest approach, but it also delivered the most data to future ages, and data are particularly crucial in the case of the extraordinary life reported in the New Testament. Nor should the Gospels be faulted for failing to constitute critical biographies in the modern sense, since *no* such biographies were ever written in the ancient world.

The fourfold traditions also provide the rich perspectives and view-points expressed in the New Testament. Although various scholars have argued that Matthew, or Mark, or Luke, or even John was the earliest Gospel, the current consensus assigns priority to Mark's brisk record—he loves the word *immediately*—and, reflecting Peter's memoirs, this evangel stresses more the extraordinary deeds than the teachings of Jesus. Both Luke and Matthew seem to have read Mark's record while forming their own, Luke aiming his Gospel principally to Gentiles, whereas Matthew's copious use of Old Testament prophecies he saw fulfilled in Jesus shows that he had a Jewish audience in mind.

Whereas the Gospels of Mathew, Mark, and Luke see Jesus' life within a similar framework and are thus called "synoptic," the Fourth Gospel introduces a dramatically different perspective in its philosophical beginning and the fresh material it unveils in Jesus' discourses. John's Gospel, probably the last to be written, also focuses on the Passion story in greatest detail.

For all their welcome variety, however, are the Gospels historically reliable? Not at all, the so-called higher critics argued. Their ultimate spokesman proved to be one of the most influential New Testament scholars of this century, Rudolf Bultmann, who claimed, in a famous passage:

> I do indeed think that we can now know almost nothing concerning the life and personality of Jesus, since the early Christian sources show no interest in either, are moreover fragmentary and often legendary; and other sources about Jesus do not exist.[1]

Such skepticism, however, has been drastically undermined in the years since 1926, when the above comment was first published, and almost every phrase has been disproven in the decades since, particularly through archaeological and historical research. Much closer to the mark is Princeton Professor James H. Charlesworth's observation in 1988 that we now know more about Jesus "than about almost any other Palestinian Jew before 70 C.E. [A.D.]"[2] Whereas Bultmann disdained even to visit Palestine and, like so many of his German colleagues (until recently), ignored the results of archaeology, Charlesworth and many others have visited, dug, and deciphered.

Jesus' Public Ministry

It was an astounding event that Sabbath day when the widow Mary's son stood up in the Nazareth synagogue to read from the scroll of the prophet Isaiah. Yeshua (later hellenized to "Jesus") was a little over thirty years old, this carpenter who not long before had submitted to a sacred washing called baptism at the hands of his cousin John. Jesus had survived a lonely spiritual contest with Evil in the desert, but now prepared to go public with the words of his favorite prophet:

> The Spirit of the Lord is upon me, because he has anointed me to
>   preach good news to the poor.
> He has sent me to proclaim release to the captives and recovery of
>   sight to the blind, to let the oppressed go free, to proclaim the year
>   of the Lord's favor. (Luke 4:18)

Jesus closed the scroll, handed it back to the attendant, and then declared, in syllables stupendous with significance, *"Today this scripture has been fulfilled in your hearing."*

The worshipers were awestruck: only the Messiah could make such a claim! It was an appropriate beginning for Jesus' ministry, since the rest of it would only enlarge on that statement in word and deed. His family was shocked, particularly his four half-brothers and two half-sisters, who even debated his sanity. Only later, after the resurrection, would they fully convert to his cause.

He became an itinerant rabbi, teaching publicly in the synagogues of Galilee or privately in the homes of friends, in the natural theaters provided by hillsides or on the grasses of the plain. Once he even embarked on a boat to avoid pressure from crowds lining the shore of the Sea of Galilee. He spoke with unparalleled eloquence and authority, and his invitation to discipleship proved irresistible to eleven Galileans and one Judean named Judas, as well as to a wider circle of some seventy members. Women were also prominent among his followers, and some of them provided financial support for his ministry.

The crowds that heard Jesus were divided. Some rejected his message outright, usually those with vested interests in the religious and political status quo or the socioeconomic establishment. Others, probably a majority, were deeply impressed with his teachings, and even more so with the signs or miracles that accompanied them. Reports about his granting hearing to the deaf, sight to the blind, locomotion to cripples, or health to the diseased swept the land, and crowds soon followed him at every turn. He dined with the wealthy or broke bread with the poor. His words resonated with fishermen and tax collectors alike, high officials in government or lepers in hovels, those with open minds and those possessed.

Travels took him from the shores of the Sea of Galilee to the coasts of the Mediterranean and the borders of Lebanon. Some Jewish festivals he celebrated in Jerusalem, necessitating trips through the somewhat alien countryside of Samaria on one trek, the valley of the Jordan through Jericho on another. At the northerly city of Caesarea Philippi he heard Peter, his prime disciple, confess that he was "the Messiah [Christ], the Son of the living God," but at the southerly city of Jerusalem he would hear this statement labeled as sheer blasphemy.

His Message

Jesus taught the fatherhood of God in a manner that accentuated both the strict demands of the God of the Old Testament—the Sermon on the Mount, for example—yet also his forgiving tenderness. In calling God his father, Jesus asserted not only the common relationship between Creator and creature, but claimed divine Sonship in a special sense. His mission was to announce the oncoming "kingdom of God" implemented by his ministry, by which he meant not God's realm but rather his rule in the lives of people, who were to repent and believe the glad news that God had indeed loved the world so much as to send his only Son—Jesus— to atone for the sins of humanity and to save the race. This divine affection was to be reflected, on the human level, in a relationship of love and concern among people, a love strong enough to extend even to enemies. Such a faith, active in love, would equip his followers not only for this life but for that which was to come.

Jesus used both parables and discourses to convey this message. The parables were illustrative stories, with plot and symbolic characters running parallel to the lessons he wished to communicate. A familiar example is the Prodigal Son as an analogy to sinners who receive pardon at the hands of God as the forgiving Father (Luke 15). Many of Jesus' parables begin with the words, "The kingdom of God is like . . . ," and the parallel, from practical, everyday situations, usually made ready sense to his hearers, though not in every instance.

His discourses, public (as in the Sermon on the Mount) or private (as in the Upper Room on Maundy Thursday), aimed to liberate his hearers from some of the unnecessary stringencies of those rabbinic traditions that, in "building a fence about the law," had gone beyond the Torah and too heavily encumbered people with restrictions. His statement "The sabbath was made for man, not man for the sabbath" (Mark 2:27, RSV) illustrates the new freedom he proclaimed. Jesus also alerted his hearers to the crucial future dimensions of existence, when God's reign would be perfected in their lives through the resurrection of the dead and the life "everlasting."

His Miracles

Only the most credulous of Jesus' hearers would have credited cosmic claims like these had it not been for the extraordinary phenomena accompanying his message, namely, the miracles. The Greek of the New Testament styles these astonishing deeds variously as *terata* (wonders), *dynamis* (power), *erga* (works), and especially *semeia* (signs).

The miracles fell into four categories. Over half were therapeutic—healings of vast numbers of diseased or handicapped men, women, and children. The Gospels give well over a score of specific examples, and then let these represent the rest. Another form of these "signs" was exorcism and the psychological healing of those possessed. Four instances of raising the dead comprise the third category, and the physical, or "nature" miracles the fourth, as when Jesus stilled a storm on the Sea of Galilee, walked on its waters, or delivered a desert lunch to five thousand hungry hearers from only five loaves and two fish.

Spectacular and faith-compelling though the miracles may have seemed at the time, the modern is entitled to ask, "But did they really happen?" History and archaeology are unable to *prove* the miraculous, of course (although they come close in one instance reported in Chapter 15). David Hume's *Essay on Miracles* is usually quoted by skeptics at this point, in which the Scottish philosopher rules out miracles on the basis of natural law that cannot be violated—a view shared in one way or another by all who deny the miraculous. While certainly valid in terms of the natural sciences, Hume's skepticism overlooks *the* quintessential issue, namely: the *only* way that the supernatural dimension, if such exists, could ever demonstrate itself in the natural realm would be, in fact, by intrusion into natural law.

Jesus' miracles always served a specific purpose: they were never performed in order to astound or mystify or entertain, but to help. Jesus was no magician. Current attempts to compare him to other presumed wonder-working Galileans of that day—Honi the Circle-Drawer or Hanina ben Dosa—founder on the overwhelmingly superior quality and quantity of documentation on Jesus.

Archaeological Aids

Jesus moved about in a real world. Almost all the sites named in his travels have been identified today, and some have been excavated. More will be. The opening scene in his public ministry at the Nazareth synagogue, for example, has been doubted by some critics because no first-century synagogues had been discovered in Israel. Now three have been found, with evidence for a fourth.

A fifth could well be the site of the very synagogue that Jesus attended while in Capernaum, the fishing-industry town beautifully situated on the northwestern shore of the Sea of Galilee. Jesus moved here from Nazareth, and it was here that he called his first disciples and based his ministry of teaching and healing. The imposing, columned remains of the synagogue visible at Capernaum today date no earlier than the third century A.D., but this structure was erected over a prior base of the first-century synagogue familiar to Jesus. Some of its black basalt stones have been excavated.[3]

South of the synagogue and nearer the lakeshore stand the newly excavated ruins of the "House of St. Peter." One is surely prone to greet any such "sensational" identification with a massive dose of skepticism, the prevailing mood of most scholars a few years ago. Now it is the scholars themselves who are arguing for its authenticity! While final proof is necessarily lacking, we may consider the evidence. The basal remains of a fifth-century octagonal church were first exposed at this location, an important clue that this was a long-venerated sacred site: the church that Constantine had erected over the Grotto of the Nativity at Bethlehem was octagonal. Under the center of this structure a first-century *house* was discovered, doubtless the very place the pilgrim nun Egeria identified as Peter's house (c. 382 A.D.) and the locus of early Christian worship. Beneath the crushed limestone floor, fishhooks were found, and the walls of the house are etched with a boat, crosses, and a host of Aramaic, Hebrew, Greek, Syriac, and Latin graffiti from other second- and third-century pilgrims who visited the place. A spacious central room apparently had been converted for some larger use during the first century A.D., since the walls of the place were plastered—the only plaster discovered at Capernaum to date. No general household pottery has been found in this large room, so the sum of the evidence points strongly to *the* earliest Christian house-church ever discovered, and, in view of its location, quite probably Peter's house.[4]

If so, this is also the place where Jesus stayed while in Capernaum, and is the scene of his healing the paralytic whose stretcher had to be lowered into the house through a hole fashioned in the roof when the crowd prevented normal access (Matt. 9, Mark 2, Luke 5). Incidentally, that cure caused no great damage to the roof. The walls of the excavated house are too weak to support tiles, so the roof was likely fashioned out of branches, palm leaves, and caked mud that could easily be replaced.

Air view of the excavations at Capernaum along the Sea of Galilee (bottom). The synagogue stands at the upper end of the exposed ruins in the center of the enclave, and Peter's house inside the octagonal structure at the lower end.

Has a *boat* belonging to Simon Peter been found also—one in which Jesus sailed? Hardly. And yet, a wooden hull, dated by its construction and carbon-14 to 40 B.C. (plus or minus eighty years) was discovered in 1986 on the shores of the Sea of Galilee near Kibbutz Ginnosar, about four miles southwest of Capernaum. A severe drought had lowered the level of the lake that year, exposing sections of sea bottom that were usually covered with water. The oval outline of a buried boat appeared, and extremely careful marine archaeology liberated the craft from its muddy tomb.

The boat is 26.5 feet long, 7.5 feet wide, and 4.5 feet high, with a rounded stern. Originally, the craft had a mast block and a mast, so it could be sailed or rowed, probably with two rowers on each side. The boat was probably used for fishing but could also have provided transportation for passengers and freight. The capacity of the boat was about fifteen men, Galilean males of that era averaging only 140 pounds in weight and 5.5 feet in height. Jesus and all twelve disciples, then, could have fit inside such a ship, and *could* even have sailed in this one, though any proof for that is lacking, of course.[5]

This find, however, helps clarify the famous episode of the Tempest, in which Mark reports Jesus "in the stern, asleep on the cushion" (4:37). To haul in the large draft of fish recorded on another occasion, the disciples probably used seine nets that had to be tended from a rounded stern platform, missing from this boat only because the upper strakes and gunwales are missing also. While the helmsman stood on this exposed platform, the most sheltered area of the boat would be immediately *under* the platform, and it was here that Jesus slept "on the cushion." Use of the direct article in this phrase—*the* cushion—indicates that it was part of the boat's regular equipment and most probably was a sandbag used for ballast or balance that was stowed in the stern when the boat was not under sail.

Other examples of how archaeology is parting the curtains of the biblical past will be presented subsequently. Such material, tangible, tactile contacts with antiquity help us recover the world of Jesus in the hard dimension of reality. The Gospel accounts are not set in some never-never land. This is especially true of their more detailed coverage of the culmination of Jesus' ministry.

14

Up to Jerusalem

> The great crowd that had come to the festival heard that
> Jesus was coming to Jerusalem. So they took branches of
> palm trees and went out to meet him, shouting, "Hosanna!
> Blessed is the one who comes in the name of the Lord—
> the King of Israel!"   JOHN 12:12–13

I T was, quite literally, "the week that changed the world." A later age would call it Holy Week and bestow names like Palm Sunday, Good Friday, and Easter on its days. But, soon after it happened, the crucial character of Jesus' final visit to Jerusalem was realized. Three of the Gospels devote a full third of their content to reporting on this week, while the Fourth dedicates its entire last half.[1]

And rippling across the rest of these records is a sense of inevitability about this life: Jesus of Nazareth was a man born to die—not merely in the normal sense, but with some special significance—an overtone, a leitmotiv that begins in the Christmas story and recurs throughout the three and one-half years of his public ministry.

Sometimes it was only a veiled hint. On other occasions, Jesus spelled it out directly, like the time he gathered his disciples together and announced their Passover plans: "See, we are going up to Jerusalem, and everything that is written about the Son of Man by the prophets will be accomplished. For he will be handed over to the Gentiles; and he will be mocked and insulted and spat upon. After they have flogged him, they will kill him, and on the third day he will rise again" (Luke 18:31–33).

As at other times, the disciples greeted this statement with a collective sag of the jaw. They simply could not grasp the Teacher's intent, and the

106

positive note on which Jesus' statement ended was merely obscured by the almost suicidal nature of the rest of it.

The Unteachable Twelve

The even dozen who followed Jesus from his earliest public ministry in Galilee seemed to have one thing in common despite their varied backgrounds: a reliable dullness that hardly ever failed to misinterpret Jesus' message and that usually asked him the naïve question at the wrong time. Occasionally the disciples even interfered with his mission, blocking children from access to him, or trying to dissuade him from his course. If Socrates chose a Plato as disciple, and Plato an Aristotle, might Jesus of Nazareth not have been a shade more selective in his choice of followers?

Perhaps it was just as well that he chose as he did. The Twelve represent all of inquiring humanity, not just the sages, and their reactions—however plodding or puzzled—are our own. Particularly their very human emotions of fear or wonder, sorrow or elation at various times in Jesus' ministry add a convincing touch to the New Testament records. Were the disciples, then, really dolts? Not unless mankind itself is doltish. And after the overpowering experience of the first Easter, something transformed these men into brilliant and courageous apostles of the new faith, a change so dramatic that it must be dealt with later in these pages.

Biographies of the Twelve are hardly possible. There were two pairs of brothers who were fishermen: Peter and Andrew, James and John. A government official named Matthew was a tax collector, while, quite oppositely, another disciple, named Simon, had probably been active *against* the government in the Zealot movement, though there is no indication that he continued these activities as a disciple. All were Galileans except for Judas Iscariot, the later traitor, who was probably from Judea. The empirical Thomas, who had a skeptic's mind—or was it a scientist's?— had a twin brother who has vanished from history. Philip has a few lines in the Gospels, but the other disciples are as transparent as the breezes of Galilee: Bartholomew, James Ben-Alphaeus, and Thaddaeus.[2]

Whatever they may have thought of Jesus' announced Passover plans, there was no thought of opposing them once the Teacher had "set his face to go to Jerusalem," as Luke puts it (9:51). Probably Jesus was only speaking in riddles again or in metaphor, they reasoned, an old habit of his. They had all been to Jerusalem before and he returned safely to Galilee. So it would be again.

A Base at Bethany

Their eighty-mile journey south took them via the Jordan valley to sunny Jericho, the last halting station for pilgrims from the north country who traveled to Jerusalem for the great Jewish festivals. Here Jesus had his famous appointments with dwarfish, tree-climbing Zacchaeus, the overeager tax collector, and a blind beggar named Bartimaeus. The New Testament reports both of them cured—in their separate fashions. And so the week that altered history had a rather ordinary prelude, typical of other days in Jesus' career.

Since Jericho lay 825 feet *below* sea level near the Dead Sea, while Jerusalem was perched on the hilly backbone of Palestine some 2,500 feet above sea level, Jesus' statement about going *"up* to Jerusalem" was quite literally true. The final leg of their journey was a dusty trek that twisted its way upward through barren hills and ravines in the Judean badlands surrounding the Holy City. Usually the roadway was desolate enough to attract highway robbers, and it was no accident that Jesus had chosen exactly this setting for his parable about the Good Samaritan. But now it was becoming choked with crowds of Passover pilgrims who were singing the traditional "songs of ascent" as they trudged upward toward Jerusalem behind their snorting and smelly beasts of burden.

Jesus and the disciples were aiming for one of the eastern suburbs of Jerusalem, a town called Bethany, which would serve as their lodging place and base of operations for the coming week. There were several important reasons for staying here rather than in the capital. For one thing, finding accommodations in the Holy City would have been next to impossible. Jerusalem, which normally had a population of some 50,000 was at least tripling in size because of the vast influx of pilgrims celebrating the Passover, and the city was ringed with tents. Then, too, Jesus, who was popular with the crowds, was quite vulnerable apart from them, and his adversaries might have come by night to arrest him earlier than they did, had they been able to locate his place of lodging inside Jerusalem.

The Teacher also had friends living in Bethany, very intimate friends. The sisters Mary and Martha, along with their brother Lazarus, had played host to Jesus and his entourage several times earlier, and this is the one spot in Judea where he could truly relax. A short time earlier, Jesus had even worked the ultimate sign on Lazarus, according to the Fourth Gospel, raising him from the dead after four days' entombment.

Since Bethany lay just on the other side of the Mount of Olives from Jerusalem, the still-fresh news of this event had a direct and double effect on the events of Holy Week. Those who believed that Jesus had truly raised Lazarus planned a delirious welcome for him in Jerusalem. But those who thought Jesus a sorcerer or imposter quickly set into high gear their plans to capture him, lest the pseudo-Messiah attract too large a following and compel Roman intervention.

While news of Jesus' approach was going from mouth to mouth in Jerusalem, he himself spent one of his last happy nights in Bethany at a dinner party given by his friends.[3] The scene of Mary anointing the feet of Jesus after supper and wiping them with her hair is familiar enough, particularly because of Judas Iscariot's grumbling reaction: "Why was this perfume not sold for three hundred denarii and the money given to the poor?" (John 12:5).

"To poor Judas" may have been more appropriate, since, as treasurer of the Twelve, he regularly pilfered from the group purse and was not at all concerned about the poor. In reprimanding Judas for his misplaced charity, Jesus closed with an amazing statement: "Truly, I tell you, wherever the good news is proclaimed in the whole world, what she has done will be told in remembrance of her" (Mark 14:9). To suggest that news of the event would ever extend this far would seem presumptuous, whether Jesus himself said it or, as some critics claim, Mark put the words into his mouth. But about a century ago, with the full missionary expansion of Christianity, this prophecy was quite literally fulfilled.

A Royal Reception

Early Sunday morning, Jesus made his baldly public entry into Jerusalem. It was the end of all privacy and safety, and the beginning of what would be an inevitable collision course with the priestly and political authorities in the land. His irrevocable step was taken deliberately, with every consideration for the consequences, for otherwise he might simply

Palm Sunday procession entering the Via Dolorosa in Jerusalem.

have slipped unceremoniously into the city along with the thousands of Passover pilgrims.

The word was out. Crowds had started gathering even in Bethany for a glimpse of the rabbi from Galilee as well as of the Lazarus whom he had revived. In the neighboring hamlet of Bethphage, a donkey was waiting to transport Jesus, according to his own specifications. And then the triumphal procession began, accompanied by shouting and singing from the throngs of people lining the roadsides. They threw down their garments on the pathway to cushion his ride—an Oriental custom still observed on occasions—as well as palm fronds, the symbol of triumph, paving his way with nature's green.

"Hosanna to the Son of David! Blessed is he who comes in the name of the Lord! Hosanna in the Highest!" The exultant shouts accompanied Jesus along the entire route down the Mount of Olives, which is still used each Palm Sunday by a procession of Christians carrying palm branches. Just skirting the Garden of Gethsemane, Jesus and his entourage finally crossed the Brook Kidron and entered Jerusalem, probably via the Golden Gate, the northeastern portal of the Temple enclave, which has since been walled up.

What did it all mean? Had Jesus perhaps arranged for the donkey because he was tired? Hardly. It was morning, and on other occasions he was a tireless walker. It was a gesture of humility, many have suggested, for the ass was the common beast of burden of the time, in contrast to the superior horse or gilded chariot used in Roman triumphs.

If so, the gesture quickly conferred a quite opposite flavor to the occasion. The prophet Zechariah had foretold the arrival of the Messianic King in Jerusalem via this humble conveyance (9:9), and here the crowd was according a wildly triumphant reception to one whom they hailed as "the son of David," a loaded name used at a loaded place, for many Jews expected the Messiah figure to be declared as king on that very Mount of Olives.

The priestly establishment in Jerusalem witnessed the procession also, catching and perhaps enlarging on any political overtones in the demonstration. Might not the waving of palm branches be symbolic, since the palm was the national emblem of an independent Palestine? These were Jewish flags! What if Jesus should actually claim to be heir of King David in a restored Judean monarchy? After all, the multitude was lavishing such dizzying phrases on him as "the King of Israel."

Caiaphas, the high priest, must have cast a worried glance westward in the direction of Herod's palace, where the Roman governor, Pontius Pilate, had just arrived to be on hand for the Passover in case any demonstration—*such as this one*—might get out of hand. He must also have marveled at the brazen effrontery of the rabbi from Galilee: the very man for whom arrest notices had been posted across the land was coming directly into Jerusalem in the most obvious manner possible.

Joseph Caiaphas will play a major role as "the Passion story" unfolds, but it may be important to emphasize again that this is history, not simply story. Lest the biblical account be deemed a saga involving legendary characters rather than authentic personalities, the recent discovery of what are doubtless the very bones of Joseph Caiaphas demonstrates otherwise.

In November, 1990, workers constructing a water park on a slope south of the Old City of Jerusalem accidently uncovered a burial cave with twelve ossuaries inside. These limestone bone chests were used primarily in the first century A.D., and one of them, magnificently carved, bore the name in Aramaic *Yehosef bar Qayafa,* "Joseph, son of Caiaphas." Among the bones inside were those of a sixty-year-old man. In view of the time frame and the lavish decoration on this ossuary, there is the probability that these are the very bones of the high priest of the Gospels—*the first remains of a biblical personality ever discovered.**

The newly discovered limestone ossuary inscribed with the name of Joseph Caiaphas. The two great circles of this extravagant carving include five whorl rosettes surrounding a center rosette, all carefully bordered with superb craftsmanship.

*For further information, see Zvi Greenhut, "Burial Cave of the Caiaphas Family," and Ronny Reich, "Caiphas Name Inscribed on Bone Boxes," *Biblical Archaeology Review,* 18 (September/October 1992), 28–44.

15

Intrigue and Conspiracy

"It is better for you to have one man die for the people
than to have the whole nation destroyed." . . . So from that
day on they planned to put him to death.   JOHN 11:50–53

ACCORDING to the usual story of Holy Week, the high priests,
Pharisees, Sadducees, Herodians, scribes, and other opponents of Jesus suddenly decided to seize the opportunity of arresting him
now that he had been foolhardy enough to show up in Jerusalem, and
they began plotting in earnest. This is incorrect. The conspiracy against
Jesus had been building for at least three years, and the sources record
seven instances of official plotting against him, two efforts at arrest, and
three assassination attempts before the events of Holy week.[1]

A formal decision to arrest Jesus had in fact been made several months
earlier, probably at a secret session of the Sanhedrin, the great Judean
senate. Jerusalem had been rocking with news that Jesus had supposedly
raised Lazarus of Bethany from the dead, and people were feverish with
excitement over the fact that Jesus was performing exactly the great signs
expected of the Messiah, that religio-political figure who, in the popular
interpretation, was to deliver the land from foreign domination.

"So if Jesus is allowed to continue performing his signs, however he
does them," opined one Sanhedrist, "he will win over our entire population, and then the Romans will come and destroy our Temple and our
nation."

It was the high priest, Joseph Caiaphas, who quickly raised his hands
to silence the growing hubbub that followed this comment, and now he
skewered the mood of alarm with pontifical authority: "You do not understand, my brothers, that it is better for you to have one man die for the

people than to have the whole nation destroyed." For the public safety, the sacrifice of a single troublemaker was not too high a price to pay.

The Fourth Gospel concludes this crucial scene with a revealing statement: "Now the chief priests and the Pharisees had given orders that anyone who knew where Jesus was should let them know, so that they might arrest him" (11:57).

We may, in fact, have some idea of how the arrest notice read. A rabbinical tradition recorded in the Talmud spells out the indictment against Yeshu Hannozri (Hebrew for "Jesus the Nazarene"). Combined with the New Testament evidence, the notice can be reconstructed as follows:

WANTED: YESHU HANNOZRI

He shall be stoned because he has practiced sorcery and enticed Israel to apostasy. Anyone who can say anything in his favor, let him come forward and plead on his behalf. Anyone who knows where he is, let him declare it to the Great Sanhedrin in Jerusalem.[2]

The reference to "stoning" rather than crucifixion is very credible. Jesus had not yet been arrested, and had he been seized anywhere or anytime that Romans were *not* present, he would likely have been terminated by stoning if deemed guilty. (This was the fate of the martyr Stephen, as recorded in Acts 7.) And the mention of "sorcery" is quite remarkable. By definition, sorcery is something extraordinary or supernatural accomplished with help "from below." A miracle is the same, though achieved with help "from above." This admission in a hostile source, then, very nearly becomes outside evidence for the miraculous.

According to legal custom at the time, a court crier had to announce publicly or post such an official handbill in the larger towns of Judea about forty days prior to a trial. Small wonder that there was some debate over whether Jesus would dare to appear in Jerusalem for the next Passover. But the discussion ended abruptly on Palm Sunday.

As the Passion story has been retold through the centuries, the picture has become more and more "contrasty" in the telling. Jesus and the disciples are the gleaming protagonists marching resignedly into the jaws of mortal danger, while their opponents are painted in progressively ugly hues: Pilate is a muddy russet (due to admixture of coward's yellow),

Caiaphas is murky sepia, and Judas is Devil's black. But where are the grays and medium tones that certainly existed among the enemies of Jesus?

They opposed him for various reasons, and some, it must be admitted, were acting in good faith. The high priest Caiaphas was a worldly-wise Sadducee whose overriding policy was to maintain the uneasy compromise between Jewish and Roman authority in Palestine. Now in his fifteenth year as high priest, Caiaphas, like any Jew, would have preferred an independent Judea controlled by God and his vicegerents, the priestly establishment, but he had the political sense to realize that Rome's was not a passing power in the eastern Mediterranean, and the road to success lay in continuing cooperation with the Empire and its representative, Pontius Pilate.

Because a dozen uprisings had shaken Palestine since Pompey first conquered the land in 63 B.C.—most of these revolts had been subdued by Roman force—another messianic rebellion under Jesus of Nazareth would only shatter the precarious balance of authority and, bleeding Rome's patience dry, might lead to direct occupation by Roman legions. For *political* reasons, therefore, Jesus would have to be dealt with.

There were, of course, important *religious* reasons as well: people were hailing the Teacher from Galilee as something more than a man, and Jesus was not blunting this blasphemous adulation. The wonders he supposedly performed to mislead the multitudes were either hoaxes, they reasoned, or of demonic origin.

Many of his opponents also had corrosive *personal* reasons for hating the Nazarene: the Pharisees and Sadducees in particular had been bested by Jesus in public debate and then been called such epithets as "whitewashed tombs," "vipers," and "devourers of widows' houses." Rankling with humiliation, they only too happily conspired with the scribes, elders, and chief priests.

A Monday Housecleaning

And finally, now, there were even *economic* motives for opposing Jesus. The great, gleaming Temple in Jerusalem, King Herod's one great favor to the city, was Jesus' most tangible connection with the Old Testament and his own past. Here he had been presented as a baby and

A reconstruction of the great Temple, in the model of ancient Jerusalem designed by Prof. M. Avi-Yonah at the Holyland Hotel in Jerusalem.

redeemed by Joseph and Mary. Here, too, he had displayed dazzling brilliance as a twelve-year-old prodigy, and just now the Temple enclave was in the final stages of completion.

Despite the terrible, repeated destructions of Jerusalem over the centuries since that time, great blocks of Herodian masonry—original stones from Jesus' day—are *still* supporting the vast Temple platform at the southeast and southwest corners, on which the Muslim Dome of the Rock now stands. The blocks are instantly recognizable because they are not only enormous, but handsomely dressed with flat, raised faces and sunken margins about six inches wide. The disciples thought even Jesus should have been impressed. Said one of them, "Look, Teacher! What massive stones! What magnificent buildings!" (Mark 13:1, NIV).

But what impressed Jesus was the commercialization taking place inside the Temple. Some of it was inevitable. The half-shekel contributions to the Temple required conversion from foreign currency, so there were various banking and money-changing tables in the outer courts of the Temple to accommodate worshipers. And who would prefer dragging a lamb down from Galilee for the Passover sacrifice when one could be purchased more conveniently from livestock dealers at the Temple? There were also stalls with caged pigeons for those who could afford only the minimum sacrifice, and a hodgepodge of tourist shops and sidewalk merchants also infested the premises, as in today's Jerusalem.

Yet this profiting on holy ground infuriated Jesus. The boisterous haggling, the clinking of coins, the groaning and bleating from oxen and sheep, to say nothing of the endless clucking of the doves, was, if anything, distracting from the solemnity of worship, quite apart from the inevitable stench. Jesus made a whip out of cords and lashed away at the dealers and their livestock, probably causing an animal stampede out of the Temple courts. Then he overturned the tables of the money changers with the famous cry, "It is written, 'My house shall be called a house of prayer'; but you are making it a den of robbers" (Matt. 21:13).

Easily one of the most graphic pictures of Holy Week, Jesus' cleansing of the Temple is also one of the more controversial. Scholars have divided themselves into three camps on this episode. Some insist the entire scene is mythical and could never have happened, since the many Temple police in the precincts would quickly have dealt with so obvious a troublemaker. Yet, by the time the guards arrived in any force, the whole affair was a *fait accompli*, and they would not have dared apprehend Jesus at the time

The southeastern corner of the Temple platform in Jerusalem, showing great blocks of Herodian masonry nearly to the top. The walls continue underground in a vast substructure 24 meters below the present surface.

because of his popularity with the thousands of Passover pilgrims, who were likely cheering him on from the sidelines.

Critics have also objected that such larger animals as sheep and oxen would never have been permitted in the Temple area. Recent excavations at the Hulda Gates in the southern perimeter of the Temple, however, have reaffirmed the historicity of this episode. The immense stone stairways uncovered here constituted one of the main entrances to the Temple, and the money changers were likely stationed just inside the Hulda Gates on the lower level of the spectacularly columned *Hanuyot*, or Royal Portico, which Herod the Great had erected along the entire southern edge of the Temple precincts. The money changers also had access via newly discovered passageways to "Solomon's Stables," a vast series of Herodian animal stalls beneath the present Temple platform.[3]

Other writers find in this violent cleansing the act of a Zealot and would make Jesus a member of that revolutionary political resistance movement. But flailing away at merchants, money changers, and animals, rather than at Roman auxiliaries, was a pathetic way to start a rebellion. And so the balance of scholars conclude that this was an isolated act of Jesus that happened more or less as described in the New Testament, which certainly seems that most logical conclusion.

The Verbal Snares

News of this scene cut the priestly establishment to the quick. What might well be called "Annas, Caiaphas, and Co." controlled all concessions on the Temple premises, and, while one day's loss was not that significant, Jesus was setting a precedent that might well rouse the rabble to future assaults on the Temple and disrupt worship and sacrifice. He would have to be dealt with—immediately.

But how? Arresting him by daylight was not feasible because of his obvious popularity with the throng of pilgrims. Insulated by them, Jesus was even showing up at the Temple on a daily basis, teaching crowds that seemed to hang on his every word. But precisely here he might be vulnerable, the authorities surmised. If he could be publicly tripped up in his words or defeated in argument—that is, proved to be a false prophet— then his popular support would vanish.

This was the reasoning behind the astonishing confrontations in the Temple between Jesus and emissaries from the Pharisees and the Saddu-cean aristocracy on Monday, Tuesday, and Wednesday of Holy Week. They might almost be called "Jesus' final press conferences," for he had to field a withering fusillade of questions from bright minds that, however, were aiming not for news so much as to discredit what they thought to be a pseudo-prophet.

Yet Jesus parried each challenge with devastating success. Questions about his own authority to teach, and teasers on multiple remarriage and the greatest commandment of the law were answered to the embarrass-ment of the interrogators. The most loaded query of all, certainly, was this: "Tell us, Teacher, is it lawful to pay taxes to Caesar, or not?"

It was a cruel alternative. A *yes* would have prevented any trouble with the political authorities but reduced Jesus in the popular mind to a Rome-serving lackey. A *no* would have pleased the crowd, but word of Jesus' treason would have been reported immediately to Pontius Pilate.

Like the best of teachers, Jesus was not above using visual aids. Calling for a coin, he asked whose image and inscription it bore. At the expected answer he merely replied, "Render therefore to Caesar the things that are Caesar's, and to God the things that are God's" (Matt. 22:21, RSV).

Prizes for everyone! Rome could hardly find the remark seditious, while the Jews knew the statement meant not 50 percent to God but more like 99 percent, since the human being belonged to God as his creation.

The attempts to humiliate Jesus before the multitudes had failed. His opponents would now have to use other means.

16

A Last Supper

Judas, who betrayed him, said, "Surely not I, Rabbi?"
He replied, "You have said so."
While they were eating, Jesus took a loaf of bread, and
after blessing it he broke it, gave it to the disciples, and
said, "Take, eat; this is my body." Then he took a cup, and
after giving thanks he gave it to them, saying,
"Drink from it, all of you; for this is my blood. . . . "
MATTHEW 26:25–28

JUDAS Iscariot occupies a wholly unique place in history: deservedly
or not, he ranks as the greatest popular villain of all time. In his
Divine Comedy, Dante places him in the deepest chasm of the inferno,
where Satan munches on him as a steady diet. If this seems too medieval,
modern opinion on Judas is not much more sophisticated in some parts
of the world. Each Good Friday in Mexico, the people ignite firecrackers
that sizzle and pop until the burning fuse reaches a hideous, powder-
stuffed Judas doll that finally blows up. And Greeks on the island of
Corfu, in a swelling chorus of curses, pitch great quantities of crockery
down a steep hill in an imaginary stoning of Judas.

He was the son of Simon Iscariot, about whom nothing is known.
Scholars have puzzled over the meaning of Iscariot, and one of the most
frequent definitions is *ish-Kerioth*, Hebrew for "man from Kerioth." But
the location of this village is uncertain, and another explanation is gaining
some currency: Iscariot may be a corruption of the Latin *sicarius*, which
means "assassin" or "murderer." The Sicarii were a radical, terrorist sect

of anti-Roman Jews who felled their enemies by mingling with them in crowds, thrusting a quick dagger into their ribs, and then vanishing.[1]

Whatever his background, Judas was one of the leaders of the Twelve, even though his name is cited last in the list of the disciples, for the Gospels were written only after his betrayal had degraded his memory. In fact, Judas was treasurer of the group, and was probably reclining next to Jesus in a place of honor at the Last Supper. But by this time he had already approached the chief priests with his infamous offer to betray Jesus.

The Need for an Insider

What were Judas' motives? Was it because Jesus had discovered his pilfering from the treasury and had planned to expose him? Was he disappointed in Jesus' failure to declare himself a political Messiah who would free Palestine from Roman control? Was he disillusioned enough to deem him a false prophet? Or, in a masterpiece of strategy, was he trying to force Jesus into a vulnerable position in which he would have to display his messianic powers in order to deliver himself? The Teacher had eluded arrest before, and now could do so in a great public show of supernatural force in the Holy City that would convince the nation once and for all.

Perhaps it was a combination of all these motives, or it could have been something so simple as avarice. After all, Judas did want to be paid for his information, and thirty pieces of silver was the agreed price, enough to buy a suit of clothes. Judas would profit, however pettily, and Jesus could always save himself if he chose.

But what intelligence could Judas possibly deliver to the priestly authorities? Some critics doubt that the betrayal story is historical, because Jesus was not in hiding: on the contrary, he was delivering daily lectures in the Temple. Since apprehending him before the crowds would have caused an uproar, however, the arrest would have to take place by night.

Yet where in the tent city surrounding Jerusalem was Jesus staying? And how could he be seized at night without arousing his fellow Galileans encamped round about? And how could they be sure to arrest the right person when all men at that time wore a beard, dressed approximately the same, and were blanketed by darkness? This was long before the day

An ancient flight of stairs leading from the Upper City of
Jerusalem down to the Kidron Valley. Jesus and the disciples
may have used these very steps on the way to Gethsemane.

of wire-service photos and their universal identification of the famous. Consider also the condition of ancient eyesight, which was poorer than ours and was not corrected by glasses of any kind. However, Judas' agreement to identify Jesus' nocturnal whereabouts, even to the point of singling him out with a kiss of greeting, nicely solved all these problems, and the pact was concluded.

Now it was Thursday, April 2, 33 A.D., a date that best corresponds to the various chronological clues in the sources.[2] For the first time during Holy Week, it seems that Jesus stayed in Bethany rather than going into Jerusalem. How did he spend his final hours of freedom? Doubtless in the company of his intimate friends, including his mother Mary, who must have been on the scene, since she stood at the foot of the cross the next day.

No later than noon, Jesus sent Peter and John into Jerusalem to make arrangements for their Passover meal. "A man carrying a jar of water will meet you," Jesus told them, and this man would identify the house with an upper guest room where they would keep the feast. The recognition sign would be unusual enough, since in the East it was women who usually drew the water and carried it from wells in pitchers perched precariously on their heads, a common sight in Israel and Jordan to this day.

A Passover Seder?

At sundown, the Twelve gathered with Jesus for dinner in the upper room. But what they ate has been vigorously debated across the centuries since then, because the synoptic Gospels—*Matthew, Mark,* and *Luke*— state quite clearly that this was the Passover Seder or meal, whereas *John* insists that this was the day *before* the Passover. Numerous attempts have been made to harmonize these differences, some suggesting that the Passover may have been observed on two consecutive days that year, due to variant reckonings by the Pharisees and Sadducees, or by the Judeans and Galileans. Others claim that Jesus celebrated an intentionally early Passover, knowing what would happen the next day.

Following the Johannine tradition, the Eastern Orthodox churches to this day celebrate Holy Communion with regular leavened bread, whereas the Roman Catholic sacrament uses *un*leavened bread, wafers similar to

125

what would have been eaten at a Passover meal. Lutherans and Anglicans generally follow the synoptic tradition also, while the rest of Protestantism uses either form.

But there can be no doubt that the mind of every Jew at this time was focused on the Passover festival, so the discrepancy may be nothing more serious than, for example, opening presents on Christmas Eve or Christmas Day. The Passover itself commemorated the liberation of the ancient Hebrews from their enslavement in Egypt. While the firstborn male Egyptians were dying in the dreadful tenth plague, the Israelites were secure behind doorways marked with lamb's blood, as they ate a dinner of unleavened bread, bitter herbs, and roast lamb, which had been cooked over an open fire on a spit made of pomegranate wood (Exod. 12).

The supper shared by Jesus and the disciples must have been similar—up to a point. Then a note of tension broke the happiness of the dinner, as the Teacher enlarged on a point he had already made while giving the Twelve an object lesson in humility by washing their feet. He had said, "Not all of you are clean." Then, after another hint, he came out directly, "Very truly, I tell you, one of you will betray me" (John 13:21).

Innocently, they all inquired, "Is it I, Lord?" Judas joined in the question, lest he incriminate himself by silence.

Looking him coolly in the eye, Jesus replied, "You have said so. Do quickly what you are going to do" (Matt. 26:25; John 13:27).

Hot with embarrassment, Judas rose from his reclining position at the table and skulked out of the room. Probably Jesus had only whispered the identification, since the rest of the disciples merely thought Judas off on an errand.

Toward the close of the supper, Jesus introduced a momentous alteration into the usual Passover Seder. He took some of the remaining bread, blessed it and broke it, and then distributed it among his colleagues with the words "This is my body, which is given for you. Do this in remembrance of me." Wondering at his language, the disciples ate the bread.

Then he reached for the cup of red Passover wine standing in front of him. According to custom, it had been diluted, two parts of water to one of wine. Again he offered thanks and passed the chalice among them, saying, "Take this and divide it among yourselves. . . . This cup that is poured out for you is the new covenant in my blood" (Luke 22:17ff.).

With these words, Jesus inaugurated what became the longest continuous meal in history, for soon his followers would start celebrating

The Brook Kidron, looking south toward an olive grove in the
Gethsemane area and the lower reaches of the Mount of Olives.
Jesus and the disciples crossed this stream on the way to
Gethsemane.

what they later called The Lord's Supper or Holy Communion, in which someone, somewhere in the world, has been offering up bread and wine in a similar manner nearly every moment since.

The meaning of Jesus' words stems from a complex of ideas that lie at the very heart of Christianity. Just as in Old Testament worship, the flesh and blood of a sacrificed victim were offered separately, so Jesus was to be the new Paschal Lamb offered in sacrifice for sin. This new covenant was intended to be a direct fulfillment of the old, which had been established after the Passover liberation from Egypt. God was offering man a fresh contract or agreement in Jesus: his sacrifice on the cross would bring liberation, not from Egypt, but from the slavery of sin. The supper also foreshadowed the messianic banquet he would share with his followers in the future kingdom.

But all this was scarcely comprehended by the disciples at the time, and not until later would they reflect on Jesus' words and understand their meaning in full. For now, all they could do was wonder at the fresh tack taken by the Teacher and listen to his last discourses, which focused on the new commandment of love that he specified for all who would follow him. His closing words, which seemed strangely attuned to the future, promised the coming of a Comforter—the Holy Spirit—who would attend them.

Finally, they all sang a closing Passover hymn, and then Jesus uttered his magnificent concluding prayer, which began with ominous import: "Father, the hour has come. . . ." It had indeed. They filed out of the room and walked eastward through the darkened streets of Jerusalem toward the Mount of Olives.

17

In the Garden

Then Jesus said to them, "Have you come out with swords
and clubs to arrest me as though I were a bandit?
Day after day I was with you in the temple teaching,
and you did not arrest me. But let the scriptures be
fulfilled." MARK 14:48–49

CERTAIN ancient traditions place the upper room in the elevated
southwestern corner of Jerusalem, although the present
purported site for the Last Supper, an upper chamber of gothic arches,
is easily the least convincing holy place in Israel. But if Jesus and the
disciples did dine somewhere in this quarter of the city, they would
doubtless have made their way over to Gethsemane via a roadway winding
around the southeastern corner of Jerusalem. An ancient flight of steps
descending toward the Kidron Valley has been excavated, and these could
very well have been used by Jesus and the Eleven who filed after him.

There was some dialogue as the party made its way in and out of the
stark shadows cast by the full Passover moon, which had now risen
gloriously over the Mount of Olives to the east.[1] With what must have
been a resigned sigh, Jesus said, "You will all become deserters because
of me this night. . . . But after I am raised up, I will go ahead of you to
Galilee."

Simon Peter, the big beloved fisherman who always managed to get
in the first word after Jesus said something, did not fail him now. With a
slightly demeaning gesture toward his colleagues, he said. "Even if *they*
all fall away because of you, *I* will never desert you."

Shaking his head sadly, Jesus told him, "This very night, before the cock crows, you will deny me three times."

"Even though I must *die* with you, I will not deny you," Peter objected. Not to be left out, and more than a little resentful at Peter's presumption, the other disciples quickly added their own promises of loyalty to the death (Matt. 26:31ff.).

Now they were crossing the Kidron, a brook that cuts through the valley separating the Temple platform from the Mount of Olives. Most of the time, this celebrated stream is nothing more than a dry ditch littered with boulders, but after a heavy rainfall the rivulet spumes with roiling waters that soon find their way into the Dead Sea. In Jesus' day, when the valley was several yards deeper, the brook would gurgle all spring.

They were walking toward a grove of olive trees nestled in the lower reaches of the Mount of Olives, a favorite haunt of Jesus and the Twelve. It was called Gethsemane, meaning "oil vat" or "oil press" in Aramaic, and somewhere in the garden the contrivance likely stood, its stone wheels reflecting a ghostly blue-white in the moonlight. Ancient olive presses are commonplace in Israel to this day, for olive oil production was a major industry in biblical times. A vertical stone wheel, driven by human or donkey power, rolled over the olives spread out on a flat, horizontal stone, which was grooved to let the oil trickle into a basin.

The Psychological Agony

When Jesus and his party entered the garden, the stage was set for the most human scene in the entire Passion story. Lenten preaching so often makes Jesus a larger-than-life figure who is completely in control of the tragic events swirling about him, as if playing out his role from a divine scenario whose glorious ending he knew well enough. Jesus the man is too often obscured by the messianic Christ.

But Gethsemane shows the humanity of Jesus with astonishing fidelity. He told his followers to stay in the grove while he went off a stone's throw to pray, for he had to be alone. Completely alone? Perhaps misery did love company, for he took the inner three disciples with him: Peter, James, and John. At any moment Judas and the arresting party were due in the garden, so he told them to warn him of their approach while he went a little farther off and prayed.

130

Falling on his face, he agonized, "My Father, if it is possible, let this cup pass from me; yet not what I want but what you want" (Matt. 26:39). For an omnipotent God, wasn't some alternate plan possible rather than the horror that lay immediately ahead? In fact, Jesus was wavering in his mission, because he was a man, too, and men waver when they stare into the jaws of death. If the story of Holy Week were a pious invention of writers who wanted to portray a superhero, this scene would never have been included. But, almost breathing with realism, it shows Jesus distractedly trying to interrupt his own agony by going over to check on the trio of disciples three different times. With unfailing consistency, they were sleeping each time.

Luke, the doctor, adds a medical detail in his account. During the psychological struggle of wills being waged in Jesus' mind, his perspiration "became like great drops of blood falling down on the ground" (22:44). Because of the simile, too much should not be made of this statement, although, in cases of extreme stress, it is physiologically possible for the human body to sweat blood.

It was now between 10 and 11 P.M. Orion, the great winter constellation, was just setting in the northwest, its first-magnitude stars still visible through the bright moonlight. But the privacy of the Passion story ended at this moment. A clanking of men and arms was starting to shatter the hush of night. Quivering daggers of orange flame began stabbing the horizon to the west, and soon a procession of torches filed into the grove. Judas, at the head of an armed company of Temple guardsmen, walked over to Jesus and said, "Greetings, Rabbi!" Then he gave him a kiss of salutation—whether on the hand or the cheek is not known—the agreed signal identifying Jesus.

In his familiar reply, spoken contemptuously or sadly, Jesus asked, "Judas, is it with a kiss that you are betraying the Son of Man?" Revulsion at the traitor's hypocritical gesture makes one almost instinctively wipe one's skin on reading the account.

The next moment, Simon Peter lunged for his sword to defend Jesus. Much derision has been heaped on the poor, impetuous fisherman for resorting to violence and then making such a mess of it, flailing away with one misguided thrust that merely slashed off the right ear of the high priest's servant Malchus. And yet the hopeless swipe is almost refreshing in a sense, the one token act of courage by any of the disciples in their otherwise dismal record of cowardice.

131

The gnarled trunk of an ancient olive tree, perhaps 900 years old, standing in the traditional Garden of Gethsemane.

"No more of this!" Jesus quickly interposed, before everyone began swinging. "Put your sword back into its sheath. Am I not to drink the cup that the Father has given me?" Again, only Luke adds the medical touch that Jesus then healed the wounded man. An early tradition claims, understandably, that this incident converted Malchus, who was likely of Idumaean extraction.

In his last free moment, Jesus could not resist taunting the crowd for clutching cudgels and swords as if hunting out a robber, when just hours earlier they had not arrested him in the Temple. "But if you are looking for me, let these men go," he said, pointing to the disciples.

Huddling together in a shivering pool of fear at the edge of the grove, the Eleven took their cue and promptly fled from Gethsemane, abandoning their Teacher just one hour after their brave promises to the contrary. Then Jesus was seized, bound, and led back into Jerusalem.

The Sites Today

More than any other episodes in the Bible, the events of the Passion story transpire against a definite background of time and place in one locality—Jerusalem and vicinity—so the various movements of Jesus should be traceable today. Each Holy Week, in fact, thousands of Christian pilgrims stream into Jerusalem and recapitulate the memorable events by trying to follow Jesus' footsteps from site to sacred site.

Some visitors return home disappointed, but these probably went to Jerusalem in the hopes of seeing Herod's Temple intact, Roman soldiers still milling about, the true cross standing at Calvary, and, if it could be scheduled, a miracle or two, if not an apostle's autograph inside their Bibles.

Others criticize the somewhat drab beige landscape of the countryside, with only rare patches of verdant green. Modern Israel, indeed, is no longer the Canaan flowing with milk and honey, thanks to several millennia of deforestation, erosion, and the root-devouring appetites of the sheep and goats who seem to own the land. And yet the topography remains essentially that of Jesus' day, though with seven to thirteen feet more altitude because the dust of centuries and the debris of conquests have settled on the land.

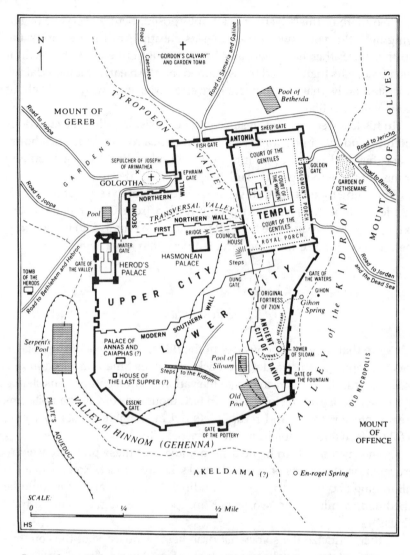

Jerusalem at the time of Jesus.   In the New Testament era, the southern half of Jerusalem lay outside the present Old City and skirted the Hinnom Valley. Question marks indicate those sites that are uncertain.

134

Today's tourist in Israel and Jordan must carefully distinguish between the authentic sites—as absolute as the River Jordan or the Sea of Galilee—such as the Mount of Olives, for example, or the location of the great Temple; probable traditional sites, as the Garden of Gethsemane; and on down to such pious but futile guesses as the "Well of the Magi," touted as the "precise spot" where the Wise Men supposedly saw the guiding star again after they had left Jerusalem for Bethlehem!

The sites of Holy Week seem to grow with authenticity and prove more locatable as the days move on. The place where Mary and Martha lived in Bethany, for example, is not really known, nor is the exact route used by Jesus on Palm Sunday. The site for the Last Supper is hazy, but the location of Gethsemane, Pilate's praetorium, and Golgotha can be pinpointed with some precision.

To be sure, today's visitor has the choice of four different Gethsemanes, at shrines belonging to Greek Orthodox, Latin, Armenian, and Russian Orthodox Christians. But all of these lie close to one another on the lower slopes of the Mount of Olives and above the Kidron ravine, and all might have been included in the larger olive grove that was Gethsemane. Most visitors prefer the Latin Gethsemane, where the Church of All Nations is erected over fourth-century ruins surrounding the traditional rock where Jesus prayed. Adjacent to it lies a grove in which eight ancient, gnarled olive trees, which may be 900 years old, still bear a few shriveled olives every other year.

The grove is walled in and planted with an attractive garden of flower beds. A few guides occasionally test the credulity of tourists by claiming that "these very trees witnessed Christ's suffering when they were seedlings." But even if the olive trees lived twice as long, all the ancient groves around Jerusalem were destroyed when the Roman general Titus besieged and conquered the city in 70 A.D. If, however, a botanist were asked: Might such trees have grown from the root systems of olive trees standing two thousand years ago? he or she would have to answer yes.

18

Annas and Caiaphas

When day came, the assembly of the elders of the people,
both chief priests and scribes, gathered together,
and they brought him to their council. . . . All of them asked,
"Are you, then, the Son of God?" He said to them, "You
say that I am." Then they said, "What further testimony do
we need?"   LUKE 22:66, 70–71

TRACING the events immediately after Jesus' arrest is made somewhat difficult by the variant accounts given in the four Gospels.
Their testimony may be schematized as follows, with each reporting Jesus'
appearance before the priestly authorities at the following times and
places:

	MATTHEW	MARK	LUKE	JOHN
Time:	Night*	Night*	Day	Night
Place:	House of Caiaphas	House of the high priest	House of the high priest	Annas, then Caiaphas

*however, with official proceedings the next morning

The issue is further complicated by both Annas and Caiaphas being called
the high priest at various places in the New Testament. And yet all the
accounts contribute to the total picture of the hearings and are not mutually
exclusive.

Jesus was first brought by night into the southwestern Upper City
to the house of Annas, who had been high priest from 6 to 15 A.D.—the
pontiff in charge at the time Jesus appeared in the Temple as a young

prodigy.[1] Although deposed from that office by the Romans, Annas continued as the wealthy power-behind-the-scenes in the sacerdotal aristocracy at Jerusalem, since five of his own sons, and now his son-in-law Caiaphas, had eventually succeeded to the high priesthood.[2] It was not only as a mark of respect to his authority, but possibly also in the nature of a preliminary, lower court hearing that Jesus was first brought before the patriarch Annas, who could still be called "high priest," much as ex-governors today are still called Governor So-and-so out of courtesy.

Jesus was not very cooperative before Annas, for he knew that the major confrontation would come later before Caiaphas and the Sanhedrin. The patriarch questioned Jesus about his followers and his teaching, but Jesus blunted the query. "My teachings are a matter of public record," he replied. "I taught openly in the synagogue and in the Temple. Ask the people what I said."

One of the guards thought this attitude impertinent. "Is *that* how you answer the high priest?" he demanded, and gave Jesus a smart slap on the cheek.

Jesus turned to him and said, "If I have spoken wrongly, testify to the wrong. But if I have spoken rightly, why do you strike me?"

So ended any hopes of a preliminary hearing. Annas sent Jesus, shackled, over to his son-in-law Caiaphas, the current high priest (John 18:19–24). Probably the two pontiffs lived at the same palace in southwestern Jerusalem, with only a courtyard separating the apartments.

Before Caiaphas

By now it was midnight. Ordinarily, no further action would have been taken in the case of Jesus until morning, for any proceedings involving a man's life had to take place in full daylight, according to Jewish law. Caiaphas, however, knew that a lengthy, daytime trial that would have attracted Jesus' popular following, once news of his arrest broke, was extremely undesirable. It could spark the kind of uproar that would require Pilate's troops. Why not another nocturnal hearing now, which could hear all the facts in the case and so facilitate a quick Sanhedral decision, passing formal judgment, as soon as day broke on the morrow? The prisoner would then be in Pilate's hands before the case could become a *cause célèbre*. This, in fact, is what most probably happened, which would explain New Testament references to nocturnal as well as daytime proceedings.

The chief priests and members of the council had gathered in the assembly hall of Caiaphas' palace upon urgent summons from the high priest's messengers. There could be no indictment unless at least two witnesses testified on a given charge, so Caiaphas opened the proceedings by soliciting such witnesses.[3]

Numbers were no problem, but the testimonies were: they simply did not agree. The evidence—probably isolated acts in which Jesus had allegedly violated the Sabbath—did not jibe with the kind of precision demanded under Jewish law. In the haste of the affair, the chief priests had not had time to interview witnesses beforehand and screen out any worthless testimony.

Eventually, it seemed that two men could agree on a solid charge: they claimed that Jesus had said, "I am able to destroy the temple of God and to build it in three days." But their testimony fell apart when it was plain that Jesus referred to the "temple" of his own body.

Disgruntled at the lack of progress, Caiaphas stood up and tried for one last time the ploy of the previous days: snaring Jesus in his own words. Fixing his gaze on the defendant, he asked, "Have you no answer? What is it that they testify against you?"

Jesus did not reply. Legally, he did not have to, since no proven evidence had yet been introduced into the proceedings.

Finally, with his case falling completely apart, Caiaphas managed to score a brilliant thrust into the very core of the issue by posing his fateful demand: "I put you under oath before the living God, tell us if you are the Messiah, the Son of God!"

A ruler of God's people had charged the demand with the most solemn oath known to the Hebrews. Jesus did not try to evade it. History, quite literally, was hanging on his response. Jesus said, "I am"—this, according to Mark's version (14:62). Matthew has it, "You have said so" (26:64), while Luke reads, "You say that I am" (22:70).

Much has been made of the apparently indirect replies, and the slogan is often heard, "Jesus never claimed to be the Messiah." But this is not true, for all three answers are really identical. Even though the wording in Matthew and Luke may sound evasive, Jewish custom discouraged a bald *yes* or *no* to questions of grave import. Just six hours earlier at the Last Supper, Jesus had also replied to Judas' question, "Is it I?" with a sad, "You have said so" (Matt. 26:25).

Underlining his affirmation of Messiahship, Jesus added, "From now on, you will see the Son of Man seated at the right hand of Power and coming on the clouds of heaven."

Tearing his high priestly robe "the length of the palm of the hand"—the inches required when blasphemy was heard—Caiaphas struggled to be heard above the rising commotion. *"Blasphemy!"* he cried. "Do we need any further witnesses? You have now heard his blasphemy: *you* are now the witnesses!—What is your verdict?"

A chorus of voices offered a unanimous opinion: "He deserves death" (Matt. 26:59–66).

But was it really blasphemy? Jesus' claim to be Messiah was either true or false, and should have been examined in detail by Caiaphas. Yet even if it were proven false, the claim itself was not necessarily blasphemous. According to the Talmud, blasphemy technically occurred only when the sacred name of God as he revealed it to Moses—Yahweh—was uttered. Whether or not Jesus said it is not known, since the Gospels were written in Greek, but it seems he did not. The entire hearing, however, had violated so many other provisions in Jewish law that no technicality at this point could stand in the way of the high priest's virtually directed verdict of Guilty in a surcharged emotional atmosphere.

Some scholars have questioned the accuracy of the New Testament in this section: a hearing with so many violations could never have occurred, they claim. Since our information on standard Jewish legal procedure comes from the Talmud, compiled two or three centuries after Christ, there is no absolute proof that all the same legal usage applied then. Yet, even if it did, everything we know about Annas, Caiaphas, and their clan would suggest that in the present emergency the end would easily justify the means, in their estimation.

Is this being too hard on the chief priests? Apparently not. Some very negative opinions about the high priestly family appear also in Jewish traditions. "Woe to the family of Annas! Woe to their serpentlike hisses!" warns the Talmud, while Josephus describes Annas' son Ananus as "very insolent."

Aerial view looking eastward across the Old City of Jerusalem, with identifications on the opposite page numbering Jesus' final movements on Maundy Thursday and Good Friday. The early morning meeting of the Sanhedrin likely took place at the Council House on the Temple mount (3), while Pontius Pilate had his tribunal at the Palace of Herod (4, 6), the site of which is now occupied by the Citadel. Jesus' appearance before

Peter's Denial

In this section of the Passion history, there is a tug of war for the reader's attention between the dramatic scene unfolding inside the high priest's palace and the incredible performance of Peter standing outside in the courtyard, warming himself before a charcoal fire flaming in a brazier. At the beginning of April, nights are still cool in Jerusalem, and the Passover moon was offering no warmth whatever.

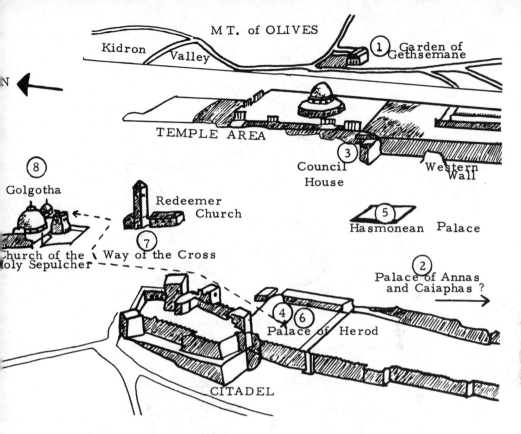

Herod Antipas took place at the Hasmonean Palace (5), of
which nothing remains today. The route to Golgotha, indicated
in (7), is *far* more likely than the traditional Via Dolorosa, which
leads from the northwestern end of the Temple area westward
to Golgotha (8). The Western Wall of the Temple mount is
sometimes called the "Wailing Wall."

Of the disciples who had fled from Gethsemane, nine continued in
hiding, but two of them—John and Peter—cautiously followed Jesus at
some distance. John, who evidently had friends among the high priest's
staff, was able to gain their admittance inside the palace. While Peter was
warming himself before the fire—and unintentionally illuminating his
face—a doormaid came up to him and challenged, "You also were with
Jesus the Galilean."

Before Peter could even think about it, the lie was out. "I don't know
what you're talking about," he snapped.

Bronze

Obv. Lituus; inscription: ΤΙΒΕΡΙΟΥ ΚΑΙCΑΡΟC
(Tiberius Caesar).
Rev. Within a wreath, the date: L IZ (17=A.D.
30/31).

Roman denar, silver; tribute money

Obv. Head of Tiberius; inscription: TI CAESAR
DIVI AUG F AUGUSTUS (Tiberius Caesar, son
of the divine Augustus, Augustus).
Rev. Pax seated, holding branch; inscription:
PONTIF MAXIM (High priest).

Syrian tetradrachma, silver

Obv. Head of Augustus; inscription: ΚΑΙΣΑΡΟΣ
ΣΕΒΑΣΤΟΣ (Caesar, Augustus).
Rev. Tyche of Antiochia; at his feet, the river-god
Orontes; inscription: ΑΝΤΙΟΧΕΩΝ ΜΗΤΡΟ-
ΠΟΛΕΩΣ (Capital of the Antiochian); date: ΔΝ
(54; after Pharsalus), ϛ Λ (36 after Actium=
A.D. 5).

The thirty pieces of silver paid to Judas were most probably
thirty shekels coined in Tyre or Antioch, a specimen of which is
the Syrian tetradrachma at the bottom of the illustration above.
The tribute money shown to Jesus in the famous "Render to
Caesar" confrontation is in the center, while a coin minted by
Pontius Pilate in Judea is shown at the top.

Later on came a more serious challenge. A relative of Malchus, the servant whose ear Peter had severed, sauntered over to him and said, "Didn't I see you in the garden with him?"

"I do not know the man!" Was that straining, high-pitched sound a cock crowing? Peter may not have noticed it—yet.

An hour later, when he finally thought himself wrapped in a cozy blanket of anonymity, somebody made fun of Peter's Galilean twang. It was a standing joke that you couldn't tell if a Galilean were talking about an ass, a lamb, or a jug of wine, since they pronounced *hamor, immar,* and *hamar* just about the same. "Certainly you are also one of them," he sneered, "for your accent betrays you."

Like a caged animal prodded by tormentors, Peter furiously lashed back at his accusers, adding curses and swearing to emphasize his denials. This time he heard the cock crow distinctly, piercingly. Tears flooding his eyes, he dragged himself out of the courtyard and indulged his private remorse.

Jesus, meanwhile, was abandoned to the whims of the Temple guard. While being led to the cell where he would spend the few remaining hours of the night, he suffered the indignities and abuses common in ancient prisons each time the authorities turned the other way. He was blindfolded and subjected to jeers, spittle, slaps, and blows. "Prophesy to us, you Messiah!" they screamed. "Who is it that struck you?"

A hopeless prophet! He wasn't saying a thing (Matt. 26:67–75).

The Sanhedrin Convenes

At dawn the next morning, Jesus was brought before an official session of the Great Sanhedrin, which had convened on the Temple mount. After bare formalities, which included asking Jesus the momentous question once more and getting his reply, Caiaphas again requested a verdict from the Sanhedrists. Since many of the members had already spent much of the night at the high priest's palace during the previous conclave, their action merely served to ratify what they had already decided.

Attention now focused on the youngest of the seventy members of the Sanhedrin, who was seated at the edge of the semicircle of benches. According to custom, the voting would begin with him—lest he be influenced by his superiors—and end with the eldest member, the high priest casting the final vote. The youthful Sanhedrist stood up in the hushed chamber and said, "He is worthy of death."

The next member arose and said the same. Whispering in the hall rose steadily as the count continued, "Guilty," "Death."

The final tally, if all members were present, would probably have been 69 votes for condemnation and two abstentions. The abstentions came from Sanhedrists named Joseph of Arimathea and Nicodemus, who were secret followers of Jesus.

If Judea were not a Roman province, Jesus would now have been executed by stoning, probably below the east wall of Jerusalem. But the *jus gladii*, or "law of the sword"—the right to execute capital punishment—was now reserved for the Roman prefect of Judea, Pontius Pilate, who would have to review the Sanhedrin's verdict and pronounce sentence or dismiss the case.[4]

A brief, tragic note closes this phase of the proceedings. Too late and too pathetically, Judas suffered his pangs of remorse. With a desperate but honest naïveté, he appeared at the Temple, clutching a bag with thirty unspent pieces of silver chinking inside. "I have sinned by betraying innocent blood," he said, handing the priests the bag as if to buy back Jesus' freedom. However ingenuous, it was the last right thing Judas ever did.

"What is that to us?" the priests replied. "See to it yourself."

Throwing the coins onto the marble floor of the Temple, Judas hurried out of the sacred precincts in total despair. Finding a rope and a convenient tree standing just under the south wall of the city, he hung himself. And this at a time when, in Christian theology, Jesus would literally be dying to forgive him.

Later, the priests took the money and bought a small plot with it in which to bury Judas and other strangers. The so-called Field of Blood is still shown south of Jerusalem on the other side of the Hinnom Valley. But any precision in such a matter, of course, is impossible (Matt. 27: 1–10).

19

Pontius Pilate

They bound Jesus, led him away, and handed him over to
Pilate. Pilate asked him, "Are you the King of the Jews?"
He answered him, "You say so." MARK 15:1–2

D URING the smoldering summer of 1961, some Italian archaeologists were excavating an ancient theater at Caesarea, the
Mediterranean port that served as the Roman capital of Palestine, when
they unearthed a two-by-three-foot stone that bore some kind of inscription. Antonio Frova, who was in charge of the dig, cleaned out the lettering
with a brush, and suddenly his eyes widened in disbelief while his face
was cut by a vast grin. The left third of the inscription had been chipped
away, but Frova reconstructed it in short order. The following Latin had
originally been cut into the stone in three-inch lettering:

CAESARIENS. TIBERIÉVM
PONTIVS PILATVS
PRAEFECTVS IVDAEAE
DÈDIT

"Pontius Pilatus, Prefect of Judea, has presented the Tiberiéum to the
Caesareans."[1] The Tiberiéum, evidently, was some kind of public structure
named in honor of the Roman emperor Tiberius.

This simple but proud sentence marked the first archaeological evidence
for the existence of Pontius Pilate ever to be discovered, and it added
dramatically to our knowledge about one of the most fascinating yet
enigmatic figures from the past. His name is repeated every moment at
Masses being conducted across the world, and each Sunday by nearly a

billion Christians as they recite the words of the Creed. In that sense, he is easily the most famous Roman of them all, for many who know little about a Caesar or Augustus or even Nero still confess the words, "I believe in Jesus Christ . . . who . . . suffered under Pontius Pilate."

Surprisingly, Pilate is termed Prefect of Judea in this inscription. Under the entry "Pontius Pilate" in nearly every encyclopedia or reference work on the Bible, this Roman is invariably styled a procurator, a mistaken term based on what has now proven to be anachronisms by the first historians who refer to Pilate. It was only later, under the emperor Claudius, that the title of Roman governors of Judea shifted to procurator. The Roman prefect had more military responsibilities than the procurator, and the New Testament very accurately labels Pilate as governor, not procurator.

Hardly due to any personal achievement, Pontius Pilate became the pin in a hinge of destiny simply because he presided at a trial that would become one of the central events in history. Aside from the Caesarea inscription, a more accurate portrait of Pilate can be drawn also from a careful rereading of the historical sources.

His very name provides two valuable hints as to his background and ancestry. Pontius, the family name, was that of a prominent clan among the Samnites, hill cousins of the Latin Romans who lived along the Apennine mountain spine southeast of Rome. A scrappy breed, the Samnites had almost conquered Rome in several fierce wars. The Pontii were of noble blood, but when Rome finally absorbed the Samnites, their aristocracy was demoted to the Roman equestrian or middle-class order.

But it is Pilate's personal name, Pilatus, that proves almost conclusively that he was indeed of Samnite origin. Pilatus means *Armed-with-a-javelin*. The *pilum*, or javelin, was a balanced missile six feet long, half wooden handle and half pointed iron shaft, which Samnite mountaineers hurled at their enemies with devastating effect. The Romans quickly copied the weapon, and it was the *pilum*, in fact, that had made the Roman Empire possible.

Roman versus Jew

Pilate ruled as prefect of Judea from 26 to 36 A.D., the second-longest tenure of any first-century Roman governor in Palestine. The very length of his office contradicts the usual impression of Pilate as an incompetent

A two-by-three-foot stone discovered at Caesarea in 1961, the first epigraphic evidence of Pontius Pilate ever found. The left facing of the stone had been chipped away for reuse so that only "TIVSPILATVS" remains of Pilate's name in the middle line. This stone is now in the Israel Museum at Jerusalem.

147

official, for it is doubtful that the emperor Tiberius, who insisted on good provincial administration, would have retained Pilate in office so long had he been the political cripple of popular repute. Nor was the prefecture of Judea a petty post staffed by dissatisfied officials, an impression almost universal among biblical novelists: in that case, Pilate need never have accepted the office.

He did, however, find the governorship of Judea a most taxing experience, and several vignettes of Pilate show the remarkably "modern" problems an ancient administrator had to face. Aside from his familiar role on Good Friday, there are five other incidents involving Pilate that are reported by the first-century authors Josephus and Philo. Because it seems that Pilate blundered in each of these instances, he has been roundly faulted for his performance as governor in most histories since that time. Yet a close study of these episodes would suggest that Pilate, while hardly a master of diplomacy, was at least trying to make the best of very difficult administrative situations.

In what came to be called "the affair of the Roman standards," Pilate's troops once marched into Jerusalem carrying medallions with the emperor's image or bust among their regimental standards. This action provoked a five-day mass demonstration by Jews at the provincial capital, Caesarea, which protested the effigies as a violation of Jewish law concerning engraved images (Exod. 20:4–5). Pilate finally relented and ordered the offensive standards removed.[2]

Later in his administration, he built an aqueduct from cisterns near Bethlehem to improve Jerusalem's water supply, but paid for it with funds from the Temple treasury. This sparked another riot, which was put down only after bloodshed, even though Pilate had cautioned his troops not to use swords.

While this seems a grotesque example of malfeasance, a case could be made that Jewish sacred writings permitted expenditure of surplus Temple funds for such civic needs as water supply, and it would seem that Pilate must have had some cooperation from priestly authorities in Jerusalem. He could not simply have plundered the sacrosanct Temple treasury: Gentiles were forbidden, on pain of death, to enter the Temple interior, where the sacred treasure was stored. Any such violation would have led to Pilate's immediate recall. And since the aqueduct fed cisterns below the Temple, building operations could hardly have been undertaken in that area without at least tacit approval of the religious authorities.

Apparently, the subsequent outcry was a protest of the people, not their leaders, who may even have warned Pilate in advance of the approaching demonstration.[3]

On another occasion, Pilate set up several golden shields in his Jerusalem headquarters that, unlike the standards, bore no images whatever, only a bare inscription of dedication to Tiberius. And yet the people and their spokesmen—Herod Antipas and his brothers—protested even the imageless shields, but this time Pilate refused to remove them. He could, and perhaps did, point to the precedent of Jews in Alexandria, who adorned the very walls of their synagogues with gilded shields in honor of the Roman emperor. But Alexandria was not Jerusalem, and Herod, who was trying also to embarrass Pilate politically, formally protested to Tiberius. In a very testy letter, the emperor ordered Pilate to transfer the shields to a temple in Caesarea, and ominously warned him to uphold all the religious and political customs of his Jewish subjects.

It was only a few months after this bizarre affair that Pilate made his entry on the stage of history as judge of Jesus of Nazareth, and *the episode of the golden shields is critically important in understanding Pilate's conduct at the trial,* as will be noted in the next chapter. Indeed, the Roman viewpoint in the "greatest story ever told" has been remarkably neglected, and yet it offers an important key to understanding the events of Holy Week.

The episode of the golden shields also provides a valuable (and strangely overlooked) clue as to where Jesus stood before Pilate on Good Friday. The traditional location shown to most visitors in Jerusalem—the ancient pavement of the Tower Antonia northwest of the Temple area and now under the Sisters of Zion convent—seems erroneous, even if it is the starting point of the Via Dolorosa, the "Sorrowful Road" along which a mournful parade of Christians passes each Good Friday. Rather, the Jewish philosopher Philo, who recorded the episode of the golden shields, wrote that Pilate hung the shields "in Herod's palace in the holy city," which he further identified as "the house of the governors."[4] The lavish palace constructed by Herod the Great on the western edge of old Jerusalem was indeed preferable to the Spartan accommodations at the Antonia fortress, and Jesus' trial undoubtedly took place there.

It is further unlikely that Pilate's wife, Procula, who accompanied him to Jerusalem that fateful week, would have been subjected to quarters in a military barracks. The New Testament merely says that the trial took place at Pilate's praetorium, which was anywhere a Roman magistrate

Prof. Avi-Yonah's model of the Palace of Herod in western
Jerusalem, where Jesus stood before Pontius Pilate. The two
wings of the palace within the fortified enclave were named the
Caesareum and the Agrippeum, for Herod the Great's Roman

friends. The three large towers guarding the northern end were called (*l* to *r*): Phasael, Hippicus, and Mariamme. In the upper right stand the four towers of the Fortress Antonia, looming over the Temple area just off the picture to the right.

decided to hold court. But according to the Jewish historian Josephus, the Roman governor Gessius Florus as late as 66 A.D. was still setting up his tribunal just outside Herod's palace, *exactly as Pilate did.*[5] The evidence, then, would seem conclusive.

Judging the Judge

Finishing Pilate's story, however, takes us to events three years after Good Friday. Strangely, it was no imbroglio with his Jewish subjects that ended Pilate's term in Judea, but rather a furor involving Samaritans, those half-breed cousins of the Jews who lived in Mid-Palestine. An obscure pseudo-prophet with messianic ambitions promised the Samaritans that he would uncover some sacred temple utensils that Moses had supposedly buried on their sacred Mt. Gerizim, and a host of credulous Samaritans gathered to witness the spectacle. Because the multitude had come armed with weapons—perhaps also to prevent the people from being exploited—Pilate ordered his troops to block the route of ascent. It came to a pitched battle. Pilate's forces won, and the leaders of the uprising were executed. Here again, Pilate's action, while certainly harsh, was not more than what other Roman governors had done under similar circumstances to subdue what had developed into armed sedition astride the main artery of Palestine.

The Samaritan Senate, however, complained to Pilate's superior, the proconsul of Syria, who ordered Pilate to return to Rome to answer the charges against him. With no choice in the matter, Pilate departed for Rome late in 36 A.D. Was Judge Pontius Pilate himself judged in Rome? Probably we shall never know. Josephus' record, our principal source, breaks off with this intriguing sentence: "But before he reached Rome, Tiberius had already died" (*Antiquities* 18:85ff.). Gaius Caligula, the successor emperor, either heard Pilate's case or, more probably, quashed it, as he did most of the cases carried over from Tiberius' administration.

The traditional view of Pilate's fate, however, is extremely negative. Although early Christianity intended the wording of the Creed ("suffered under Pontius Pilate") merely to document the event and not necessarily to assign guilt, the blame developed anyway, and for the last seventeen centuries Pilate has had an unusually bad press. The most terrifying—and certainly imaginative—punishments were invented for him: torture, insanity, exile, compulsive handwashing, suicide, drowning, decapitation, being swallowed by the earth, and even that ancient punishment for parricide—being sewn up in an ox hide with a cock, a viper, and a monkey, and pitched into a river. Medieval legends would add tales of his restless corpse, accompanied by squadrons of demons, disrupting localities from France to Switzerland, causing storms, earthquakes, and other havoc.

On the basis of the earliest sources, however, it is clear that nothing of the sort ever happened to Pilate, let alone to his corpse. Although the tradition of Pilate's suicide dates back to the fourth-century church historian Eusebius, there are difficulties in his evidence. And the more important testimony of the earlier church father Origen, plus conclusions from first-century historians, decidedly contradict the suicide story. Nothing grossly negative, it seems, ever befell Pilate.

What, then, did happen to him? Much later Lenten preaching to the contrary, the Early Church father Tertullian claimed that Pilate "was a Christian in his conscience." Greek Orthodoxy canonized his wife, while the Ethiopian church even recognizes a St. Pilate and St. Procula's Day on June 25. Saint or sinner, Pilate most probably spent the rest of his days as a retired government official, a pensioned Roman magistrate emeritus, enjoying a less than sensational fate. He may even have spent his time looking for an answer to the question he once asked, under circumstances he may well have forgotten, "What is truth?"[6]

Yet all this lay in the distant future. When he arose early Friday morning on April 3, 33 A.D., Pontius Pilate could hear no drumroll of destiny as he prepared to adjudicate the cases waiting at his tribunal. But his appointment with history was waiting for him in the person of a manacled prisoner being brought by a huge throng into the paved esplanade in front of Herod's palace.

20

A Roman Trial

Then the priests accused him of many things. Pilate asked
him again, "Have you no answer? See how many charges
they bring against you." But Jesus made no further reply,
so that Pilate was amazed.   MARK 15:3–5

UNDOUBTEDLY, Pilate had some advance notice from Caiaphas
that the case of Jesus of Nazareth would be coming before his
tribunal. The governor ordered his ivory *sella curulis*, the magistrate's
official chair, moved outside the palace to a raised dais overlooking the
plaza to the east, which had filled with a vast multitude. This was to
accommodate the people, who would have defiled themselves for the
Passover Seder that night had they entered a pagan headquarters.

Turning to the prosecution, Pilate asked, in common Hellenistic Greek,
"What accusation do you bring against this man?" It was the opening
formula for a Roman trial, the *interrogatio*.

Several of the chief priests, who were acting as principal *accusatores*
or prosecutors, presented a formal bill of indictment: "We found this man
perverting our nation, forbidding us to pay taxes to the emperor, and
saying that he himself is the Messiah, a king." The charges were superbly
tailored to alarm a Roman governor, for they fairly glowed with sedition
and treason. Of the religious grounds on which Jesus had been condemned
by the Sanhedrin there was not a word, since the priestly authorities knew

that Pilate could hardly put a man to death for the purely theological offense of blasphemy.

Since no one seemed ready to defend Jesus, Pilate thought it fair to give him a brief, confidential hearing before proceeding with the trial, in order to learn something more about the defendant apart from the glare of his accusers. Summoning Jesus inside the palace, he inquired *"Are* you the King of the Jews?" In other words, "How do you plead?"

Jesus looked up at him, his face showing the abuse of the past hours and the lack of sleep. "Do you ask this on your own," he replied, "or did others tell you about me?"

"I am not a Jew, am I? Your own nation and the chief priests have handed you over to me. What have you done?"

"My kingship is not of this world. If it were, my followers would be fighting to keep me from being handed over to the Jews. But as it is, my kingdom is not from here."

"So? You *are* a king?"

"You say that I am a king. For this I was born, and for this I came into the world, to testify to the truth. Everyone who belongs to the truth listens to my voice."

"A kingship of *truth*, you say?" Pilate wondered. "What *is* truth?"

Evidently the private hearing convinced Pilate that Jesus' claims for kingship—his visionary "kingship of truth"—had no political implications, so it would hardly be possible to construct a case of treason against him. Ordering the defendant back to his outdoor tribunal, Pilate announced, "I find no case against Jesus thus far. What evidence do you have to substantiate your charges?"

Now far better organized than at the Sanhedral hearing, the prosecution chose its witnesses well—witnesses who made much of Jesus' messianic claims and probably added new evidence, such as Jesus' violence in the Temple. According to early sources outside the New Testament, there may also have been testimony indicting Jesus for magic and sorcery in the case of so-called miracles.[1]

When the prosecution rested its case, Pilate turned to Jesus, who had remained silent the whole time, and asked, "Have you *nothing* to say in your own defense? Don't you hear all this evidence against you?"

Jesus said not a word, supplying no defense of any kind, not even to a single charge. Pilate was astonished at his conduct, and probably asked the crowd, "Can anyone offer evidence favoring the defendant,

Jesus of Nazareth?"—for so he would have been obliged under Roman law.

Whatever response there may have been, it was hopelessly submerged by calls for condemnation from the multitude. Most of the vast throng, which was composed of the priestly establishment as well as the staff, police, and servant corps of the Temple, had marched directly westward from the Temple to Herod's palace, and they were starting to get restless. The prosecution now enlarged on Jesus' alleged sedition: "His teachings are inflaming the people throughout all Judea, starting from Galilee and spreading even as far as this city."

"Beginning in Galilee?" Pilate wondered. "Is the defendant a Galilean?"

The *accusatores* happily confirmed that Jesus had grown up in Galilee and recently lived in Capernaum, for Galileans had a reputation for rebellion, and this could undergird their indictment.

But Pilate had other ideas in mind with this information. Stated simply, he wanted to unload this troublesome case, which was really religious and not political in essence. Yes, he had likely heard how Jesus had roasted the Temple aristocracy in his preaching, but there had been no intelligence on Jesus' supposed political treason. So now he announced, "The defendant, then, is clearly a Galilean, and, as such, he is under the authority of the tetrarch Herod Antipas. And since Herod is in Jerusalem at this very moment, I think it eminently proper to remand this case to his jurisdiction."

Waving aside all protests, Pilate invoked what would later be called change of venue and sent Jesus under armed guard to the Hasmonean palace, which lay due east about two-thirds of the distance back to the Temple, for this is where Herod Antipas and his entourage were staying at the time (Luke 23:1–7). Legally, Pilate *did* have the authority to try Jesus in Judea as the *forum delicti* of his alleged crime, the place of the offense. But he also had the option of remanding the case to the jurisdiction of the sovereign of the accused, since Galilee was his *forum domicilii*, the place of residence.

The shift was logical enough for several important reasons. Herod Antipas certainly understood Jewish religious law better than Pilate did, and if it came to prophet-killing, why should Pilate bear the opprobrium? A specialist in that trade was now in Jerusalem: Antipas had already stained his hands with the blood of John the Baptist, and now he could do so again if he were so minded.

Before Herod Antipas

The tetrarch—"ruler of a quarter [of Palestine]"—was one of the sons of Herod the Great, the Temple builder and king in the Christmas story, and his domain included Galilee, as well as lands east of the Dead Sea. His brother Archelaus had originally ruled Judea but had made such a mess of it that Rome exiled him in 6 A.D. and then dispatched a series of its governors to rule Judea, the latest of whom was Pilate.

There was, then, divided authority in Palestine, and the ambitious Antipas had brutally embarrassed Pilate by forwarding a letter of protest over his head to the emperor in the case of the golden shields. Since this episode had virtually placed Pilate on probation, he thought an olive branch waved in Herod's direction might be more suitable than revenge for the moment, and sending Jesus to his tribunal would be an unmistakable courtesy. Kill the cur with kindness, and perhaps he would stop barking. In fact, it was yet another reason for the change of venue.

Herod Antipas could not have been more pleased. For many months he had wanted to meet Jesus, that miracle-worker about whom tongues were wagging across the land. It was getting almost embarrassing: a native of Galilee was supposedly performing wonders, and yet the *ruler* of Galilee had never seen any! Herod eyed the prisoner with obvious interest and then must have said something like, "Do a miracle, Jesus."

The prisoner did nothing, said nothing. He would stage no spectacle for the man who had beheaded his close friend, forerunner, and cousin, John the Baptizer. He would not entertain the sly opportunist whom he had once called "that fox"; nor his painted wife, Herodias, who had previously been married to Herod's brother; nor her dancing daughter, Salome, who was probably also in Jerusalem for the annual Herodian family Passover reunion.

The priestly prosecution repeated their formal indictment against Jesus, but this time they did not demur at also introducing the religious issues that had led to Jesus' conviction before the Sanhedrin, since Herod had very nobly led their complaint against Pilate in the case of the golden shields. Certainly in an issue of much greater significance, he would support them once again.

Herod prodded Jesus for some reaction, but got nothing. Embarrassed and at the limit of his patience, he invited his troops to wade in for a round of derision and contempt. Dressing Jesus in a brilliant white robe—the Messiah was expected to wear such—they performed their mock reverence.

"All right, that's enough," Herod must finally have directed. "Now take this magnificent prophet-Messiah-monarch back to Pontius Pilate."

Even though Luke made no reference to it, the prosecution must have felt bitterly betrayed by Herod Antipas. They had expected easy cooperation, an ideal shortcut to their goal, but now it had eluded them. The tetrarch's motives, however, were obvious: he was still enduring the popular odium for having killed one prophet—John—so he would not tackle a second, especially when his chief steward, Chuza, and his adviser, Manaen, were followers of the Nazarene, not to mention numerous of his Galilean subjects.

But it was very decent of Pilate to make such a conciliatory gesture, and so, as Luke puts it, "That very day, Herod and Pilate became friends with each other; before this they had been enemies" (23:12). The New Testament does not explain their enmity, but the episode of the golden shields certainly does, a good example of how the biblical and secular sources sometimes blend seamlessly.

Back to Pilate

The return of the prisoner to his jurisdiction was a bitter, though hardly unexpected, surprise for Pilate. But perhaps he could use it as an excuse to quash the case. Seizing the initiative, he announced,

> You brought me this man as one who was perverting the people; and here I have examined him in your presence and have not found this man guilty of any of your charges against him. Neither has Herod, for he sent him back to us. Indeed, he has done nothing to deserve death. I will therefore have him flogged and release him." (Luke 23:14–16)

This provoked a general outcry from the crowd for the first time, a rising rumble of disapproval punctuated by shouts of "Away with him! Crucify him!"

The rest of the story is painfully familiar: Pilate lamely tried to offer the multitude a Passover amnesty for either Jesus or the insurrectionary Bar-Abbas, assuming they would easily choose Jesus—but they surprised him. Next, Pilate's wife added an ominous overtone with her famous note,

"Have nothing to do with that innocent man, for today I have suffered a great deal because of a dream about him" (Matt. 27:19). A modern might dismiss this as a housewifely intrusion with bad timing, but dreams were very important to the Romans, for they were thought to predict future events. Everyone knew about Calpurnia's dream of Caesar's torn and bloodied toga on the eve of the Ides of March.

Amid further shouts for the death sentence, Pilate had Jesus brought inside the palace courtyard for scourging. Troops gathered around the prisoner, stripped him, and then administered a brutal flogging that, Pilate hoped, might yet win the people's sympathy for the accused. Playing on the idea that this wretch should be a king in general, and *of the Jews* in particular, the anti-Semitic troops laughingly planted a crown of thorns on his head and shoved a reed into his right hand as a scepter, then did him mock homage.

Pilate halted the fun and brought Jesus back before the multitude. Surely it had been punishment enough. "Behold the man!" he said, in a tone of condescending compassion.

"Crucify! Crucify Him!" the shouts returned.

Pilate lost his patience. "*You* crucify him, then," he snarled, "for I've found no case against him." He now decided to close the trial.

It was then that the prosecution shifted the charges back to religious grounds, since they were making no headway on the political. "We have a law," said their spokesman, "and according to that law he ought to die because he has claimed to be the Son of God."

Disturbed, irritated at the new charge, and perhaps a little superstitious, Pilate drew Jesus back inside the palace for a second private hearing. He led off with a frankly metaphysical question, "Where have you come from?"

Jesus made no reply.

"You won't speak to me? Don't you know that I have the authority to release you or to crucify you?"

"You would have no authority whatever over me if it had not been given you from above," Jesus replied. "Therefore the prosecution has the greater sin."

Pilate now returned to his tribunal outside and declared Jesus not guilty. He was on the point of releasing him when, in understandable desperation, the prosecution played its trump card. Perhaps it was Caiaphas himself who said, "If you release this man, you are *not* a Friend of

When the trial of Jesus was transferred to the tribunal of Herod
Antipas, Jesus was led eastward to the Hasmonean Palace,
where Herod was staying at the time. This palace, reconstructed
in the model at the Holyland Hotel, is at the upper right center,
the building crowned by the columned twin towers. Below it is
a staircase leading to the Temple from the Tyropoeon
("Cheesemakers") Valley, and in the foreground stands the
hippodrome or stadium built by Herod the Great for chariot races.

Caesar. For anyone who would make himself a king *treasonably* defies Caesar!"

It was a brilliant thrust that hit the mark cleanly, directly. Implied was every syllable of the following:

> If you set this man free, we will send a delegation to Tiberius Caesar, accusing you of condoning treason in one who would set himself up as subversive counter-king to Rome, and also of failure to uphold our religious law. Do you recall Tiberius' threatening letter to you five months ago? If he supported us then in the case of the golden shields, he'll surely support us now in a far more serious matter. You, Pilate, will lose your membership in the Friends of Caesar club. Your golden membership ring with Tiberius' image will be pulled from your finger, and you will make your exit via the usual means for disgraced members: exile, or compulsory suicide.

The club existed. High officials in the Empire and some members of the Senate were privileged to join the elite fraternity of *Amici Caesaris*, the Friends of Caesar, and no one left it except under mortal disgrace.[2] Pilate's resistance crumbled: It was Jesus or himself, and he opted for self. His final feeble attempts to defend Jesus and the bowl in which he tried to wash his hands of responsibility in the matter were all retreating actions in the face of the mounting riot conditions that rattled cries of "Away with him! Crucify him!" across the plaza. The trial was over—also for the judge.

Drying his hands, Pilate gestured toward Jesus and said, "*Staurotheto*" to a centurion of the Jerusalem cohort: "Let him be crucified."

The Question of Responsibility

Except for the last sentence, much of the above *never happened*—according to a flurry of recent books on the life of Jesus, some by pseudo-scholars but others by very serious biblical specialists.[3] Despite a dozen different interpretations of Jesus' arrest and trial, they agree on two basic hypotheses: (1) that Jesus *was* indeed deemed some sort of political revolutionary, perhaps even a Zealot, and Pilate really *wanted* to crucify so dangerous a rebel; and (2) that the New Testament documents have falsely shifted the moral responsibility for Jesus' death from Pilate to the Jewish Sanhedrin. Some scholars fault the Gospel writers for outright anti-Semitism in reporting the events of Holy Week as they did, while others suggest they were merely tampering with the truth for political reasons: unless a reluctant Pilate were made to appear pressured by Jewish authorities, how else could Romans be converted to believe in someone who was crucified by a Roman governor?

If these two hypotheses are true, then, of course, a very serious question mark is superimposed over the entire New Testament so far as its historicity, and even veracity, is concerned. But these theses have not been proven, and can easily be disproven. No firm link between Jesus and the Zealots has ever been established aside from the fact that one of his disciples, Simon Zelotes, had evidently been related to the movement at one time. Once, in symbolic fulfillment of prophecy, Jesus did suggest that his disciples buy swords, but when two were produced, he termed that armament program "enough" (Luke 22:36ff.). In any case, two swords are certainly a minuscule arsenal, and Jesus' later advice to Peter to sheathe one of them—"for all who take the sword will perish by the sword"—is hardly the remark of a political revolutionary.

The second thesis, that the Gospels falsely portray a Jewish prosecution, is far more serious. However, there is a very important, yet little known, support for the New Testament accounts from a surprising source: even purely Jewish rabbinical sources and traditions require the death penalty for Jesus of Nazareth, such as Sanhedrin 43a of the Babylonian Talmud, which states that he "shall be stoned because he has practiced sorcery and enticed Israel to apostasy."[4] And in 62 A.D., only twenty-nine years after Good Friday, a stunning near-parallel occurred: the high priest and the Sanhedrin in Jerusalem stoned to death James, the half-brother (or relative) of Jesus and first Christian bishop of Jerusalem in the absence of the Roman governor Albinus, who was later so angry at this execution that the high priest was deposed.[5]

The Talmud, moreover, heartily agrees with the New Testament in its evaluation of Annas and the priestly aristocracy of Jerusalem in the time of Jesus. Early Jewish traditions about Jesus were later gathered also in a fifth-century compilation called the Toledoth Jeshu, which freely assigns all responsibility for Jesus' conviction to the priests, hardly even mentioning Pontius Pilate. And finally, long before it supposedly became necessary to "sweeten" Pilate's role on Good Friday in order to gain Roman converts, Paul was writing the same version of the events at Jerusalem in his epistles, as would the Gospels later on. Unless these and similar facts are refuted

162

by hard evidence—not the flimsies of sensational theory—the New Testament records of the trial and conviction must stand as historical in essence.

Who, then, *was* responsible for crucifying Jesus? An incredible amount of bad thinking has gone into answering this vexed query, with very tragic consequences. Obviously, Pilate had the final responsibility for executing sentence, but he could very well have been pressured into it, as the Gospels claim. Were the Jews, then, morally responsible? The priestly prosecution, yes. Other Jews, too, then and since? Categorically *no!* Medieval Christianity erred tragically in developing an anti-Semitic attitude from Jewish involvement in Jesus' trial, which must stand as one of the supreme instances of illogic in Western history.

The prosecution, acting in good faith, did believe Jesus a dangerous religious terrorist and possible seditionist, but that prosecution represented only a small fraction of the Jewish populace at the time, and their specific responsibility is *not* transferrable. Indeed, Luke reports "a great multitude of the [Jewish] people . . . who bewailed and lamented" Jesus on his way to the cross (23:27, RSV), a verse too often overlooked in this connection. And in view of the fact that the founder and early membership of Christianity was Jewish, and that many of his own countrymen did indeed sympathize with Jesus, it is clearly ridiculous to pin any collective responsibility for Good Friday on "the Jews" then or since. If some bigot wishes to make much of the people's famous challenge, "His blood be on us and on our children!" it should be noted that Matthew records no sudden voice booming down from the sky in reply, "So be it!" (27:25).[6]

Responsible Christian theology emphasizes that it was God—not any Jewish prosecution—who was ultimately responsible for the Crucifixion, since all mankind was involved in, and affected by, the events swirling around the cross, not just one or another ethnic group. Finally, to be anti-Semitic because of Good Friday would be as ridiculous as hating Italians because Nero once threw Christians to the lions. The only final blunder would be to try to claim that Nero never persecuted Christians, because the records that claim he did must have a hopelessly anti-Italian bias!

21

At Skull Place

So they took Jesus; and carrying the cross by himself, he
went out to what is called The Place of the Skull, which in
Hebrew is called Golgotha. There they crucified him, and
with him two others, one on either side, with Jesus
between them. Pilate also had an inscription written and
put on the cross. It read, "Jesus of Nazareth,
the King of the Jews." JOHN 19:17–19

PERHAPS crucifixion was not *the* most painful death a person
could suffer—there are records of human torments that exceeded
in duration and intensity what a crucified victim would endure—but it
was one of the slower and more brutal forms of execution known to man,
and certainly the most public. From the moment the judgment went
against him, the condemned victim was *on display:* he had to shoulder his
thirty- or forty-pound wooden *patibulum,* or crossbeam, and carry it in a
hideously public parade out to the place of execution, where it would be
fastened to one of the upright stakes already standing there. The victim's
extremities were bound or nailed to the cross, and he was left to hang,
sometimes for several days before he died, as a public example and
warning to others to avoid *his* crime, which was plainly stated in the
titulus, a placard posted above his head.

Crucifixion was invented in the ancient Near East, and one of the
earliest accounts of mass execution via the cross was Darius I's crucifixion
of 3,000 political enemies in Babylon in 519 B.C. The Romans learned it
from their blood enemies the Carthaginians, who regularly used to crucify
their admirals for losing sea battles to Rome. Cicero termed it "the cruelest

and most hideous punishment" possible, and it was never inflicted on Roman citizens but reserved for slaves, pirates, and those political or religious rebels who had to suffer an exemplary death. Tortured by cramped muscles, unable to swat crawling and buzzing insects, hungry, thirsty, and naked before a taunting crowd, the victims had painfully few ways to retaliate. They might curse back at their tormentors, try spitting on them, or urinate triumphantly in their faces, as in the case of the slaves crucified after the Spartacus revolt.

Some writers have doubted that victims were ever nailed to the cross, claiming that the spikes would have torn through their flesh and failed to support them. But in the summer of 1968, archaeologist V. Tzaferis excavated some stone ossuaries in northeastern Jerusalem dating from the first century A.D. These were chests in which bones of the dead were reburied after the flesh had decomposed following original burial in a cave. One of these ossuaries, inscribed with the name Yehohanan Ben-Hagakol, contained the bones of a man who had obviously been crucified, the first such victim ever discovered. A large, rusty iron spike, seven inches long, had been driven through both heel bones after first penetrating an acacia wood wedge or plaque that held the ankles firmly to the cross. The nail must have encountered a knot on being driven into the cross, for the point of the spike had been bent directly backward. Slivers still clinging to it show that the cross was made of olive wood.

Israeli pathologist Dr. Nicu Haas further examined Yehohanan's bones and announced the following conclusions: the victim was between twenty-four and twenty-eight years old, with a triangular face, curved nose, robust chin, and good teeth, but he had a cleft palate on the right side. In addition to the iron spike, evidence of crucifixion included a deep scratch on the right radius bone, showing that a nail had penetrated between the two bones of his lower forearm just above the wrist, which abraded them as the victim writhed in agony.

Yehohanan, at any rate, had his lower arms pierced with nails, not his hands, but there were numerous variations of crucifixion. Even the detail of the two criminals (on crosses flanking Jesus) having their legs broken at the close of Good Friday to induce death—the *crurifragium*—has an exact parallel here: Yehohanan's right tibia and the left tibia and fibula were all broken in their lowest third segment at the same level, indicating a common crushing blow, probably from a mallet or sledge.[1]

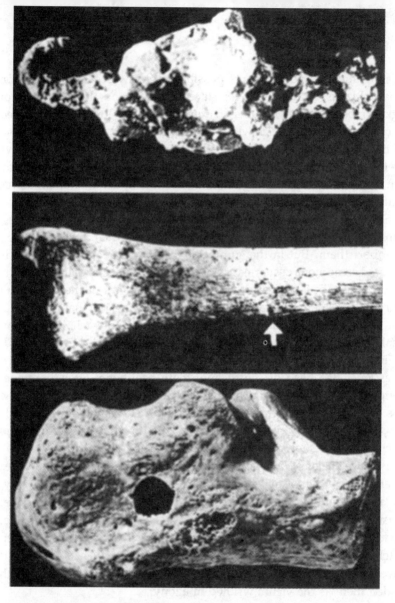

Recently discovered bones of the victim Yehohanan crucified in
Jerusalem at the time of Jesus. The upper photograph shows
the heel bones as discovered, coated with calcareous crust and
pierced by the seven-inch iron spike whose tip encountered a
knot and was bent back. In the center is the distal end of the
right arm bone, the arrow indicating where a nail scratched the
radius. The lower view is of the left heel bone, showing where
the spike penetrated from the lateral side.

Breaking legs, then, appears to have been "standard operating procedure" for crucifixion. The victim was deprived of stance to support his diaphragm and the mechanics of breathing, resulting in exhaustion and asphyxiation.

What was Yehohanan's crime? Something doubtless political, although we shall never know precisely what sent this probable contemporary of Jesus to the cross.

The Via Dolorosa

The route Jesus was forced to take on his final journey to the cross came to be called, long ago, the "Sorrowful Road." A centurion, dressed in Roman uniform, preceded him, even though the centurion was probably a Syrian or Samaritan auxiliary. Four soldiers formed the execution detail itself, but probably all of the 600 in Pilate's Jerusalem cohort were lining the roadsides to control any demonstrations.

Those that did break out were peaceful enough. Evidently a great crowd of people, including numerous women, bewailed and lamented his fate. By now news of Jesus' arrest and condemnation was spreading through Jerusalem, but too late for his followers to try to save him. Turning to them, Jesus said, "Daughters of Jerusalem, do not weep for me, but weep for yourselves and for your children," continuing with his prophecy of the destruction of Jerusalem, which would take place thirty-seven years later.

This is a very important scene that is too often overlooked. How many sermons have excoriated "the fickle mob that could shout 'Hosanna!' on Palm Sunday and then 'Crucify him!' on Good Friday." This interpretation, however, would seem faulty. To be sure, some people may have changed their minds about Jesus, but the shouting multitude in front of Pilate's tribunal consisted primarily of the priest-controlled Temple staff— their police alone numbered 10,000—whereas some of the Palm Sunday people were just now getting the news about Jesus' conviction and rushing to the roadside in tears, as in this scene.

By now it was high noon. Two other condemned men were also grunting under their crossbeams on the way out to Golgotha, a pair of felons about whom nothing is known. Jesus' scourging must have been more brutal or more recent than theirs, because he stumbled and collapsed under his crossbeam, and the troops had to impress a bystander, Simon from Cyrene in North Africa, into carrying the beam for him. Some have thought Simon a black, others a Jew attending the Passover in Jerusalem, but the experience of carrying the cross may have converted him. Mark says that he was "the father of Alexander and Rufus," who were obviously known to Christian readers of his Gospel (15:21), and Rufus' name crops up again at the close of Paul's letter to Rome (16:13).

When they reached Golgotha, the execution detail offered the condemned men a drink of wine mixed with myrrh as a narcotic. Jesus tasted it but would not swallow it. Perhaps he alone remembered that now, at the end of his life, came several incredible reminders of its beginning: myrrh had been given him by the Magi at the Nativity, and they had come to this very city asking for a newborn "King of the Jews." Astonishingly, this was precisely the charge that was now being nailed onto the central vertical post that would form his cross.

Where Was Golgotha?

Just as two different sites have been suggested for Jesus' trial before Pilate, so two locations are offered for Skull Place, yet only one of these has any historical support. Many current tourists prefer the other—the so-called Gordon's Calvary—since there is a somewhat skull-shaped hillock overlooking the Damascus Gate of Jerusalem, which British General Charles "Chinese" Gordon assumed was the crucifixion site, in 1883, just two years before he was killed at Khartoum. But, attractive as the location is, Gordon's Calvary and the nearby "Garden Tomb," in which Jesus was presumably buried, have no ancient historical traditions to authenticate them.

The traditional site, the Church of the Holy Sepulcher, does. As in the case of the Nativity at Bethlehem, the story goes back to the Roman emperor Hadrian (117–138 A.D.), who tried to romanize Jerusalem by obliterating its sacred sites. Over the precincts of Golgotha and the sepulcher in which Jesus was buried he erected a temple to Venus, patroness of Rome, but in trying thereby to erase the locations he merely preserved their identity.

In 325 A.D., while attending the first ecumenical council at Nicea, Bishop Macarius of Jerusalem persuaded Constantine the Great, first Christian emperor of Rome, to assist him in restoring the sacred sites. In the following year, the emperor's mother Helena made a pilgrimage to

Jerusalem and directly contributed to the work, which finally saw several structures erected where the Church of the Holy Sepulcher now stands. Although the complex of buildings around Golgotha has been destroyed and rebuilt several times, and the present structure gathering them all under one roof dates back only to Crusader times, the sites of Calvary and the tomb are the same as those uncovered seventeen centuries ago.

The present Church of the Holy Sepulcher, however, is usually disappointing to the modern visitor because almost nothing seems right about it. It stands squarely inside the present Old City of Jerusalem, while the crucifixion certainly took place outside. Moreover, the Church would seem to link Calvary and the sepulcher much too closely together, barely fifty yards, and the aesthetic disappointment inside the structure is almost suffocating. And yet all these objections are easily explainable.

It must be remembered that Jerusalem has certainly expanded since Jesus' day to include inside it what used to be the execution hillock standing originally outside the Ephraim gate in the northwestern wall. Excavations by Kathleen Kenyon in 1967 have uncovered an ancient quarry south of the Church of the Holy Sepulcher, further indicating that this general sector stood beyond the walls of Jerusalem in early New Testament times, since ancients went outside their closely packed towns to quarry stone.[2] And other tombs discovered just west of the Holy Sepulcher prove that this site lay outside Jerusalem at one time, since burials were never permitted within the walls.

But could the sepulcher have been located only a scant 150 feet northwest of Golgotha? Would the wealthy Joseph of Arimathea have had his new tomb, in which Jesus was buried, hewn so close to an area of public execution? Astonishingly, yes. Execution and burial grounds lay very close to each other in ancient towns, and this location, near one of Jerusalem's principal gates, would have been prestigious.[3] According to the Fourth Gospel, "Now there was a garden *in* the place where he was crucified, and in the garden there was a new tomb in which no one had ever been laid. . . . The tomb was *nearby*" (19:41–42, italics added).

Constantine's engineers constructed a great marble basilica around and to the north of the Golgotha hillock, and then built a separate monument over the Easter tomb. Originally, Joseph's sepulcher was a simple excavation in living rock, but the Roman engineers cut the surrounding matrix away from the tomb and erected a great domed *tholos,* or circular colonnade, around it. Finally, the Crusaders linked Golgotha, the basilica,

The Church of the Holy Sepulcher in Jerusalem, built over the
traditional sites of Golgotha (approximately under the small
cupola in the foreground) and the tomb of Joseph of Arimathea
in which Jesus was buried (under the largest dome).

The entrance and southern facade of the Church of the Holy Sepulcher in Jerusalem. A Good Friday procession is about to enter the basilica, whose right doorway has been walled up since the time of Saladin.

and the resurrection *tholos* under one roof, which is the present Church of the Holy Sepulcher.

Western visitors are usually disappointed by the potpourri of garish votive lanterns and chapels that cluster about the sacred sites. After entering from the south portal of the Church, the traditional site of Calvary is reached by climbing up some natural rock to a sanctuary sixteen feet above the floor of the basilica, the rise of Golgotha. At the end of the sanctuary stands the Altar of the Cross, constructed over outcroppings of living rock that still show a fissure caused by the earthquake attending Jesus' death, according to tradition. Under the altar is a silver disk with an opening in the center, presumably marking the spot where Jesus' cross was erected, but such locational precision, of course, is extremely doubtful.

Fifty yards to the northwest, under an ancient rotunda, stands the sepulcher. The excessively ornate edicule erected over the tomb and the artificial setting in general seem a poor contrast to vivid mental impressions of the first Easter. But during Holy Week each year, the entire basilica quivers with worshipers who recapitulate Jesus' final journey, death, and resurrection in an atmosphere of burning wax and incense, while the vast reaches of the structure reecho the chanting and singing of many thousands of pilgrims. The most spectacular moment is the lighting of the Holy Fire on Easter eve, when the Greek Orthodox patriarch hands a burning candle out from the sepulcher and into the basilica, where worshipers light their own tapers from his in expanding jubilation.

The Seven Last Statements

Back in time to the first Good Friday, Jesus had just refused the narcotic wine, and now the execution detail stripped off his clothes. They divided his garments into four shares, one for each auxiliary, but they had to cast lots for his cloak, since it was seamless. Perhaps it was the white robe Herod Antipas had awarded the mock king. At any rate, they shook knucklebone dice for it, and we have no idea who won.

Jesus' hands or wrists were nailed to the crossbeam, which was then lowered onto a vertical stake at Golgotha, and his feet were spiked onto it. He was probably made to straddle a wedge placed between his legs, as in other crucifixions, which would have borne his weight sufficiently so that the nailed hands would not, in fact, have torn apart.

173

Jesus maintained this agonizing position "from the sixth . . . until the ninth hour" (Matt. 27:45, RSV), that is, from noon till about 3 P.M. Sneers from the claque gathered around the crosses focused on a rather obvious theme: the wonder-worker who supposedly saved others could not even save his own skin. The soldiers mocked him in similar vein, "If you *are* the King of the Jews, save yourself!" (Luke 23:37).

The New Testament records seven final statements that Jesus made from the cross. There may well have been more, but these are the only ones reported. Not one of them was vindictive, yet the first did address itself to the taunts from below: "Father, forgive them; for they do not know what they are doing."

One of the felons crucified next to Jesus harped on the same, rather unimaginative theme as the voices below: "Are you not the Messiah? Save yourself—*and us!*" But his misery was seizing on anything—*anything*—to make him forget the present horror, even for a moment.

What happened next is familiar, but never ceases to amaze. The comrade of the felon proceeds to tell him off for this impertinence, admits their common guilt and Jesus' innocence, and then turns to the center cross with the plea, "Jesus, remember me when you come into your kingdom."

Jesus replies, "Truly I tell you, today you will be with me in Paradise."

Of all the disciples, John alone had the courage to show up at Golgotha, and he was standing near the foot of the cross with the three prime Marys in Jesus' life: his mother, whose heart must have been slowly breaking; his Aunt Mary, wife of Clopas; and Mary Magdalene. From the cross itself he made final provision for his mother in the famous statement, "Woman, here is your son." And then to John, "Here is your mother." From then on, John did indeed treat Mary as a mother, for earliest Christian traditions link Mary and John from Jerusalem to far-off Ephesus.

By now the sky had darkened ominously, as if the eastern Mediterranean were shadowed by a solar eclipse. Because of the full Passover moon, however, it could not possibly have been an eclipse. Glowering April skies are not unknown in Palestine, and sometimes dark siroccos or windstorms blow in from the desert, plunging the countryside into an uncanny darkness. Did the meteorological mood affect even Jesus? For he cried out, in the daily Aramaic spoken in Palestine, the opening words of Psalm 22: "*Eli, Eli lema sabbachthani?* My God, my God, why have you forsaken me?"

174

Most of Israel, Jordan, and the Negev are visible in this photograph
taken by the *Apollo 7* mission in October, 1968, with astronauts Schirra,
Cunningham, and Eisele. The Sea of Galilee, half beclouded, the
Jordan River, and the Dead Sea are in the left center of the picture. The
Mediterranean lies at the extreme left, just above the Sinai Desert.

An aerial view of Bethlehem, looking eastward over the Church of the Nativity in the center toward the hills of Judea.

(*Above, opposite*) A fourteen-pointed silver star in the Grotto of the Nativity marks the presumed place where Jesus was born.

 (*Below, opposite*) Christmas Eve illumination, looking from the Church of the Nativity out to Manger Square in Bethlehem.

The city of Nazareth in Galilee, where Jesus spent his boyhood years. Peeking just over the ridge at the left center is the summit of Mt. Tabor, where the Transfiguration presumably took place. To the right is the Plain of Esdraelon.

(Above) The excavations at ancient Capernaum along the Sea of Galilee. The octagon in the left foreground marks the presumed site of Peter's house, while to the right *(and below)* are the remains of the synagogue.

Hull of a first-century boat similar to the kind used by Jesus and his disciples, which was excavated from the bottom of the Sea of Galilee.

Jerusalem today, from the Mount of Olives. The golden Dome of the Rock marks the location where the Temple once stood.

View over the Dome of the Rock toward the Mount of Olives at Jerusalem.

The earliest know mosaic map of Jerusalem discovered at Madaba in Jordan, showing the colonnaded main street running left to right past the Church of the Holy Sepulcher at center.

The Jordan River, at the point where it flows out of the Sea of Galilee.

One of the towers of the Citadel in western Jerusalem, whose lower half shows surviving Herodian masonry that once constituted the base of the Tower Phasael, the largest of the three towers at the northern end of the Palace of Herod. Since Roman governors of Judea regularly held court in this palace, these great blocks of stone undoubtedly witnessed Jesus' condemnation by Pontius Pilate.

(Above) The Mount of Olives with the Church of All Nations in the foreground, sheltering olive trees at the reputed site for the Garden of Gethsemane. Onion domes in the upper right mark the Russian Orthodox Church of St. Mary Magdalene. The pathway to the left may have been used by Jesus on Palm Sunday.

A first-century, rock-hewn Jewish sepulcher at Abu-Gosh, west of Jerusalem, similar to the one in which Jesus was buried.

Sheep and goats grazing along the western shore of the Sea of Galilee near Magdala, home of Mary Magdalene. The Gospels record several resurrection appearances of Jesus in this vicinity, including the fish breakfast on the shores of the Sea (John 21) and the mountain appearance (Matthew 28), traditionally associated with the hills around Safad on the peak to the right.

(*Above*) The Sea of Galilee. One traditional site for the Mount of the Beatitudes is to the left.

The Jordan River, as it leaves the Sea of Galilee.

From the Pnyx Hill at Athens, a panorama to the east shows Mars' Hill on the left, where Paul addressed the Athenians (Acts 17), and the Acropolis on the right, crowned with the Parthenon.

View of Mars' Hill from the Acropolis, looking northwestward over Athens across the Agora toward the Temple of Hephaestus.

(Right) The great theater at Ephesus, scene of the silversmith's riot (Acts 19), with the Arcadian Way at the upper right.

(Below, right) The reconstructed facade of the library of Celsus at ancient Ephesus to the left, and the Gate of the Mithridates to the right.

(Below) Ruins of the Temple of Apollo at Corith.

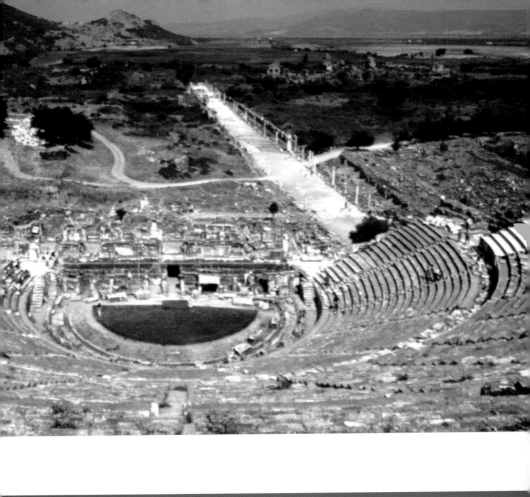

(Top) The Roman aqueduct that brought water from Mt. Carmel to Caesarea, where Paul was imprisoned for two years.

Rome, the final destination of Paul and Peter. The ruins of her ancient Forum still stand amid the modern city. To the left are the columns of the Temple of Castor and Pollux, at left center is the Arch of Septimius Severus, and at right center, the squarish, reconstructed Senate House.

Shortly afterward he uttered his fifth comment from the cross, the only slight complaint that entire Friday, "I am thirsty." The soldiers stuck a sponge on a reed, dipped it in a bowl of their common military *posca*—a sour but thirst-quenching combination of vinegar and water—and held it up to Jesus' lips. After sucking a little of it, Jesus announced the consummation of his mission: "It is finished." In Christian theology, this meant that God's great plan for saving man- and womankind had now been accomplished. The Messiah, the Christ, was also the Suffering Servant who had lived the perfect life, thus fulfilling God's law, yet had taken on himself the sins of humanity—the innocent having suffered for the guilty—so that life for all would come from the death of one. It had been "accomplished" indeed.

It remained only for Jesus to articulate the sublime dedication of Psalm 31. With a loud voice, his final words were: "Father, into your hands I commend my spirit." One last breath, and he died.

The spectacular events surrounding his death—the earthquake, the torn veil of the Temple, the centurion's comment, "Truly this man was God's Son!"—do not detract from the solemnity of the moment: Jesus of Nazareth, who for three incredible years had transformed the multitudes, was dead.

Was he surely dead? So that the three victims would not have to hang on their crosses after sundown and into the Passover sabbath, the priests requested that the *crurifragium* be inflicted. The execution detail broke the legs of the two felons, inducing immediate death. But when they approached the center cross, they saw that Jesus had already died. Still, as an executioner's gesture and to make assurance doubly sure, one of the men shoved a spear into Jesus' side. Blood and water flowed out of the wound, probably pericardial fluid or extravasated blood that had separated into its constituent red cells and plasma, possibly indicating a heart rupture. Or whatever else a pathologist might judge, Jesus was dead indeed (Matt. 27, Mark 15, Luke 23, John 19).

The Burial

It was Joseph of Arimathea who asked Pilate's permission to remove the body of Jesus from the cross and bury it. Joseph was a wealthy member of the Sanhedrin who had not voted to condemn Jesus and was doubtless

The Altar of the Crucifixion within the Calvary Chapel in the Church of the Holy Sepulcher. Jesus' central cross presumably stood at the altar area. On both sides of the altar, the limestone crest of Golgotha is now exposed under illuminated glass.

a disciple in secret. Although Romans had no requirement that a victim's body be removed from the cross—indeed, they often left corpses hanging indefinitely until picked clean by vultures—Jewish law was far more humane, requiring burial of a criminal on the same day as his execution (Deut. 21:23). Bowing to local custom in the matter, Pilate readily allowed Joseph to inter the body of Jesus, wondering only that he had died so soon.

Typical Jewish sepulchers of the time—and Joseph's must have been one of these—had two chambers hollowed out of rock, the first serving as a vestibule or entranceway into the tomb proper, which was a small squarish room with a shelf built into the far wall where the corpse was laid. Outside, the doorway into the vestibule was closed by a very heavy

The silver disk under the altar of the Crucifixion in the Church of the Holy Sepulcher marks the traditional spot where Jesus' cross stood at Golgotha.

circular stone that rolled down a slightly inclined runway or channel until it shut the sepulcher.

Nicodemus, another Sanhedrist who was a disciple in secret, helped his colleague Joseph in the burial process. He brought a great bundle of spices—myrrh and aloes—and placed these between the folds of the eight-foot linen shroud that he and Joseph wound around the body of Jesus, the standard Jewish practice. There was also a separate, smaller piece of gravecloth in which they wrapped Jesus' head and then placed it on a pillow of stones, as was customary. Some of the loyal women from Galilee watched the pair at work, intending to improve the necessarily hasty job as soon as the Sabbath was past. Finally, Joseph kicked away the wedge holding the door stone in its upper channel, and the great circle of rock grumbled down its track, shutting the sepulcher.

Only the Passover Seder that evening prevented the chief priests and Pharisees from asking Pilate any earlier, but the next morning they appeared at his palace with the following request: "Sir, we remember what that imposter said while he was still alive, 'After three days I will rise again.' Therefore command the tomb to be made secure until the third day; otherwise his disciples may go and steal him away, and tell the people, 'He has been raised from the dead,' and the last deception would be worse than the first."

Amazed at a fanaticism that could hound a man not only to his grave, but beyond it, Pilate replied, "You have a guard of soldiers; go, make it as secure as you can" (Matt. 27:63ff.).

Summoning a detachment of Temple police, they went to Joseph's tomb and secured the area, sealing the stone and stationing a guard. The seal was nothing more than a cord strung across the rock and fastened at each end with clay. Like any seal, its purpose was not to cement the rock but to indicate any tampering with it. (The wire seals on electric meters serve a similar function today.)

22

Easter Dawn

When the Sabbath was over, Mary Magdalene, and Mary
the mother of James, and Salome bought spices, so that
they might go and anoint him. And very early on the first
day of the week, when the sun had risen, they went to the
tomb. They had been saying to one another, "Who will roll
away the stone for us from the entrance to the tomb? When
they looked up, they saw that the stone, which was very
large, had already been rolled back. MARK 16:1–4

WHAT *did* happen at dawn on Sunday? If it were somehow possible to get an authentic replay of an event from the past, probably more people would opt for the first Easter than for any other episode in history. Or, if Jesus had lived in the twentieth century instead, his grave would probably have been guarded in a different fashion: scientists would have installed sensory devices both inside and outside the sepulcher; medical experts would have been scanning computers recording any of Jesus' life signs—or lack of them; theologians and philosophers would have recorded their impressions on tape; while photographers would have been ready to focus anything visible on film of every kind. Or *would* any of this have happened? Possibly the hints Jesus dropped about "rising on the third day" would have gone just as unheeded today as then.

Because scientific and scholarly measurement of the events on Sunday morning did not take place, but the resurrection itself did—so the earliest narratives claim—the Easter phenomenon has been vigorously denied, doubted, disregarded, believed, or enthusiastically proclaimed ever since. The central event of history, then, is also its most controversial.

The resurrection accounts in the New Testament—magnificent, joyful, triumphant narratives that they are—do present some startling variations on a common theme. One *or* two *or* three *or* more women approach the sepulcher at Easter dawn, according to John, Matthew, Mark, and Luke respectively. One angel greets them with the resurrection announcement in Matthew and Mark, while two angels do the same in Luke and John. Luke confines the resurrection appearances to the Jerusalem area, but the other three involve Galilee as well, and there are other problems of sequence that have bedeviled conservative scholars and cheered the critics.

First of all, it is no service either to Christianity or to honesty to gloss over these discrepancies, or, as is incredibly done in some circles, to deny that they exist. A seriatim reading of the last chapter in each of the Gospels will identify them plainly enough, and burying one's head in the sands of faith to hide from their existence is merely the posture of an ostrich.

On the other hand, some critical scholars are equally mistaken in seeking to use these inconsistencies as some kind of proof that the resurrection did not take place, for this is an illogical use of evidence. The earliest sources telling of the great fire of Rome, for example, offer far more serious conflicts on who or what started the blaze and how far it spread, some claiming that the whole city was scorched while others insist that only three sectors were reduced to ash. Yet the fire itself is historical: it actually happened.

Now, if such variations in the New Testament showed up *only* in the resurrection accounts, then the problem would be far more serious than it is. But all four Gospels contain similar variations in relating previous episodes in the life of Jesus, so the accounts of the first Easter are simply more of the same.

This leads to a point that has not been sufficiently stressed: actually, the variations in the resurrection narratives *tend to support, rather than undermine, their authenticity.* They demonstrate that there were several independent traditions stemming from some event that must indeed have happened to give rise to them. Clearly, Matthew and Luke, for example, did not blindly copy from Mark or from each other, and the multiple traditions are of maximum importance in supplying separate documentation for the Easter event. And the fact that differences among them were not edited out or harmonized shows both the honesty of Early Church

The traditional site of Calvary is indicated by the small hillock at the center in this model of ancient Jerusalem designed by Avi-Yonah, although it lay somewhat farther away from the wall than the angle of this photograph would suggest. In the foreground stands the tomb of the Hasmonean John Hyrcanus, who ruled Palestine from 135 to 104 B.C., while the four towers of the Fortress Antonia command the background. Here the 600 auxiliaries in Pilate's Jerusalem cohort were barracked, and here Peter (Acts 12) and Paul (Acts 23) were taken into custody.

copyists and the fact that there was no agreed upon—and therefore partially fabricated—version.

Even eyewitnesses can report the same event differently. In a common classroom demonstration of this fact, a professor stages some episode—perhaps a "crime" being perpetrated—and then, on the next day, he asks his students to record their impressions. The variations in their reports are stunning. Certainly the Easter witnesses, in reporting something as incredibly awesome as what they claimed to see, would tell their stories in similar, yet different ways.

The Women

Women play a more enviable role than men in the events of Holy Week. In contrast to the misunderstandings, betrayals, denials, and flight of the male followers of Jesus, it was women who anointed Jesus at Bethany, who punctured Peter's pretenses in the courtyard of Caiaphas, who warned Pilate to release Jesus because he was innocent, who commiserated Jesus' fate on the way to Golgotha, and who stood loyally under the cross until the end.

And it was women who were the first witnesses to the events of Easter morning. Just before dawn that Sunday, Mary Magdalene, Mary (the mother of James), Salome, and Joanna brought aromatic oils to anoint the body of Jesus. The Sabbath had prevented their doing this earlier, and they wished to improve on the necessarily hasty burial given Jesus by Joseph of Arimathea and Nicodemus. All of these women were Galilean followers of Jesus who had supported his ministry in the north country, also financially, and had now accompanied him to Jerusalem. Salome was probably the mother of the disciples James and John, while Joanna had important political connections: she was the wife of Herod Antipas' chief steward, Chuza.

But the story focuses primarily on Mary Magdalene, the only woman mentioned in all four Easter Gospels. She came from the coastal town of Magdala at the westernmost bulge of the Sea of Galilee, a place so notorious that it besmirched also Mary's reputation, for tradition has made of her an ex-prostitute. However, there is no real evidence that Mary had actually been plying the world's oldest profession, and after Jesus cured her unidentified but serious illness, she became one of his most devoted followers. The Fourth Gospel offers her most luminous portrait: the woman weeping at the empty tomb, talking with the risen Jesus whom, in her blurred vision, she thought a gardener, and finally radiantly recognizing him.

But before this or any of the other appearances, the women approaching Joseph's tomb had a substantial problem on their hands: "Who will roll away the stone for us from the entrance to the tomb?" The circle of rock shutting off the entrance was "very large," according to Matthew and Mark, while two ancient Gospel manuscripts add that it was a stone "which twenty men could scarcely roll" (Matt, 27:60).[1] Certainly this is an exaggerated embellishment, though it is true that it would require more strength to move such a gravestone up to an open position than to close it, due to its sloping channel.

Evidently the women were also unaware that the stone had been sealed, and that the whole area was under military guard. Had nothing else happened that Sunday morning, the soldiers would simply have refused them admission to the sepulcher and the women would have returned, spices heavy in hand. Then we would probably never even have heard of one Jesus of Nazareth, and Easter would be nothing more than a pagan spring fertility festival named for Eostre or Ostara, the reputed Anglo-Saxon goddess of the dawn.

But the Gospels claim that a momentous phenomenon occurred, and the rest of this chapter is a reconstruction of the New Testament accounts. The earth shook, the gravestone was dislodged and rolled open, the guards trembled and "became like dead men," and an angel announced to the understandably terrified women, "Do not be afraid; I know that you are looking for Jesus who was crucified. He is not here; for he has been raised, as he said. Come, see the place where he lay. Then go quickly and tell his disciples, 'He has been raised from the dead'" (Matt. 28: 5–7).

With the most contrary emotions coursing through them to test their sanity, the women fled from the tomb in both fear and joy to tell the disciples. Matthew records Jesus himself intercepting them in his first resurrection appearance with the salutation, "Greetings!" Now surer of the event, they took hold of his feet and worshiped him in an ecstacy of gladness. "Do not be afraid," Jesus said. "Go and tell my brothers to go to Galilee; there they will see me" (28:9–10).

The Men

The women hurried off to the disciples with their incredible tidings, but the Eleven greeted their reports with unanimous disbelief. "Idle tales!" "Hysterical women!" or "The demons have returned to Mary Magdalene" may have been the more charitable comments.

Exterior facade of the edicule constructed over the presumed sepulcher in which Jesus was buried, now under the rotunda of the Church of the Holy Sepulcher.

Indeed, the fact that *women* served as the first witnesses to the resurrection was later something of an embarrassment for the disciples. Not that they were jealous of them for getting the first glimpse, as it were, but women did not have the right to bear witness in Jewish courts—their testimony, in that day, was deemed unreliable—so the initial reaction of the Eleven was understandably one of suspicion and disbelief. Again, if the resurrection accounts had been manufactured out of whole cloth, women would *never* have been included in the story—at least, not as first witnesses.

Perhaps for this reason there may have been a change of plans at least implied in the Gospels: Jesus, according to Luke and John, appeared to the disciples in Jerusalem even before their planned reunion in Galilee,or there might have been no reunion at all with the disciples refusing to make the trip just on the word of the women.

Two of the men, however, had reason to give some credence to the women's reports. Peter and John, after hearing Mary Magdalene tell of the missing body, raced to the tomb—John got there first—and they both went inside the sepulcher. There they saw the linen gravecloths in two parts: the main linen bands lying flat, pressed down by the eighty-pound weight of the spices,[2] and the separate napkin, which had covered Jesus' head, still in a bunched-up, rolled condition at the end of the stone slab on which his body had lain, retaining its shape because of its smaller size. According to this literal interpretation of the Greek, in which John was written, it seemed as if the body simply vanished from its grave wrappings, leaving them exactly in place except for gravity flattening the main shroud.[3]

Peter and John, at any rate, knew for a fact that Jesus' body was missing, even if they did not yet believe in its revivification. Their doubt, however, lasted no longer than twelve hours, because on Easter evening came the first general appearance of Jesus to his disciples. In despair over the evident failure of Jesus' mission, and in fear that the priestly aristocracy in Jerusalem might persecute them too, ten of the Eleven were huddled behind locked doors when suddenly Jesus appeared to them and said, "Peace be with you." Evidently he had materialized through the walls, and the disciples—in their usual posture in such instances—were merely terrified. Only spirits behaved in that fashion.

But this was only the same "ghost" that had once scared them while walking on the Sea of Galilee. "Why are you frightened?" Jesus asked. Then, showing them his pierced extremities, he said, "Look at my hands and my feet; see that it is I myself. Touch me and see; for a ghost does not have flesh and bones as you see that I have."

The mood among the disciples was shifting instantaneously from disbelief to radiant joy. As a kind of final visual aid, Jesus even asked them, "Have you anything here to eat?" They gave him a piece of broiled fish, a dish appropriate enough for a partial crew of ex-fishermen. Jesus took the fish and ate it, hardly the gesture expected of a specter. None of the Gospels was fully able to convey the incredible happiness at the reunion between the Teacher and his disciples.

Then it was time for one of Jesus' final discourses with them, in which he directly keyed his mission to Old Testament prophecy, adding, "Thus it is written, that the Messiah is to suffer and to rise from the dead on the third day, and that repentance and forgiveness of sins is to be proclaimed in his name to all nations, beginning from Jerusalem. You are witnesses of these things" (Luke 24:46ff.).

Indeed, in view of his own prediciton that he would rise on the third day—so specific that the Temple authorities tried to forestall a grave robbery—and against the background of his already demonstrated success in dealing with death, perhaps the event at Easter dawn should not have been *that* surprising to the Eleven.

One of the disciples, however, was missing from this glad reunion: Thomas the Twin. The sources do not tell us what had detained him. Conceivably, Thomas was out, trying to shape a new life for himself after three years he may have thought wasted in the wrong cause. Then, when his colleagues broke the happy news to him, "We have seen the Lord!" Thomas simply balked. Evidently they also mentioned Jesus' marks of identification, the crucifixion scars, for Thomas challenged that point directly: "Unless *I* see the mark of the nails in his hands, and put *my* finger in the mark of the nails and *my* hand in his side, I will not believe" (John 20:24–25, italics added).

For this remark, future ages would call Thomas a fool, a dullard, a doubter, or, more charitably, a skeptic. Germans in the Middle Ages used the ass as the sign of this apostle, in ridiculing his disbelief, but the modern era tends instead to applaud Thomas' demand for empirical proof. His was a scientific challenge, a demand for direct and objective, not hearsay, evidence that would reach his five senses. The tales of excited women were not enough. The supposed apparition deluding his colleagues was not enough. But his personally touching the scars would indeed be enough—if that were possible.

A week later, the disciples were gathered at the same place, only this time Thomas was with them. Again Jesus appeared to them with the Hebrew greeting, "*Shalom!*"—"Peace be with you!" Then he walked purposefully over to Thomas and met him on his own terms: "Put your finger here and see my hands. Reach out your hand and put it in my side. Do not doubt but believe."

Overcome, Thomas could only manage to stammer, "My Lord and my God!"

"Have you believed because you have seen me?" Jesus chided him gently. "Blessed are those who have not seen and yet have come to believe" (John 20:26ff.).

Other Appearances

That comment focused largely on the future. For the present, most of those who believed had also, like Thomas, seen the risen Jesus, for he made other climactic appearances—Luke calls them "convincing proofs"

Interior of the edicule in the Church of the Holy Sepulcher, the marble slab marking the traditional place where Jesus lay. Nothing, however, remains of the original tomb but the rock foundation, since the caliph Al Hakem brutally demolished the Church of the Holy Sepulcher in 1009 A.D., and a successor razed the tomb to the ground.

(Acts 1:3)—over the next forty days. Sometimes Jesus came in a very unobtrusive and casual manner, as he already had on the afternoon of Easter Sunday, when he appeared to two of his followers on the road to Emmaus. Cleopas and his unnamed friend, both probably members of the larger group of seventy of Jesus' disciples (Luke 10:1), were walking the seven-mile trip from the Holy City when Jesus joined them as a fellow traveler. They failed to recognize him until they had supper together in Emmaus, after which they raced back to Jerusalem and told the disciples.

There were specialized appearances to individual followers for a specific purpose: to Simon Peter, apparently as a reconfirmation in apostleship after his denial, as well as to his half-brother James, the future bishop of Jerusalem.

There were additional appearances to the disciples, including two unforgettable scenes among their familiar haunts up in the north country. In one, a poignant recapitulation of their first meeting with the Teacher, the disciples were again fishing on the Sea of Galilee when they followed piscatorial directives from the Man on shore and brought him 153 fish for their breakfast. In another, on a mountain in Galilee, Jesus appeared not only to the Eleven but also to at least five hundred in a broader circle of his followers. And at the final parting on the Mount of Olives, the disciples witnessed Jesus' ascension, i.e., his withdrawal into another dimension.

In one of the earliest records of the Easter event, written before any of the Gospels, Paul would pen these words to readers in the city of Corinth:

> For I handed on to you as of first importance what I in turn had received: that Christ died for our sins in accordance with the scriptures, and that he was buried, and that he was raised on the third day in accordance with the scriptures, and that he appeared to Cephas [Peter], then to the twelve. Then he appeared to more than five hundred brothers [and sisters] at one time, most of whom are still alive, though some have died. Then he appeared to James, then to all the apostles. Last of all, as to one untimely born, he appeared also to me. (1 Cor. 15:3–8)

The "last," of course, referred to the episode on the Damascus road. Paul wrote this statement only a score of years after the first Easter.

23

Doubts and Skepticism

If Christ has not been raised, then our proclamation has
been in vain and your faith has been in vain. . . . If for this
life only we have hoped in Christ, we are of all people most
to be pitied.   I CORINTHIANS 15:14,19

P AUL'S belief in the resurrection, shared by early Christianity,
was absolute and categorical. Anything less than Jesus' actual,
physical, historical triumph over death would have vitiated the cause to
which he had staked his life, and rendered Christians in general a pitiable
lot.

Nevertheless, the apostle's exuberant faith has not been universally
shared since the first Easter, and a literal resurrection of Jesus' body has
been denied not only by non-Christians but generally also by liberal
theology. The opposition stems from this basic argument: a physical resurrection, like the other so-called miracles in the Bible, could never have
happened, since natural laws simply cannot be suspended. The dead are
not raisable today; nor were they then.

Since, however, *something* must have taken place on Easter morning
to have ignited that spiritual explosion called Christianity, critics have
advanced the following hypotheses to explain some of the phenomena
noted at the first Easter.

The "stolen body" theory. The oldest and simplest explanation for an
empty tomb is that Jesus' body was removed by the disciples either to
protect it from possible desecration or to hatch the myth of a risen Christ.
Or Joseph of Arimathea, who had first hastily buried Jesus in a cave near
the execution site, later gave the body permanent, secret burial in his own

189

tomb. Conversely, he may have had second thoughts about his charitable action in burying a criminal and therefore removed the body so it would not contaminate his tomb. Or Pontius Pilate may have ordered its secret removal to forestall any cult of martyrdom at the grave site. At any rate, when the women came to the original tomb at Sunday dawn, they would have found it empty.

The "wrong tomb" theory. Because of Jesus' hasty burial and the fact that they came in dim morning light, the women were not sure exactly which of the many rock-hewn tombs in the area was Joseph's. When they examined the wrong one, which was empty, they were startled by a gardener or grave worker (whom they thought an angel), who guessed their mission and tried to correct their mistake. "He is not here," the gardener advised, and then pointed to the correct sepulcher, "See the place where he lay." But the women panicked, fled, and later announced an empty tomb.

The "lettuce" theory. This is an alternate of the conjecture above. The gardener was so piqued at curiosity-seekers trampling over lettuce seedlings he had planted in the garden around Joseph's tomb that he removed the body of Jesus and reinterred it elsewhere. But visitors still came to the now-empty sepulcher and proclaimed the resurrection. Crude as this hypothesis sounds, it was, in fact, one of the early non-Christian explanations for the resurrection, and the second-century Church father Tertullian himself records it.[1]

The "swoon" theory. Jesus never really died, in this hypothesis. He only appeared to die, but, perhaps due to the effect of some deep narcotic administered to him on the cross, he lingered on in a state of suspended animation. After his burial, the cool of the tomb and the healing effect of the spices wrapped around his body revived him. Exchanging his grave clothes for those of a gardener, he somehow managed to crawl out of the sepulcher and then encountered Mary Magdalene. After her glad recognition, he made his way to Joseph or the disciples, who nursed him back to health and presented him as the risen Lord. Forty days later, his wounds got the better of him, but just before he expired, he assembled the disciples on a mountain and parted from them by walking into a cloud. Though he was crawling off to die, the Eleven believed he had ascended into heaven. Various forms of this theory have been suggested ever since the pagan philosopher Celsus first proposed it in the second century A.D.[2]

The "psychological" or "hallucination" theory. The various visions or appearances of Jesus were merely the psychic effects of profound wish fulfillment, according to some critics. When one of the women claimed to see the resurrected Jesus, the experience became contagious, and soon others "saw" him, too, including finally the disciples also. Jesus' prophecies of his triumph over death had primed his followers to expect exactly that, and so the whole myth began with "the visions of a half-frantic woman," according to Celsus.

Others, such as the nineteenth-century German critic David Strauss, have suggested that one of the disciples, perhaps Peter, sustained the original hallucination. According to this scenario, the Eleven fled to Galilee after the crucifixion, where they finally calmed down and reflected on Jesus. The impulsive Peter, in particular, was meditating on his dead master when suddenly he had a sensation or vision of Jesus' surviving presence. Peter himself could not know that this was just a fantasy of his own imagination because, like his contemporaries who believed in ghosts and spirits, he would have been unable to distinguish between a real incursion from another dimension and a subjective hallucination. Peter's enthusiasm quickly became contagious, and when confused and exaggerated reports were received from the women in Jerusalem, the disciples, clutching at every resurrection rumor, returned joyously to the Holy City and proclaimed the new faith. Unconsciously, they began pushing back the date of Peter's vision until it was fixed at the third day after the crucifixion, influenced by such prophecies as Hosea 6:2: "On the third day he will raise us up. . . ." They did all this not as frauds or liars but in good faith.

The "twin brother" theory. Jesus had an exact twin brother, in this scenario, who substituted for him on occasion but generally stayed out of sight. When Jesus truly died on Friday, the twin emerged triumphantly from seclusion on Sunday, and people beheld the risen Lord.

Other theories, such as the rapid-decay hypothesis, are not worth the listing. In Palestine's hot climate, supposedly, the process of organic putrefaction was accelerated, and the sepulcher was not visited until the body had fully decayed. But in only three days, this would have been manifestly impossible.

191

The Garden Tomb in northern Jerusalem, showing the channel in which the circular doorstone—now missing—moved. This Jewish sepulcher, probably from the seventh century B.C., is partially walled in.

A Critique of Criticism

Certainly these various theories stand as tributes to human ingenuity. And they have surely stood the test of time: although most of them are still in current use, nearly all were advanced in one form or another many centuries ago. The different explanations also have this in common: they all require at least as much faith to believe in their validity as in the resurrection itself. For the overpowering weight of all the sources, all circumstantial evidence from the first Easter, and logic itself stand against them.

The "stolen body" theory founders on two insurmountable obstacles: the problem of motive and the problem of execution. To plan a tricky grave robbery of a closely guarded tomb would have required an incredibly strong incentive by a daring and extremely skillful group of men. But who had this incentive? Who had the motive and then the courage necessary to bring it off? Certainly not the dispirited disciples, huddling and hiding in their despair over Jesus' evident failure and in fear of the Temple authorities—hardly a pack of calculating schemers enthusiastically planning to dupe their countrymen. Certainly not their discredited leader, Peter, who, unable to stand by Jesus in life, could not possibly have had the audacity to snatch his body in death. Certainly not Joseph of Arimathea or Nicodemus, who were probably already suspected by their Sanhedral colleagues for their attention to Jesus' body. If, as is sometimes argued, they were merely showing charity to a criminal that they later regretted, why did they not bury and then reinter all three victims that Friday? And certainly Pontius Pilate would have been the last to disturb the body: after permitting the sepulcher to be sealed and guarded, he was glad to be done with the sorry business.

But even if the disciples did have the overpowering motive and the incredible courage to steal a body and then—with total cynicism—to announce a resurrection, how could they hope to achieve it? The grave area was crawling with guards specifically instructed to forestall any such attempt. Certainly there were not so many as "thirty Romans and a thousand Jews," as the Slavonic version of Josephus has it,[3] but it would have been ridiculous for any guards to go to the trouble of sealing the sepulcher and setting a watch if they were not more than adequate to handle any attempted theft by night or riot by day. Later on, Peter would be guarded by four squads of four men each when imprisoned by Herod

193

Agrippa (Acts 12), so sixteen would be a minimum number expected *outside* a prison. Guards in ancient times always slept in shifts, so it would have been impossible for a raiding party to step over all their sleeping faces, as is sometimes claimed. The commotion caused by breaking the seal, rolling the stone open, entering the tomb, and lifting out the body would surely have awakened the guards even if they had all been sleeping.

Admittedly, there was indeed a period of time when the sepulcher was unguarded: the approximately twelve or thirteen hours between the burial of Jesus on Friday evening and the priests' request for a guard from Pilate early Saturday morning. A raiding party *could* have removed the body Friday night while everyone was sleeping off wine from the Passover Seder. Although the New Testament does not record whether or not the guard first rolled back the stone on Saturday morning to make sure the body of Jesus was still inside before sealing it, the most primitive logic would have dictated that they do just that. They would hardly have sealed and guarded an empty tomb. That they did in fact open the grave can easily be concluded from the reaction of the priests when the shaken guards reported the missing body to them: "You must say," they were instructed, "'His disciples came by night and stole him away while we were asleep'" (Matt. 28:13). Obviously they would have had a *much* better excuse had they found the tomb empty already on Saturday morning, which would not have compromised the soldiers.[4]

The "wrong tomb" theory is interesting enough, but Matthew tells of Mary Magdalene and "the other Mary" directly observing the burial of Jesus on Friday evening, when they had specifically gauged the size of the stone, so it seems extremely unlikely that they would have erred. If they had, Joseph of Arimathea or the guards assigned to the sepulcher would certainly have corrected them in the ensuing furor.

The "lettuce," or "salad," theory introduces a note of humor and nothing more, for the versatile gardener (who evidently transplanted bodies as well as lettuce) would have had some answering to do to the owner of the sepulcher, to say nothing of his having been prevented by the guards in the first place.

The "swoon" theory is very ingenious, but it rides roughshod over all evidence from the sources—so much so that there was no hint of this theory by any of the early opponents of Christianity. True, there is a recorded instance of a victim being taken down from a cross and surviving. The Jewish historian Josephus, who had gone over to the Roman side in

Interior of the Garden Tomb, showing a broken stone slab on which the body of the deceased was placed.

the rebellion of 66 A.D., discovered three of his friends being crucified. He asked the Roman general Titus to reprieve them, and they were immediately removed from their crosses. Still, two of the three died anyway, even though they had apparently been crucified only a short time.[5] In Jesus' case, however, there were the additional complications of scourging and exhaustion, to say nothing of the great spear thrust that pierced his rib cage and probably ruptured his pericardium. Romans were grimly efficient about crucifixions: victims did *not* escape with their lives.

And even if Jesus were history's great exception in this instance, how could a crawling, wounded near-cadaver inspire in his followers the founding of a faith based on his resurrection? Even David Strauss, the critic who propounded the hallucination theory, wrote:

195

It is impossible that a being who had stolen half-dead out of the sepulcher, who crept about weak and ill, wanting medical treatment, who required bandaging, strengthening, and indulgence, and who still at last yielded to his sufferings, could have given the disciples the impression that he was a conqueror over death and the grave, the Prince of Life: an impression which lay at the bottom of their future ministry.[6]

The "psychological" or "hallucination" theory would be attractive if only one person had claimed to see a vision of the risen Christ, perhaps Mary Magdalene, who formerly may have had psychological problems anyway. But the disciples were a hardheaded and hardly hallucinable group, especially Thomas. And, if the sources have any validity, there would have to have been collective hallucinations for different groups of up to five hundred in size, all of them seeing the same thing—a virtual impossibility in the case of a phenomenon that is usually extremely individualistic. Many different people will *not* see the same thing at different places in any general hallucination, mirage, daydream, or mass hysteria.

Such visions, moreover, are generated only when the recipients are in an agitated state of expectancy and in hopes of seeing their wishes fulfilled, a mood diametrically opposite from that of the disciples, who were hopelessly saturated in sorrow and despair. In fact, news of the resurrection nearly had to be forced on them in the face of their obvious disbelief.

And why, incidentally, did such visions ever end? The New Testament records of Jesus' appearances stop abruptly after forty days with the Ascension, whereas such hallucinations might have continued for decades, centuries. Finally, this theory does not even touch the problem of an empty tomb.

The remaining hypotheses are so weak that they need no commentary.[7] None of these theories, then, offers any solid base for historical reconstruction of what happened on the first Easter morning. If honestly examined, they appear quite fanciful, and all of them raise far more difficulties than they solve. No one theory explains all the phenomena reported at the time, and it would take an incredible combination of several of them to begin to do so. This much must be admitted, not merely on any basis of Christian apologetic, but of sober historical inquiry.

24

An Empty Tomb

They found the stone rolled away from the tomb, but when
they went in, they did not find the body.   LUKE 24:2–3

C AN history tell us what actually *did* happen on that crucial
dawn?

Many facts from antiquity rest on just one ancient source, while two
or three sources in agreement generally render the fact unimpeachable.
In the case of the first Easter, there are at least *seven* ancient sources—
the four Gospels, *Acts*, and the letters of Paul and Peter—but this has
not led to universal acceptance of the resurrection as a datum of history.
Why not? Because the more unlikely the episode, the stronger the
evidence demanded for it. So if something supernatural were claimed,
the evidence required to support it would have to be of an unimpeachable, absolute, and, indeed, direct eyewitness nature. Quite obviously,
however, such categorical evidence disappeared with the death of the
last eyewitnesses nineteen centuries ago.

Nevertheless, important historical evidence—quite apart from the
Gospels—can be assembled to show that *the tomb, at any rate, was empty
on Easter morning.* It should be added immediately that an empty tomb
does not prove a resurrection, although a resurrection would require an
empty tomb. Its occupancy, indeed, would effectively disprove it.

What happened in Jerusalem seven weeks after Easter could have
taken place only if Jesus' body were missing from Joseph's sepulcher.
For, beginning at the festival of Pentecost and continuing thereafter, Peter
and the other apostles sustained personality transformations inexplic-
able apart from their blazing faith in the resurrection. Abandoning their

craven fear of the Jerusalem authorities, they began preaching a resurrected Christ with almost reckless boldness from no less a forum than the Temple itself.[1] To Christians, what changed these men is itself a proof of the resurrection, and a chapter could be devoted to this phenomenon alone. But it is the reaction of the priestly authorities that, even for the neutral historian, must constitute evidence for an empty tomb. The Temple establishment did *not* do the obvious to counter the apostles' preaching: they did not lead an official procession out to Joseph's tomb, where, for all to see, they could have given the death blow to the dramatically growing kernel of Christianity by opening Joseph's sepulcher and revealing the moldering body of Jesus of Nazareth. They did not do so because they knew the tomb was empty, even if they had an official explanation for this: the disciples had stolen the body. But in offering this, their admission was implicit: the sepulcher was vacant.

Some have tried to defeat this point by claiming that the disciples preached only a spiritual resurrection of the soul, with the body so unimportant that no one would have bothered to check a still-occupied tomb. This theory would be attractive in a Greek context, where philosophers taught the immortality of the soul, but not among Jews, who believed that resurrection was nothing if it did not involve the physical body.

This objection must now inevitably arise: But the record of the apostles' preaching a resurrected Jesus and the supposed failure of the authorities to produce the body rests only on New Testament sources biased in favor of Christianity. True, it rests on them, but not *only* on them. Some important, yet long overlooked, evidence derives also from purely Jewish sources and traditions.

Jewish Evidence

Understandably, this was hostile to Christianity, yet in none of the early Jewish writings is the statement made that the body of Jesus was still in its tomb that Sunday morning. Rather, Jewish polemic shared with Christians the conviction that the sepulcher was empty, but gave natural explanations for it. And such positive evidence within a hostile source is the strongest kind of evidence and becomes self-authenticating. For example, if Cicero, who despised Catiline, admitted that the fellow had

Tombs of the wealthy in this era were hewn out of rock and closed by a cylindrical stone, often a millstone, set in a channel. The tomb of Joseph of Arimathea in which Jesus was buried was undoubtedly very much like this sepulcher at Abu-Gosh west of Jerusalem, the ancient Kiriath-Jearim where the Ark of the Covenant remained for a time (I Sam. 7).

one good quality—courage—among a host of bad ones then the historian correctly concludes that Catiline was at least courageous.

Some Jewish sources treat the matter neutrally. One of the earliest and most authoritative historians of this age was Flavius Josephus, whose celebrated reference to Jesus in *Antiquities* 18:63–64 states, in part, "He was the Messiah . . . for he appeared alive again on the third day." Since it is extremely unlikely that any non-Christian Jew could have written this statement—and Josephus did not convert—it is properly regarded as an early Christian interpolation today. In 1972, however, Professor Schlomo Pines of Hebrew University in Jerusalem announced his finding of an Arabic manuscript with a differing and probably original version of this passage, which states: "His disciples . . . reported that he had appeared to them three days after his crucifixion and that he was alive; accordingly, he was perhaps the Messiah. . . ." This is language a Jew might have written with less difficulty, but what no one has yet pointed out is the remarkable fact that Josephus does *not* seek to scotch the resurrection claim by any information at his disposal that Jesus' body still lay in its grave. Certainly this is an argument from silence, but the silence is especially eloquent in view of Josephus' known habit of roasting false Messiahs elsewhere in his histories, in contrast to the near-favorable reference here. The complete, *un*interpolated passage in Josephus is as follows:

> At this time there was a wise man called Jesus, and his conduct was good, and he was known to be virtuous. Many people among the Jews and the other nations became his disciples. Pilate condemned him to be crucified and to die. But those who had become his disciples did not abandon his discipleship. They reported that he had appeared to them three days after his crucifixion and that he was alive. Accordingly, he was perhaps the Messiah, concerning whom the prophets have reported wonders.[2]

Well into the second century A.D. and long after Matthew recorded its first instance, the Jerusalem authorities continued to admit an empty tomb by ascribing it to the disciples' stealing the body. In his *Dialogue with Trypho*, Justin Martyr, who came from neighboring Samaria, reported c. 150 A.D. that the Jewish authorities even sent specially commissioned emissaries across the Mediterranean to counter Christian claims with this explanation of the resurrection.[3]

Early Jewish traditions regarding Jesus were later gathered also in a fifth-century compilation called the *Toledoth Jeshu*, which offers a garbled but interesting version of Jesus' burial. The disciples planned to steal the body of Jesus so they could claim a resurrection, the *Toledoth* states. But Juda, a gardener, overheard their plans, and so he dug a grave in his own garden, stole Jesus' corpse from Joseph's tomb, and then laid it in the newly dug pit. When the disciples came to the original sepulcher and found it empty, they proclaimed Jesus' resurrection in Jerusalem. The Jews, who also found the tomb empty, were perplexed and in mourning until Juda wondered why everyone was so long-faced. Upon learning the cause, he smiled and conducted them to his garden where he unearthed the body of Jesus. Overjoyed, the priestly authorities asked Juda to give

Fishermen on the Sea of Galilee, looking north toward
Magdala, home of Mary Magdalene.

them the body, but he said, "No, I'll sell it to you." "How much?" they asked. "Thirty pieces of silver," came the reply. The priests gladly paid it, and then dragged the body of Jesus through the streets of Jerusalem.[4]

It must be stated that Jewish scholars today regard the *Toledoth Jeshu* with total disdain, but the fact remains that this compilation, which reflects early traditions, the Talmud, and the fourth-century Jewish historian Josippon, agrees that Jesus' original tomb was empty.

Roman Evidence?

Provincial governors in the Roman Empire had to dispatch *acta*—annual reports of their activities—to the emperor, and Justin Martyr claims that Pilate mentioned the case of Jesus in his records prepared for Tiberius.[5] But these have never been found, possibly due to the destruction of government archives in the great fire of Rome in 64 A.D.

Some scholars think that Pilate *may* have included in his *acta* a reference to the empty sepulcher along with a natural explanation for it—Jesus' body having been stolen—because a fascinating inscription was found in Nazareth on a 15-by-24-inch marble slab that might have been prompted by Tiberius' reply to Pilate. The inscription is an edict against grave robbery, and was written in Greek (italics added):

> Ordinance of Caesar. It is my pleasure that graves and tombs remain perpetually undisturbed for those who have made them for the cult of their ancestors or children or members of their house. If, however, anyone charges that another has either demolished them, or has in any other way *extracted the buried, or has maliciously transferred them to other places in order to wrong them, or has displaced the sealing or other stones,* against such a one I order that a trial be instituted, as in respect of the gods, so in regard to the cult of mortals. For it shall be much more obligatory to honor the buried. Let it be absolutely forbidden for any one to disturb them. In case of violation I desire that the offender be sentenced to capital punishment on charge of violation of sepulture.[6]

All previous Roman edicts concerning grave violation set only a large fine, and one wonders what presumed serious infraction could have led the Roman government to stiffen the penalty precisely in Palestine and to erect a notice regarding it specifically in Nazareth or vicinity. If only the "Caesar" had identified himself, but most scholars conclude—from the style of lettering in the inscription—that the edict derives from Tiberius or Claudius, either of whom *might* have reacted to tidings of the Easter enigma in Jerusalem. Nothing conclusive, however, has thus far been discovered from Roman sources.

Other Evidence

What happened to the Christian movement itself speaks strongly for an empty tomb. The seedbed for the first budding and growth of the Church was in the city of Jerusalem itself, where, of all places, it would have been ridiculous to preach a risen Christ unless both the apostles and their hearers knew that Joseph's sepulcher was empty. Some months later, the authorities were so desperate to stop the movement that they even resorted to persecution. A far more effective tool would have been at least an elaborate counter-rumor that there was a body in Joseph's grave after all, but this was never attempted because by then, apparently, too many Jerusalemites had seen for themselves that the sepulcher was empty.

Accordingly, if all the evidence is weighed carefully and fairly, it is indeed justifiable, according to the canons of historical research, to conclude that the tomb of Joseph of Arimathea, in which Jesus was buried, was actually empty on the morning of the first Easter. And no shred of evidence has yet been discovered in literary sources, epigraphy, or archaeology that would disprove this statement.

This is as far as history can go. Pursuing any answer to the fascinating question, *Why* was the tomb empty? leads very simply to two kinds of answers: the sepulcher was empty due to (1) some natural cause, or (2) some preternatural cause.

If it were a natural cause, this must still be discovered, because none of the theories advanced thus far is in any way probable or convincing. The empty tomb, in this interpretation, becomes one of the great, unresolved enigmas in history.

Christianity holds to the second alternative, that the tomb was empty due to Jesus' resurrection, which, of course, is what the New Testament proclamation is all about. But here also there is *some* supporting evidence outside the four Easter Gospels. The psychological change of the disciples is certainly striking. What transformed Peter, the man who could be

A shallow-draft fishing boat on the Sea of Galilee at sunrise.

unhinged by questions from a servant girl, into so bold a spokesman for the faith that even the entire Sanhedrin could not silence him? Had the disciples deceitfully tried to spawn a new faith on the world, would they have gone on to give their very lives for it? Clearly, they were themselves convinced that Jesus rose, for myths do not make martyrs.

The transformation of James the Just, Jesus' doubting half-brother, and of Paul, a convinced enemy of the fledgling church, is even more striking, and the conversion of the many Jerusalem priests mentioned in Acts 6:7 equally so.

One of the Jewish beliefs held with the most tenacity is observance of the Sabbath, and yet Christian Jews transferred their worship from Saturday to Sunday, which they called "the Lord's Day." Only some drastic consideration would have introduced this change: their weekly celebration of the resurrection.

204

Finally, the birth and growth of the Christian Church itself, its survival and expansion across nineteen centuries, offers telling evidence for the Easter event. Could it all have been rooted in a fraud, or did something else happen that Sunday dawn that has anchored the belief of 1.75 billion people in the present generation alone?

The significance of the first Easter, in Christian theology, is its guarantee that Jesus did accomplish his mission of salvation and achieve the supreme "pilot project" for humanity in triumphing over the ultimate enemy—death: Jesus rose; so will other human beings. No one expressed this better than someone who was not even around that morning. Paul wrote: "Since we believe that Jesus died and rose again, even so, through Jesus, God will bring to life with him those who have fallen asleep" (1 Thess. 4:14, RSV). This, the very earliest writing in the New Testament, dates from 50 A.D., only seventeen years after the first Easter. Arguments that Christianity hatched its Easter myth over a lengthy period of time or that the sources were written many years after the event are simply not factual.

The defeat of death in renewed life, then, is the message of the first Easter, and of every celebration in the centuries since. Easter is the only festival that looks in two directions at the same time: back into history to fathom what happened in the week that changed the world, and forward into the future with the assurance that people who die will live again. Small wonder that it was the earliest festival to be celebrated by the Church, or that its message is as young as tomorrow.

The First Christians
Pentecost and the Spread of Christianity

PART III

25

The Commission

"But you will receive power when the Holy Spirit has come
upon you; and you will be my witnesses in Jerusalem,
in all Judea and Samaria, and to the ends of the earth."
ACTS 1:8

ONE would have thought that the resurrection of Jesus of Nazareth was the ultimate proof necessary to launch Christianity
upon the world. But it was not.

Had ancient novelists contrived this story, they could hardly have
resisted a scenario in which the risen Christ paid a victorious visit to
Pilate, Caiaphas, the Sanhedrin, and the Jerusalem mob, finally compel-
ling them to believe what they previously had rejected. The terror, the
awe, the hysterical pleading for forgiveness would have made high drama,
and waves of now-universal adulation would have splashed as far away
as Rome and converted the Empire. But Jesus made no such appearances
to his enemies after the first Easter, which was entirely in accord with
divine policy: God never rewards disbelief; he always rewards faith,
according to Christian theology.

Instead, then, the great Good News would have to be communicated
by people who had witnessed the Easter phenomenon, not by endless
theophanies of the risen Christ to prove the case. But could the witnesses—
unaided—handle such an assignment? One doubts. The record of the
disciples surely leaves nothing to boast about. Their somewhat naïve
question even *after* the Resurrection—"Lord, is this the time when you

will restore the [political] kingdom to Israel?" (1:6)*—shows precious little theological progress on their part.

Enter the Holy Spirit. Jesus repeatedly foresaw the problem of a message too powerful for the messengers, and so he told the disciples at the Last Supper: "I will not leave you orphaned. . . . The Advocate, the Holy Spirit, whom the Father will send in my name, will teach you everything, and remind you of all that I have said to you" (John 14:18, 25f.). That person and function of God that would convict and convert people, inspire and propel them, would shortly transform the apostles from timid, passive, dull, and generally ineffective followers of Jesus into courageously powerful heralds in his behalf.

The Spirit's arrival would be anchored to a specific time and place in the first instance. After Jesus left them, the disciples were not to leave Jerusalem but rather to wait there for the Spirit. The Day of Pentecost would mark his dramatic arrival, even if the apostles could not know that.

The Departure

Forty final days the risen Jesus spent with his followers—a number sacred since the Flood. Then he prepared to take leave of them.

Only Luke reports the Ascension in any detail. Jesus led the Eleven over the Mount of Olives toward Bethany, the village where he had lived during the week before his crucifixion. His last message to them was both blessing and assignment, a solemn commission to do what must have seemed overblown and impossible at the time: to spread his story across the entire world! The other Gospels echo this categorical goal: ". . . Make disciples of all nations" (Matthew 28:19); "Go into all the world and proclaim the good news to the whole creation" (Mark 16:15); and ". . . proclaimed in his name to all nations, beginning from Jerusalem" (Luke 24:47).

Such phrases forever set the New Testament apart from other books. Certainly, they are unparalleled in the ancient world. No dying philosopher ever uttered so all-embracing a charge to his followers, nor did any world conqueror. The best that Augustus of Rome could manage for his

*Such notes without further identification refer to the *Acts of the Apostles*.

last words was a witty borrowing from Greek theater: "Have I played my part in life's farce well enough? Then clap your hands and take me off the stage."[1] Other "famous last words" are not much more profound than this.

Jesus, however, was not dying. He was instead establishing an almost limitless objective for Christianity, and the only thing more amazing than the words themselves is the fact that they have been *fulfilled*. With the current expansion of the Christian faith across the world, the Great Commission has proved to be great prophecy as well.

When the inexorable moment arrived, Jesus raised his hands in benediction, departed majestically from all terrestrial limitations, and disappeared from view. A bright cloud interposed between Jesus and his followers—some have seen it as the same "pillar of cloud" that protected Israel from the Egyptians in the Exodus account—but when it dissolved, Jesus was gone.

The Ascension should never be interpreted in quantifying terms. Incredibly, some have speculated on Jesus' rate of ascent, on the spectacular sight of a Christ figure in the heavens getting ever smaller to human view, and whether or not this would have caused any commotion in nearby Jerusalem! This is not Luke's purpose, which was merely to tell of Jesus' transit to another dimension, in more modern terms. Even Jesus' direction "upward" serves only to emphasize his physical separation from the earth, not a specific vector away from it.

Predictably, the disciples' only reaction to the stupefying visual phenomenon was simply to stand there, gazing after it. Was it awe? Was it the realization that Jesus actually *was* parting from them? Bewilderment at their leaderless situation? The voices of two bystanders "in white robes" restored their senses: "Men of Galilee, why do you stand looking up toward heaven? This Jesus, who has been taken up from you into heaven, will come in the same way as you saw him go into heaven" (1:11).

Precisely *where* all this took place is not definite. Luke writes only that it was on the Mount of Olives, "a sabbath day's journey away" from Jerusalem, which would be about half a mile (1:12). Any point along or near the present ridge of the Mount of Olives would qualify, and only the gullible will believe that the two footprints in stone shown pilgrims today at the hilltop mark "the last steps of Jesus on earth."

211

A Unique Source

With the Ascension, Luke begins his great story of the spread of Christianity, the account of how a faith born in the hills of Judea would penetrate the imperial capital of Rome, 1,500 miles away, in a stunningly brief period of time. By many standards, our chief source for this record is unique among biblical authors. Luke is the only writer of Scripture to produce both a Gospel and the earliest Church history, known as the *Acts of the Apostles*. But more important, Luke is the *only* Gentile author in that library of sixty-four other Semitic books called the Bible. He had a personal interest, then, in telling how the faith overcame its Jewish restrictiveness to embrace also the Gentile world.

Luke, whose name was an affectionate form of the Latin *Lucius* or *Lucanus*, was a close companion of Paul and an eyewitness to many of the events he described. A trained physician, Luke seems to have sublimated his profession to what he deemed a more pressing priority, and turned to the pen instead. The Church is poorer for not having more solid information on Luke. Even his native country is uncertain, although early tradition favors either Antioch in Syria or Philippi in Macedonia as his hometown. The autobiographical details Luke could so easily have provided he did not supply, perhaps intentionally, since he wanted nothing personal to detract from his Gospel or his history.[2]

Some critical scholars have debated whether the author of *Luke-Acts* actually *was* Luke, and have substituted terms such as "the author of the Third Gospel," "the diarist," and the like. Yet no other name for the writer of these works has ever been successfully offered, and the evidence is strong that Luke was indeed the author. Other sources for the earliest spread of Christianity include the letters of Paul and the other apostles, surviving works of first-century Jewish, Greek, and Roman historians, and, to be sure, archaeology. Such evidence blends well into Luke's record, as we shall see.

"You will be my witnesses in Jerusalem, in all Judea and Samaria, and to the ends of the earth," Jesus had predicted in his last charge on the Mount of Olives (1:8). These phrases serve as the simple, solemn outline for the entire Book of Acts, and Luke begins his record with the Spirit's dramatic arrival in Jerusalem ten days after the Ascension.

26

The Day of Pentecost

*So those who welcomed his message were baptized, and
that day about three thousand persons were added.*

ACTS 2:41

B EFORE Pentecost[1] there were only about 120 Christians in Jerusalem, and their gathering place was a large "upper room,"
otherwise unidentified, but probably the same chamber where Jesus had
instituted the Last Supper. An early tradition places the Upper Room in
southwestern Jerusalem outside the present Zion Gate, but the structure shown tourists today is very disappointing: a gloomy chamber with
Gothic vaulting that could not possibly have witnessed the first Christian Pentecost, because the Gothic arch was not developed until the
twelfth century A.D., and this room was built by the Crusaders. The *site,*
however, may be authentic, since the structure has been heavily rebuilt
across the centuries.[2]

The Jewish Christians who fled across the Jordan to Pella to escape
the Roman destruction of Jerusalem in 70 A.D. returned to Jerusalem
shortly thereafter under the leadership of Simon, son of Clopas, who was
Jesus' cousin and the second Christian bishop of Jerusalem. The original
synagogue-church on Mt. Zion, erected over the site of the Upper Room,
was most probably built by this group. It was standing when the emperor
Hadrian visited Jerusalem in 131 A.D., and some reused Herodian ashlars
from that structure survive to the present day.

Who were the 120 first Christians? They included the disciples, now
twelve again with Matthias replacing Judas, who had committed suicide;
the Galilean followers of Jesus, including the Seventy (Luke 10:1); Jesus'

The eastern face of the Temple in Jerusalem, as reconstructed in a model designed by Prof. M. Avi-Yonah. To the upper left is the Palace of Herod, where Pilate condemned Jesus, and at the extreme right is one of the towers of the Antonia fortress, where Peter and, later, Paul were imprisoned.

mother, Mary, and his half-brothers (or relatives) who had now converted to the faith; Mary, Martha, Lazarus, and the rest of the Bethany contingent; plus miscellaneous Judean followers, such as the Emmaus disciples, John Mark, and Mark's mother. Small in number, they nevertheless formed the nucleus of the most powerful movement ever to develop in history. Their mood was one of prayerful waiting for the Spirit, for they could not know the time and place of his arrival.

Before the destruction of their Temple in 70 A.D., the Jews had three great "pilgrim festivals" that drew the pious from all parts of Palestine, and, indeed, from the Mediterranean world, to Jerusalem. These celebrations were the Passover, the Festival of Weeks, and the Feast of Booths. The Weeks festival was also called the Feast of Harvest, or the Day of Pentecost (Greek for "the fiftieth"), since it fell exactly fifty days after the wave offering of the sheaf of barley during Passover (Lev. 23:9). Very much akin to the American Thanksgiving Day, Pentecost was an agricultural festival celebrated seven weeks after the harvest season began— hence Festival of "Weeks"—when the first fruits of the *wheat* harvest were presented to God as the source of fertility, in accord with scriptural directives (Lev. 23:15).

It was most likely the morning of May 25 in the year 33 A.D. that Jerusalem woke to what would be a very special Pentecost. Throngs were soon converging on the Temple mount to watch the chief priests prepare not only their regular sacrifices but also the special cereal offering of Pentecost. Probably it was the high priest himself, Joseph Caiaphas, who formally picked up two loaves of bread, baked with flour milled from the new wheat crop, and solemnly waved them back and forth in front of the altar as an offering to God in behalf of his people. He was careful not to touch the altar with the loaves, because they had been baked with leaven and would therefore be eaten afterward by the priests. Two lambs without blemish were also presented as a wave offering and sacrificed to the Lord, who had made the harvest possible.

All Jewish males attending were then invited to do an altar dance in the courts of the Temple, during which they sang the *Hallel*, joyous phrases from Psalms 113 to 118. Later in the day they might make individual presentations of the first fruits from their own harvests to priests on duty in the Temple, and finally join in the communal meals to which the poor and the strangers in the city were also welcome.

Elsewhere that morning, diagonally across Jerusalem to the southwest, many in the Christian nucleus had gathered for prayer in the Upper Room. Suddenly, at about 9 A.M., the place sounded like the foredeck of a ship in a storm. A noise "like the rush of a violent wind" swept into the chamber, filling the entire house with its whistling roar. Even more astonishing was the visual phenomenon that followed the wind: "Tongues, as of fire" appeared to rest on each of the believers at the only flammable part of their bodies—the hair—and yet harmlessly (2:1ff.).

Whether the flames were actual or only apparent is not clear, but a word study on "fire" in the Old Testament shows that flames regularly denoted theophany—an appearance of God—ranging from Moses' burning bush and the protective pillar of fire in the Exodus account to the giving of the Law at Mt. Sinai. Fire signified the purifying presence of Deity.

The wind and the tongues of flame were the externals marking a profound personal revolution in each of the Christians in the Upper Room, for now at last, the Holy Spirit had made his dramatic entry into their lives. Yet how could they be certain of so subjective an experience? And even if they were sure of it, how could others believe it?

Foreign Tongues

By recourse to the supernatural, Jesus had regularly supplied credentials for his message by performing not tricks but useful miracles, and now the Spirit would do the same. Luke reports that unlettered Galilean fisherfolk and commoners started speaking fluently in foreign languages they had never learned but that would prove crucial for their future mission work. They were being understood by Jewish and proselyte celebrants of Pentecost from fourteen different countries ranging from Mesopotamia to Rome, most of whom had probably prolonged their pilgrimage from Passover to include the second great Jewish festival fifty days later. Luke's list of nationalities covers virtually all countries in the eastern Mediterranean except for Galilee, Syria, Cilicia, and Greece, but a total listing would have seemed contrived.

Critics have tried to diminish the number of languages spoken at the first Christian Pentecost to essentially two—Aramaic and Greek, which the disciples and their hearers would already have known—but this does violence to Luke's text, which records the foreigners' reaction: "In our own languages, we hear them speaking about God's deeds of power" (2:11).

Such an incredible phenomenon could only attract a growing throng of the curious in always-crowded Jerusalem. Many were able to hear their own national languages plainly above what must have been a din of foreign tongues, while others, particularly at the periphery, might well have heard only a confusing melange of sounds. They would have been the first to drench the event with soggy ridicule. "These men are filled with new wine!" they mocked.

This beverage, in the original Greek, is *gleukos*, meaning "sweet new wine," from which our word "glucose" is derived. New wine in Palestine did not convey a faster intoxication—older wine, in fact, was stronger—but it was a cheap beverage and common fare for drunks. More expensive vintages were often diluted with water, especially among the Greeks and Romans, and so the taunt might have meant, in essence, "These babblers here have guzzled the *cheap* stuff, taken *straight!*"

During Jesus' ministry Simon Peter always seemed to have volunteered the first word whenever the Master stopped teaching or preaching. That it was often a wrong word did not seem to have fazed the strong, lovable, impetuous fisherman. After a gentle scolding from Jesus, Peter would be back again, posing the first question, offering the first opinion—or drawing the first sword.

So it was absolutely in character for Peter to speak first when the disciples were taunted for drunkenness. Probably using Aramaic, the everyday language of Palestine, Peter stood up to address the multitude. He began by meeting the charge of too much alcohol head on: "These men are *not* drunk, as you suppose, since it's only the third hour of the day!" (2:15, RSV). Even drunks would hardly start indulging as early as nine o'clock in the morning. More likely they would be sleeping off the effects of the night before.

No longer groping between faith and misunderstanding now that the Spirit was inspiring him, Peter went on to deliver a masterpiece of an address. In less than a quarter of an hour he managed to root the Pentecost experience and the mission of Christ in Old Testament prophecy—the only way to convince pious Jews of anything. Without resorting to any diplomatic niceties, Peter then stung his hearers for their involvement in the events of Good Friday: "This Jesus . . . you crucified and killed by the hands of lawless men" (2:23, RSV). But in closing he announced the way of salvation with the same sublime simplicity that has always characterized it:

> Repent, and be baptized every one of you in the name of Jesus Christ so that your sins may be forgiven; and you will receive the gift of the Holy Spirit. For the promise is for you, for your children, and for all who are far away, everyone whom the Lord our God calls to him. (2:38)

Anyone reading Peter's sermon in the second chapter of *Acts* is astounded at the dramatic personality transformation it reflects. To be sure, Peter had shown moments of boldness before—the Rock, as Jesus had named him, did have some solid credits, though generally he was fissured with flaws. Waves on the Sea of Galilee, the taunts of a servant girl at the palace of Caiaphas, or Jesus' trial on Good Friday could turn the Rock into jelly, as he cursed and swore away his relationship to Jesus and then abandoned him. How could he now surmount so triumphantly the same challenges that had earlier overcome him?

The Spirit. In Luke's record the miracle of Pentecost was not primarily rushing sounds, tongues of flame, or instant linguistic genius, but the arrival of God the Holy Spirit, who could inspire and transform a person in such a way. And even this was only half the miracle.

The Response

The other half was the response. The story of Pentecost closes with an all-but-incredible statistic: "So those who welcomed his message were baptized, and that day about three thousand persons were added" (2:41). And these were not fly-by-night converts toying with Christianity for a time, but totally committed Christians, as the context makes clear—a reaction unparalleled for the fledgling faith. Not even Jesus' preaching had drawn such a response, at least not in Jerusalem, or there would have been more believers than the lonesome 120 Christians before Pentecost.

And this was only the beginning. One day soon afterward, when Peter and John went up to the Temple for midafternoon prayer, they healed a beggar at the Beautiful Gate who had been crippled from his birth forty years before. The helpless victim had been a familiar fixture at the Temple—one sees dozens of his cousins-in-misery throughout the Near East today—and so his healing caused an instant sensation and an immediate crowd.

Peter seized the opportunity to deliver an even more impressive version of the Christian message, with this extraordinary result: "Many of those who heard the word believed; and they numbered about five thousand" (4:4). Even more astonishingly, "a great many of the priests became obedient to the faith" in the weeks to come (6:7).

Is such a growth curve for earliest Christianity (120→3,000→8,000 plus) credible? Critics have challenged the figures in *Acts*, pointing out how often ancient authors tended to exaggerate numbers. Luke's statistics should be divided by a factor of ten or more, some argue, since a Jerusalem with five or ten thousand Christians would be far too high a Christian-Jewish ratio.

This may be true for the normal population of the Holy City, but many of the converts at Pentecost and the days afterward seem to have been pilgrims, visitors, or temporary sojourners who at least tripled the normal Jerusalem population of some 50,000 during the high festivals. The Jewish historian Josephus would have us believe that as many as three million were in Jerusalem at such times, but most scholars reduce his claim to several hundred thousand.[3] Against this statistic, however, Luke's figures are not that extreme.

But were there really that many converts? What is simpler than hanging a zero or two onto a statistic? Wouldn't a little padding be appropriate for Luke's success story? Not really. A fascinating datum of evidence from a purely pagan source attests to the rapid growth and spread of the earliest church. One of the most respected Roman source historians, Cornelius Tacitus, wrote the following statement about Nero's first great persecution of the Christians at Rome in 64 A.D.:

> To suppress the rumor [that he had set fire to Rome], Nero fabricated as culprits, and punished with the most refined cruelties a notoriously depraved class of people whom the crowd called "Christians." The originator of the name, Christus, had been executed in the reign of Tiberius by the governor of Judea, Pontius Pilatus. . . . First, the self-acknowledged members of the sect were arrested. Then, on their information, a vast multitude was condemned. . . .[4]

The startling phrase, of course, is the "vast multitude" of Roman Christians persecuted. For Tacitus the Latin *multitudo ingens*, while indefinite, elsewhere suggests numbers in the high hundreds at the very least, and because he detested the Christians and would thus have no interest in stretching his figures on them, ancient historians generally take Tacitus at face value. His is positive evidence from a hostile source and is therefore unusually strong and convincing.

This evidence, in turn, has an obviously important bearing on conversion claims at the first Pentecost. How could there be a "vast multitude" of Christians available for persecution *only thirty-one years later* in a Rome 1,500 miles away unless the movement had the kind of powerful ignition described in *Acts*? Any historian would have to admit that a profound religious explosion must have occurred in Jerusalem some years earlier, since its repercussions shook distant Rome with extraordinary speed. For a philosophy or teaching to spread this far, this fast in the ancient world is absolutely unparalleled, and scholars have not devoted enough attention to this fact. Clearly, the spiritual waves breaking on the shores of Italy had been building from the "rushing, mighty wind" of the first Pentecost.

Perhaps even more important than the *numbers* of converts after Peter's preaching were the *kinds* of converts. As noted, the new believers seem to have come largely from the ranks of the pilgrims, visitors, or temporary sorts sojourning in Jerusalem at Pentecost, which has obvious implications for the quick seeding of Christianity across the whole Mediterranean basin. For when these Passover-Pentecost pilgrims returned to their homelands, they would *carry their new faith with them*.

The city of Rome itself is a prime example of such a self-seeding Christianity. When some years later Paul addressed his famous letter to the Christians there, he paid them a high compliment: "I thank my God . . . for all of you, because your faith is proclaimed throughout the world" (Rom. 1:8). But who planted this vigorous faith? Neither he, nor Peter, nor any of the apostles had brought Christianity to Italy, even though both Peter and Paul would visit there in the future. Most church historians therefore suggest Pentecost pilgrims—"visitors from Rome, both Jews and proselytes" (2:10)—as the originators of the church at Rome. That church, in turn, would found many other mission stations in the West in a swelling spiritual chain reaction set off, unquestionably, from the original detonation at Pentecost.

Peter, accordingly, could not have addressed a more important audience than the crucial pilgrim Jews of the Dispersion, many of whom became human fuses igniting Christianity elsewhere in the ancient world. But if the effect was there—conversion—so was the cause: the arrival of a Spirit who would inspire both speakers and hearers to the faith, governing both ends of the communication process. This alone could explain the extraordinary success of Peter's preaching. This was the true miracle and the ultimate significance of the first great Christian Pentecost.

27

The Opposition

Then the high priest took action; he and all who
were with him, that is, the sect of the Sadducees,
being filled with jealousy, arrested the apostles and
put them in the public prison. ACTS 5:17–18

A SWIFT crackdown from the priestly authorities was inevitable. The apostles were not starting their movement in far-off Galilee, but, almost brazenly, they were proclaiming the faith from the very steps of the Temple in Jerusalem. Peter, John, and the others seem to have converted Solomon's Portico on the eastern edge of the Temple enclave into something of a primitive Christian church. Here they preached and healed the sick in a virtual continuation of Jesus' ministry, all under the very noses of the priestly establishment.

Obviously, their activities could not remain unnoticed, and the Temple authorities would hardly have prosecuted Jesus to the cross only to allow his movement to use their facilities as a breeding ground. What particularly rankled the priestly hierarchy were the repeated claims that Jesus had risen from the dead, for most in the Temple establishment were Sadducees, who denied outright any possibility of a resurrection.

The first blow fell during Peter's address after healing the Temple cripple. While he was still speaking, guards swarmed into Solomon's Portico, arrested the apostles, and put them into prison overnight. The next morning almost exactly the same cast assembled as that which Jesus had faced some weeks earlier. The high priest himself presided, with his father-in-law Annas and other relatives present. "By what power or by what name did you do this?" Caiaphas led off.

Peter replied with a humorous bit of irony: "If we are questioned today concerning a good deed done to a cripple . . . let it be known to all of you, and to all the people of Israel, that this man is standing before you in good health by the name of Jesus Christ of Nazareth, whom you crucified, whom God raised from the dead" (4:9).

The rest of his defense pursued the same daring tack, offering a fearless testimony to the risen Christ. Pre-Pentecost Peter would have found his knees buckling before any Sanhedral collection of Jesus' enemies, but this was a new or renewed Peter. Luke explains it very simply: "Then Peter, filled with the Holy Spirit, said to them . . . " (4:8). The miracle of Pentecost was continuing.

The priests at that point must have had unhappy memories of the trial of Jesus some weeks earlier, after which there may well have been a popular backlash against the Sanhedrin for its role on Good Friday. Besides, Exhibit A was standing there, a forty-year-old lifelong cripple, who was probably flexing his newfound leg muscles from time to time in another dance or leap or kick. (Physiologically, of course, his was a double cure, since even instantly regenerated joints and sinews would have required many days' therapy to control for the first time.) In any case, the crowd knew the man had been cured, and crowds were dangerous. Thus a diplomatic solution: the Sanhedrin "ordered them not to speak or teach at all in the name of Jesus" (4:18). After a few more threats the apostles were discharged.

More Clashes with Caiaphas

In succeeding weeks the Christian movement only grew. The apostles had not obeyed the authorities' order to keep quiet about Jesus, nor had they promised they would. Caiaphas ordered them arrested again, and they were thrown into "the public prison" (5:17f.).

This time Caiaphas assembled what must have been a major meeting of the Sanhedrin (5:21), and he summoned the prisoners before it. A much discomfited group of prison guards had to admit, red-faced and sheepish, that the captives had somehow vanished from their still-locked cells without leaving a trace. A second report to the Sanhedrists was even worse. Someone arrived to tell them, "The men whom you put in prison are standing in the Temple and teaching the people" (5:25). According to

Luke, it was all due to a timely visit from "an angel of the Lord" who had opened the prison doors, the sort of intervention that Simon Peter, for one, would become almost used to.

Gingerly, the Temple police arrested the apostles once again and rather courteously escorted them into the hall of the Sanhedrin. Any violence and they would have been stoned by the crowds, with whom the Christian cause was gaining in popularity.

Caiaphas' opening statement was predictable. "We gave you strict orders not to teach in this name, yet here you have filled Jerusalem with your teaching and you are determined to bring this man's blood on us."

Peter's reply has become a spiritual classic: "We must obey God rather than men," the call of conscience versus authority. Nor did he dodge the resurrection issue. "The God of our fathers raised up Jesus, whom you had killed by hanging him on a tree. . . . And we are witnesses to these things" (5:30).

The apostles had not given an inch. Caiaphas and his colleagues were enraged enough to ponder a violent solution to the impasse. In halting a dangerous movement the ancients often eliminated not just one leader but all leaders. Amid such dark deliberations, however, a much-honored Pharisee named Gamaliel stood up and asked to speak confidentially to his colleagues. The apostles were led out.

Easily the ranking theologian of his day, Gamaliel was a grandson of the great Rabbi Hillel, the talmudic sage who had pioneered some liberal interpretations of Hebrew law. Gamaliel continued the liberalizing tradition of his grandfather and went on to so great a career in his own right that he was the first to be honored with the title *Rabban* ("our Master") rather than the ordinary *Rabbi* ("my Master"). Since he is not mentioned in connection with Jesus' hearing before the Sanhedrin, it is not known if he was present or not. But he was very much in attendance at this later sitting of the Sanhedrin, and the chamber hushed to hear him.

"Men of Israel, consider carefully what you propose to do to these men," he warned. "Let them alone; for if this plan or this undertaking is of them, it will fail" (in fact, Gamaliel cited two such human failures), "but if it is of God, you will not be able to overthrow them—in that case you may even be found fighting against God!" (5:35).

Gamaliel's cool and sage advice correlates readily with the tolerant figure known so well in Jewish history.[1] His words served to calm the Sanhedrin, which accepted his suggestion—though not completely, for

223

the apostles received a beating before release. It was the first time since Good Friday that the Christian movement endured physical suffering. It would not be the last.

A First Martyr

As the Church grew, it quickly found itself involved in matters not only spiritual but also very material. For a while the Jerusalem Christians tried a collectivistic scheme by which they deemphasized private property and held everything they owned "in common" in order to aid their poor (4:32). Certain disadvantaged believers, especially widows, were well served by such an arrangement, but problems were inevitable.

Some Greek-speaking Jewish Christians, called Hellenists, felt that their widows were being slighted in the daily handouts, and they complained to the disciples. For the first time the Twelve saw the need for specialized callings in the Church. With a world to win, they could hardly abandon their efforts in the spiritual sphere, so they advised that a board of seven deacons be appointed to administer to the church's material necessities.

A man named Stephanos was one of those chosen, and his Greek name suggests that the ration for the Hellenist widows must soon have improved dramatically! At least Luke records no further complaints about the dole for charity. But Stephanos, or Stephen, proved to be more than a lay deacon. He was also a gifted teacher and preacher, "full of faith and the Holy Spirit" (6:5). We wish we knew more about this man of charisma and wisdom than his brief, meteoric appearance early in the *Acts* account.

As with Socrates, it was Stephen's wit that got him into trouble. He took on representatives from five different synagogues in Jerusalem and debated with them at the same time, the dispute likely centering on Stephen's prediction that Christ would ultimately change Jewish customs. Stephen overpowered his opponents in debate, but, as in the case of Socrates, the losers preferred charges of impiety against him in court, in this instance, the Sanhedrin.

When Caiaphas asked this latest Christian to stand before him if the charges were justified, Stephen replied with an address that at first seems frankly disappointing, for, instead of a defense, it is a lengthy tour through Old Testament history that blurs several facts, and is surely material that

224

The traditional site of the stoning of Stephen below the northeastern corner of the walls of Jerusalem above. An oratory commemorating his martyrdom is to the left, with Stephen's name in Greek lettering along its wall.

members of the Sanhedrin should have known very well indeed. But, aside from the question of Luke's reportage, early Christian preaching focused strongly on the Old Testament—the *only* Scriptures then available, it should be remembered—and, again, the only final authority for a Jew. Stephen interpreted Israel's past as a case history of disobedience to God and a continual rejection of his prophets. This set the stage for an abrupt climax in his address, when he suddenly shifted to direct discourse:

> You stiff-necked people, uncircumcised in heart and ears, you are forever opposing the Holy Spirit. As your fathers did, so do you. Which of the prophets did your fathers not persecute? They killed those who foretold the coming of the Righteous One, and now you have become his betrayers and murderers. You are the ones that received the law as ordained by angels, and yet you have not kept it. (7:51)

225

Naked rage boiled up from the ranks of the Sanhedrin, and when Stephen reported his vision of the victorious Christ in the heavens, they stopped their ears against what they deemed horrendous blasphemy. Howling with fury, the Sanhedrists did something unparalleled in Hebrew history. Members jumped up from their benches, grabbed Stephen, and dragged him out of the city to an open spot, probably just below the northeastern corner of the Temple wall. Stripping off their outer garments for the violent task ahead, they deposited them on the grass in front of a studious young Pharisee named Saul, who promised to look after them. Then they stooped down to pick up the commonest item on the fields of Palestine to the present day—rocks—and hurled them at Stephen until he collapsed and died.

The lynching was grossly illegal: Pontius Pilate alone had the authority to inflict capital punishment in Judea. But he had returned to his head-quarters at Caesarea after the close of the Jewish Passover, and the Roman cohort of 600 auxiliaries, stationed in the nearby Tower Antonia, for some reason did not intervene. The mob action was doubtless out of their view and a *fait accompli* before they even learned of it.

At the Last Supper, just before his own death, Jesus had told the Twelve, "Servants are not greater than their master. If they persecuted me, they will persecute you" (John 15:20). Stephen fulfilled that prediction directly. Poignantly, he had tried to pattern his death as close to Jesus' as possible. While the stones were pounding into him, he also forgave his enemies before crying, "Lord Jesus, receive my spirit" (7:59). With that he died, the first martyr after Jesus in Christian history.

226

28

The Dispersion

That day a severe persecution began against the church in
Jerusalem, and all except the apostles were scattered
throughout the countryside of Judea and Samaria.
ACTS 8:1

MARTYRS are protected from their future mistakes, but perse-
cutors are not. Their errors rather compound themselves,
and this earliest oppression of Christians is a classic example. Caiaphas
and the authorities had evidently decided to abandon wise Gamaliel's
policy and go the route of purge, persecution, and repression. But instead
of eliminating Christianity they only served to spread it. Rather than
nipping it in the bud, they unwittingly pruned it for healthier growth.

Saul of Tarsus, the young Pharisee who had guarded the garments
of those stoning Stephen to death, now abandoned so passive a role for
a far more active one. He became something of a fanatic in persecuting
the Jerusalem Christians, instituting a house-by-house search for all
followers of "The Way," as Christians were first identified, arresting both
men and women and committing them to prison. So effective was his
performance that the priests seem to have made him their chief agent for
this purpose in Jerusalem, even providing him with credentials for extending
the purge to Damascus.

Why was Saul so zealously anti-Christian? Had he been on the receiving
end of one of Jesus' diatribes against the Pharisees and heard himself
labeled a "hypocrite," "viper," or even "a whitewashed sepulcher"? No.
Young Saul seems never to have met or heard Jesus personally as of that
time. Was it Saul's education in Jerusalem? Again unlikely, because his

prime teacher was none other than the same liberal savant, Gamaliel, who had advised a "hands-off" policy toward the apostles. For some reason such tolerance had not rubbed off on Gamaliel's disciple Saul, which has led critics to question whether the man who would one day be St. Paul ever had Gamaliel as his teacher, as he later claimed (22:3).

Professors, however, would be the last to admit responsibility for all the opinions and actions of their students, who hardly ever emulate them in every area. One of the items the student Saul clearly did not learn at Gamaliel's feet was tolerance. The reason may be as simple as the exuberance of youth, which takes any trend or pattern laid down by the older establishment and exaggerates it. The same phenomenon that today finds young political groups at the conservative or liberal extremes would, two millennia ago, have led a young student Pharisee "educated strictly according to the law of our fathers" (22:3) to outdo even the priests in his practice of orthodoxy.

The immediate effect of persecution was dispersion, not elimination, of the church in Judea. What might have been contained to the "Greater Jerusalem" area now spread for the first time to such non-Jewish regions as Samaria and the Mediterranean coastlands. While the apostles stayed in the Holy City and served, in a sense, as board of directors to coordinate the Christian movement, most of the other believers scattered elsewhere. Exuberant about the twice-proved validity of their faith in the events of Easter and Pentecost, they could not help but become ambassadors for Christianity, and so the faith expanded. The priestly authorities had only themselves to blame.

Philip the Evangelist

One of the most prominent of the seven deacons was another believer named Philip, not to be confused with Philip the disciple. Possessed of the same evangelistic qualities as the martyred Stephen, Philip had left his wife, four daughters, and his home in Caesarea to help launch the infant church in Jerusalem. When persecution struck, Philip answered it by accelerating efforts elsewhere. Of all places, he chose Samaria as his mission field, the home of those despised religious half-breeds who were forever the targets of Jewish disdain because of their checkered, part-Assyrian ethnic background and their departure from Hebrew orthodoxy.

The holiest spot in Samaria was 3,000-foot Mt. Gerizim (the "Mount of Blessing" of Deut. 11:29), which looms over ancient Sychar. Because Pontius Pilate put down a revolt on the slopes of this hill in 36 A.D., he was recalled to Rome.

Jesus, however, had ministered to the Samaritans, and so would Philip. Arriving at an unnamed Samaritan city, he began proclaiming Christ to the multitudes who heard him there. Various clues suggest that the city was Gitta,[1] near the Plain of Sharon. Philip received an unusually warm reception from the Samaritans, and his planting of Christianity in Samaritan soil would yield one of its most important church fathers, Justin Martyr, only sixty-five years later.

Samaria was also the site of one of the strangest conversions in Christian annals. Before Philip's arrival the religious star at Gitta had been a certain Simon, a *magus*, or magician, who dealt in incantations, spells, astrology, necromancy, and exorcisms. Simon so impressed the credulous Samaritans that they regularly billed him as "The Power of God that is called GREAT"—a title that has escaped a satisfactory explanation, though scholars have surely tried. Yet when Philip announced the Good News in Samaria and confirmed it with not magic but miracles, Simon Magus (as he came to be called) was himself so impressed that he converted and was baptized. He even seems to have become Philip's disciple, but whether as genuine believer or more as "wizard's apprentice" trying to learn better magic than his own is not clear.

Peter and John now came down from Jerusalem in order to lay their hands on the Samaritan converts so that they might receive the Holy Spirit. When Simon Magus witnessed this, he assumed, with utter naïveté, that he might be able to purchase such powers from the apostles for cash. Offering Peter a bag of silver, he asked, "Give me also this power so that anyone on whom I lay my hands may receive the Holy Spirit." It was *the* miscalculation of Simon Magus' life!

Peter's brow darkened and his eyes flashed. *"May you and your money go to hell,"* he roared, "for thinking that you can buy God's gift with money!" (8:20, TEV, italics added). Then he lectured Simon on the proper approach to the faith, concluding, "Repent therefore of this wickedness of yours, and pray to the Lord that, if possible, the intent of your heart may be forgiven you."

A much shaken Simon Magus could only stammer, "Pray for me to the Lord, that nothing of what you have said may happen to me" (8:24).

Simon seems to have remained a believer after this episode, albeit a controversial, even heretical one. Early Christians wove him into countless legends that are difficult to unravel for the truth, if any, that they contain. The church historian Eusebius places Simon Magus among the founders of Gnostic heresy. Other sources claim he later went to Rome with an ex-prostitute named Helena and tried to fly from a lofty tower there, but perished in the ensuing crash—a showman to the end.[2] Actually, the only sure thing that can be told of Simon after his clash with Peter is the extraordinary fate attending his name. One of the greatest curses in medieval Christianity was the buying and selling of church offices, termed "simony" by subsequent histories in honor of Simon Magus!

A Nubian Treasurer

If Simon seemed an unlikely Christian, so did the very next convert recorded in *Acts*. Philip, that highly mobile missionary, was now inspired to take the Good News southward on the road leading from Jerusalem to

Gaza on the coast. Here, on a moving chariot, he encountered a pilgrim returning from worship at Jerusalem, reading aloud to himself from the scroll of the prophet Isaiah. Not that he was a poor reader: all ancients customarily read aloud. Luke describes the man as "an Ethiopian eunuch, a court official of the Candace, queen of the Ethiopians, in charge of her entire treasury" (8:27). In those days, however, the term Ethiopia meant the lands south of Egypt, called Nubia in ancient times and more recently the Sudan.

As to other definitions, *Candace* was the title of the Nubian queen, not her name, much as *Pharaoh* denoted the rule of Egypt. That she should have been served by an emasculate as treasurer was common in this area of the world, ever since Potiphar of Egypt in Old Testament times, who was probably a married eunuch (Gen. 39:1). Since, however, castrates were excluded from the Israelite congregation, the Nubian was doubtless either a Gentile proselyte or a "God-fearer," the pious half-believer in Judaism (Deut. 23:1).

Philip approached his chariot to inquire, "Do you understand what you are reading?"

"How can I, unless some one guides me?" he honestly confessed. Then he showed Philip the passage from Isaiah that was bothering him:

> Like a sheep he was led to the slaughter
> and like a lamb silent before its shearer,
> so he does not open his mouth.
> In his humiliation justice was denied him.
> Who can describe his generation?
> For his life is taken away from the earth.

The famed messianic prophecy from Isaiah 53, dealing with the suffering servant of the Lord, was perfect for Philip's purposes, and he used it to channel the Gospel into the life of the Nubian. Together they rode across the desert, Philip instructing the treasurer all the while. Finally, they came to a spring or pool by the side of the road. "Look, here is water!" the Nubian exclaimed. "What is to prevent me from being baptized?" (8:37). The chariot stopped, and Philip baptized the official then and there.

More is involved in this episode than the extraordinary conversion of a colorful person at a bizarre corner of Palestine. African mission work started here. The names, the places, and the connections have been lost to history, but a curiously strong Christian church developed in Nubia. Such a conversion also foreshadowed the inclusive or universal direction of the future faith in contrast to the exclusivity of its parent Judaism. People of another nation, another color, another race were clearly welcome as full members of the Church, even if they were physically maimed.

Philip, meanwhile, resumed his preaching ministry via a swing northward along the Mediterranean seacoast, beginning at Azotus, the old Philistine town formerly called Ashdod, and continuing up to his home in Caesarea. Other refugees from the Jerusalem persecution traveled even farther northward to Phoenicia; Antioch, the Syrian capital; and even the island of Cyprus (11:19). These scattered groups of Christians were never quiet about their beliefs but shared them enthusiastically.

What began, then, as a response to persecution—dispersion of the church—served to spread Christianity in a cause generating its own momentum. But the whole expansion process, so the apostles confidently believed, was directed, inspired, and fueled by nothing less than the Spirit of Pentecost.

29

Peter the Rock

Then Peter began to speak to them: "I truly understand
that God shows no partiality, but in every nation anyone
who fears him and does what is right is acceptable to him."
ACTS 10:34–35

SIMON Peter had the dual task of coordinating the Christian
movement from Jerusalem and visiting the newly missionized
towns and cities of Judea and Samaria. Sometimes he took on a third
assignment, personally serving as missionary to open up fresh areas for
the faith. So it was that he soon became "apostle to the northwest," in a
sense, traveling to Lydda, Joppa, and Caesarea.

Near the southern end of the fertile Plain of Sharon stood the town
of Lydda, where a small Christian community was already in existence,
probably deriving from Pentecost. Peter stopped there to brace up the
flock and was presently brought to the bedside of a paralytic whose name
was famous from Vergil's epic, Aeneas, but who had been bedridden for
eight years. Stretching forth his hand, Peter said, "Aeneas, Jesus Christ
heals you; get up and make your bed" (9:34). Aeneas promptly complied,
astonishing the townspeople, many of whom converted. Peter's no-
nonsense directive "and make your bed" was less a housekeeping
suggestion and more an indication that the sickbed would no longer be
needed.

Although only a modest paragraph in the *Acts* account, the incident
provides modern travelers to the Holy Land with their first biblical site.
Lydda, called Lod today, is where Israel's international airport is located.

Two men from nearby Joppa now arrived, begging Peter to come and
visit their city on the Mediterranean coast. Joppa had been the major

233

seaport of Palestine prior to Herod's building Caesarea, and it was there that Solomon had rafts of cedar logs floated down from Lebanon and then shipped overland to Jerusalem for the construction of his Temple (2 Chron. 2:16). There, too, the prophet Jonah had tried to shirk his responsibility by taking ship to Tarshish (Jon. 1:3).

Peter had been summoned because of a crisis in the new Christian assembly there. A woman named Tabitha in Aramaic (Dorcas in Greek) had just died. She had been something of a saint-in-the-flesh, "devoted to good works and acts of charity." We can almost visualize her as president of the women's society at the Joppa church, or at least chief provider for the congregation's bazaars, since her friends showed Peter "tunics and other clothing that Dorcas had made while she was with them."

Gently, Peter escorted the mourners outside. Then he knelt down and prayed beside the body of the dead Dorcas. Turning to her lifeless form, he said determinedly, "Tabitha, get up." She opened her eyes, Luke reports, and sat up. Peter summoned the weeping Christians back inside the room for a glad reunion festival.

The ultimate sign was quickly reported in the streets of Joppa, and again the wonder served far more than restoration of life to one victim, for, as an understandable result, "many believed in the Lord" (9:42). Dorcas' name would far outlast her later, second death. It lives on in the various Dorcas Societies of consecrated and gifted church women, who, like their namesake, have devoted their efforts to "good works and acts of charity."

Peter, who had now emulated his Lord even to the point of raising the dead in his name, stayed on in Joppa for some time at the Mediterranean seaside home of a man called Simon the Tanner. His name itself provides another clue to the inclusivity of the Early Church. Because their contact with the bodies of dead animals rendered them culticly unclean, tanners were in low repute among the Jews (Lev. 11:39). But if a castrate could become a Christian, so could a tanner. So could anyone else.

Cornelius the Centurion

The Roman governor of Palestine had only 3,000 troops with which to keep order in the land, five cohorts of 600 men each. And these soldiers were *not* of Roman stock, but auxiliary forces conscripted locally. Ordi-

Traditional site of the house of Simon the Tanner at Joppa,
looking northward across the Mediterranean bay.

narily, Jews would have served in such units, but they were exempted
from military service because of their dietary restrictions—the Roman
army moved on pork!—and in view of military action that might be
required on the Sabbath. The cohorts, therefore, were usually recruited
from Samaritan and Syrian mercenaries who often were less than reliable
and also nourished a cordial hatred for the Jews they were supposed to
police. This volatile combination caused several imbroglios during the
administration of Pontius Pilate, and it could well have been Pilate himself
who requested that at least one cohort of genuine Italians be sent from
Rome to his capital at Caesarea for security purposes.

At any rate, the *Acts* account now introduces a Cornelius who was
centurion in the "Italian Cohort" at Caesarea. An archaeological inscription demonstrates that there was indeed a *Cohors II Italica (civium Roma-
norum voluntariorum)* at Caesarea by 69 A.D., and probably earlier, a

235

"Second Italian Cohort of Roman Citizen Volunteers."[1] This Cornelius, while possessing a Roman family name famous since the Punic Wars, is otherwise unknown. Luke describes him as a generous, devout "God-fearer," a technical term for those Gentiles who had not become full Jewish proselytes but who still worshiped the God of the Hebrews. Although uncircumcised and not bound by Jewish dietary law, Cornelius was as much interested in Judasim as was his famous counterpart in Luke's Gospel, the centurion of Capernaum who had even built a synagogue for his Galilean friends (Luke 7:5).

During a period of midafternoon prayer, Cornelius was moved by a vision to send three subordinates to Joppa for a man he had never met—Simon Peter—at an address he had never known—the house of Simon the Tanner, by the seaside. Peter, meanwhile, had been using Simon's house as a base for his mission work along the coast.

At noon on the day after Cornelius' vision, Peter went up to the housetop to pray, feeling normal hunger pains at the time. While lunch was being prepared downstairs, he fell into a trance and saw one of the most bizarre visions this side of the *Book of Revelation:* a vast sheet was descending from the sky, freighted down with a Noah's ark load of animals, reptiles, and birds. A voice called out to the hungry apostle, "Get up, Peter; kill and eat."

"By no means, Lord," remonstrated Peter. "For I have never eaten anything that is profane or unclean."

"What God has made clean you must not call profane," the voice replied (10:13).

The same dialogue occurred twice more, after which the vision dissolved. Understandably, Peter was perplexed. Just then Cornelius' three emissaries arrived from Caesarea, at which Peter was prompted to receive them and return to Caesarea with them. When he went there and learned of Cornelius' complementary vision, the message came into focus for the apostle: Gentiles, evidently, were to receive the Good News as well, for "truly . . . God shows no partiality" (10:34).

Critics have scorned the *deus ex machina* apparatus necessary to lure Peter to Caesarea, but the visions have their inner logic: nothing separated Jew and Gentile so much as dietary restrictions, a bone of contention time and time again in the Early Church, so it was no accident that the visions concerned food of the *unkosher* variety.

The episode had a glorious conclusion. Not only Cornelius was spell-bound by the preaching of Peter, but so were the houseful of friends and relatives that the centurion had gathered in Caesarea. Peter, too, was slowly learning his most important lesson since Pentecost. "You your-selves know that it is unlawful for a Jew to associate with or to visit a Gentile," he confessed, which is why earliest Christianity had an almost exclusively Jewish membership. "But God has shown me that I should not call anyone profane or unclean." For "everyone who believes in Jesus Christ receives forgiveness of sins through his name."

Forgiveness, perhaps, but certainly *not* the preferential gift of the Holy Spirit. This would have put Jew and Gentile on the same Christian plane. But then, undoubtedly surprising the apostle himself, "While Peter was still speaking, the Holy Spirit fell upon all who heard the word . . . even on the Gentiles" (10:44). The phenomenon would later be called "the Gentiles' Pentecost" because they, too, were speaking in tongues and praising God. Baptism followed, and the first Gentile clan in Palestine had been Christianized.

The remarkable event changed not only Peter but church history too. The Christian mission field would be vastly expanded from *Jews* across the world to *anyone* across the world. Other early Christians, however, would not learn the lesson as quickly as Peter did. Indeed, when he returned to Jerusalem, Peter had to face acute criticism from what *Acts* terms "the circumcision party"—orthodox Jewish Christians—who voiced a very dietary complaint: "Why did you go to uncircumcised men and eat with them?"

Peter defended his conduct by reporting his preternatural vision in detail, and particularly the culmination at Caesarea: "As I began to speak, the Holy Spirit fell on them just as it had upon us at the beginning."

The Jerusalem church had no choice but to applaud the tolerance of God: "Then God has given even to the Gentiles the repentance that leads to life" (11:18).

The miracle of Pentecost was continuing.

Herod Agrippa I

Some years later Peter would face a more serious threat, not to his theology, but to his very life. Judea underwent a momentous change of government in 41 A.D., when Rome withdrew her provincial governor from Caesarea and replaced him with a grandson of Herod the Great whose name was Herod Agrippa I.

The story of Agrippa's rise to power reads better than a novel, but here there is space only to report that Agrippa was a brother of the Herodias who had compassed the death of John the Baptist. After an extremely checkered career, Agrippa finally attained the throne by happening to be in Rome during the critical hours when Caligula was assassinated and Claudius was hesitant to assume the emperorship. Playing a double agent's role, Agrippa firmed Claudius up in this crisis and was actually instrumental in winning the throne for him. Claudius, in turn, gratefully rewarded his friend Agrippa with nothing less than kingship in Palestine over virtually the same territory Agrippa's grandfather had once ruled.

Agrippa returned to Judea in triumph and proved far more deferential to his subjects than Herod the Great had been. He had more purely Jewish blood than his grandfather, and had served the Jewish cause well some months earlier when he dissuaded Caligula from his mad scheme to erect a statue of himself inside the Temple at Jerusalem. Small wonder that Agrippa was a vastly popular ruler, and he now looked for ways to enhance his acceptance even further. How else could he assist the religious establishment in Jerusalem?

Well, the priests must have responded, there was a certain pestilential sect gaining more and more converts to the cause of that Jesus who had been crucified eight years before. And the leaders could be found right in Jerusalem.

With no Romans around to moderate his decision, Agrippa simply arrested James, the son of Zebedee, who with his brother John and Simon Peter formed the apostolic triumvirate, the prime three who had always stood closest to Christ. There is no indication of how or why James in particular was singled out or whether he received a trial of any kind. The *Acts* record merely reports, somberly and bluntly, that Agrippa killed James with the sword—decapitation—just before the Passover of 41 A.D.

The second martyr for the faith had succumbed. It must have been a particularly bitter blow for Mother Zebedee, who had once asked Jesus for special places of honor for her two boys when he returned in glory.

Because Peter was the most notable Christian leader in Jerusalem, he easily became Agrippa's next target. The apostle was seized, thrown into prison at the Tower Antonia, and would have had a quick trial and execu-

A model of the fortress Antonia in Jerusalem, where Peter was incarcerated. Later, Paul would be imprisoned here also after being detained in the Temple courtyard (below). Designed by Prof. Avi-Yonah, this model is at the Holyland Hotel in Jerusalem.

tion but for the Passover that intervened. No matter, Agrippa decided; his case would be first on the docket after the festival. At this point the morale of the Jerusalem Christians must have approached a nadir. With two of their prime leaders killed or imprisoned, the only recourse was "earnest prayer" not only for Peter but for the shrouded prospects of the church itself.

In prison, meanwhile, Peter was clearly *over*guarded. He had been delivered to four squads of soldiers for absolute security, sixteen men in all. At night he slept chained by the wrists to two of them *behind* the bars of his cell. There were additional guards at two stations beyond that, and finally, also, thick walls that insulated the Antonia fortress from the rest of Jerusalem, breeched only by a huge iron gate. Why this excessive

guard? Might the priests have reported to King Agrippa an earlier imprisonment of the apostle, followed by his embarrassing disappearance?

What happened is a favorite Sunday school story: Peter's impossible
escape the very night before Agrippa had planned to condemn him. Luke
tells of the angel who apparently had more of a problem waking Peter up
than causing the chains to fall from his hands or opening all the necessary
prison doors, including the massive iron gate. Don't blame Peter. The
man had an unbreakable habit of sleeping through crises, ever since
Gethsemane. Besides, he had been subjected to so many visions lately
that he could only conclude this was one more of the same. And so the
angel had to walk an extra block with Peter outside the fortress to make
sure the sleepy fisherman-apostle had really grasped his senses. Only
then did the angel vanish.

Awake, finally, and understandably elated at his deliverance, Peter
made for the house of John Mark in Jerusalem, the man who would one
day write the earliest of the Gospels. Mark's widowed mother, Mary, must
have been a woman of some means, because her Jerusalem town house
was spacious enough to accommodate the large group of Christians who
had gathered there, praying for Peter's deliverance even though by now
it was midnight. She also had a maid named Rhoda, who hurried to the
door when she heard it being pounded.

"Who's there?" asked Rhoda (which is Greek for "Rose").

"Simon Peter."

It *was* Peter's voice! In her delirious elation Rhoda provided one of
the most human scenes in the *Book of Acts*. Instead of opening the door,
she had to share the joy immediately or burst. Hurrying back to the
conclave of Christians, she shouted, "Peter is standing at the gate!"

An immediate hushed silence, and then an opinion: "You're mad!"
someone commented dryly.

"No! It's Peter. I heard him!"

"No. It's his angel. Or his spirit," another suggested.

There was, however, the problem of that continual knocking. Spirits,
after all, have only spiritual knuckles. The nearest Christians made a rush
for the door and opened it. Would that photography had been available!
The film would have shown the greathearted, kindly countenance of the
big fisherman wreathed in the broadest smile his gray-bearded cheeks
could muster. He had quite a story to tell.

But the next morning it was all perplexity and consternation at the palace of Herod in west Jerusalem. The king had ordered that Peter be brought over from the Tower Antonia for trial in the same place where Jesus had stood before Pilate eight years earlier, the sprawling courtyard in front of the palace Herod the Great had built. Peter, however, was nowhere to be found. Storming across the city to the Antonia, Agrippa barked questions at the helpless sentries, who could give no decent answers to the obvious queries. In a fury, Agrippa ordered that they be put to death.

Luke tacks on an amazing sequel to the scene, for he could not resist reporting what ultimately happened to Herod Agrippa I. It was some three years after this episode that Agrippa, back home in his palace at Caesarea, suffered a very ominous fate. Because he had been having problems with the coastal cities of Tyre and Sidon to the north, Agrippa evidently slapped an embargo on grain shipments there from Palestine. It had the desired effect. Soon a rather hungry delegation arrived from the north country, pleading for an audience with the king so that they could sue for peace. Agrippa finally condescended to receive them. Donning his royal robes, he mounted his throne and gave the delegation so gracious an address that they shouted fawningly, "The voice of a god, and not of man!" Agrippa said nothing, though he doubtless smiled.

In one abrupt and violent sentence *Acts* concludes: "Immediately, because he had not given God the glory, an angel of the Lord struck him down, and he was eaten by worms and died" (12:23).

Fortunately, Josephus also reports this scene, and so the Lucan account can be supplemented with a more complete version of the grotesque episode. Agrippa's address was before a wider audience that was present in Caesarea for a festival in honor of the Roman emperor. It was on the second day of these spectacles that the king entered the theater of Caesarea at daybreak to address the people, for ancients began their days with the first glimmer of dawn.

The "royal robes" Agrippa wore that morning, according to Luke, were quite a dazzling outfit, for Josephus says the garment was "woven completely of silver so that its texture was indeed wondrous." As Agrippa mounted the dais,

> . . . the silver, illuminated by the touch of the first rays of the sun, was wondrously radiant and by its glitter inspired fear and awe in those who

The restored Roman theater at Caesarea, looking northward.
It was here that King Herod Agrippa I was seized with his
extraordinary illness. At the upper left is the Mediterranean.

gazed intently upon it. Straightway his flatterers raised their voices from
various directions—though hardly for his good—addressing him as a
god. "May you be propitious to us," they added, "and if we have hitherto
feared you as a man, yet henceforth we agree that you are more than
mortal in your being." The king did not rebuke them nor did he reject
their flattery as impious. But shortly thereafter he looked up and saw an
owl perched on a rope over his head . . .

Seven years earlier, when Agrippa had been a prisoner on Capri, an
owl alighted near him. Another captive, who was a German seer, predicted
that the bird would bring Agrippa good luck and release from imprisonment—which happened in fact. "But remember, when you see this owl
again," the German added ominously, "your death will follow within five
days."

The unnerving sight of an owl near his dais was accompanied by a stab of pain in Agrippa's heart, Josephus reports.

> He was also gripped in his stomach by an ache that he felt everywhere at once and that was intense from the start. Leaping up, he said to his friends: "I, a god in your eyes, am now bidden to lay down my life. . . . " Even as he was speaking these words, he was overcome by more intense pain. They hastened, therefore, to convey him to the palace. . . . Exhausted after five straight days by the pain in his abdomen, he departed this life in the fifty-fourth year. . . .

Medical authorities have tried to diagnose Agrippa's malady, the opinions ranging from arsenic poisoning to general peritonitis following acute appendicitis, all aggravated by roundworms in the alimentary canal. Whatever the cause, it was surely an extraordinary ending to an extraordinary career.[2]

Archaeology has added two interesting notes to the story. In 1961 the Roman theater at Caesarea was excavated and partially restored. Situated along the seashore, the rising tiers of semicircular stone benches face westward toward the Mediterranean. On the dais below, a speaker would have to face eastward to address his audience and would be directly illumined by a rising sun in the early morning, exactly as Josephus describes.

In the second century, parts of the theater were rebuilt. A two-by-three-foot stone from that reconstruction had previously stood in a public building called the "Tiberiéum" in honor of the emperor. It is cut with the two-inch Latin lettering cited previously, which translates: "Pontius Pilate, the Prefect of Judea, has presented the Tiberiéum [to the people of Caesarea]"—the first archaeological evidence for Agrippa's predecessor ever discovered.[3]

A king had challenged nascent Christianity and lost—also his own kingdom, since the Romans now reinstated governors in Palestine. Agrippa was dead; Peter was alive. After his remarkable deliverance and the warm reunion at the house of Mark, Peter "left and went to another place" (12:17). Where might that have been? Speculation focuses on Antioch in Syria, but no one knows with any certainty, and the next chapters in Peter's life remain dim. This is because Luke has another extraordinary story to tell.

30

Saul the Fanatic

Meanwhile, Saul, still breathing threats and murder
against the disciples of the Lord, went to the high priest
and asked him for letters to the synagogues at Damascus,
so that if he found any who belonged to the Way, men or
women, he might bring them bound to Jerusalem.

ACTS 9:1–2

ONE of the games some historians like to play is called "Might
Have Beens," posing hypothetical alternatives to history. For
example, how different would the map of Europe look today if Hitler had
never lived? Or Napoleon? Would the Reformation have happened
without a Martin Luther? And so on.

Carrying the game further into the past, what would have happened
to Christianity, humanly speaking, if St. Paul had never lived? Some claim
that it could never have become a world religion but would have remained
a comparatively small Jewish sect scattered at various places around the
Mediterranean. Christianity might have lasted a century or two but then
would have died out entirely. Today, it is argued, only religious scholars
would have known about that curious sect called "Followers of The Way"
or "Nazarenes," who worshiped a Jewish renegade prophet crucified as
a common criminal by the Romans.

An overstatement? Perhaps. Christians would be the first to insist
that, with the Spirit inspiring the movement ever since Pentecost, the
spread and success of the faith were inevitable, and that God would have
tapped someone else on the shoulder if it had not been for Paul. Still, in
view of the way it actually happened, the scenario just described does

244

point up the crucial importance of Paul of Tarsus, a man second only to Jesus himself in the founding of Christianity.

It is very difficult to exaggerate the role of Paul in the formation of the Christian Church. The rest of the account in *Acts* focuses primarily on his activities—about 60 percent of Luke's entire treatise—and half the New Testament books are Paul's letters to the new congregations in the Mediterranean world. His words are heard on a weekly basis when the epistle lesson is read in church services, and probably more books have been written about Paul of Tarsus than anyone else, with the exception of Jesus of Nazareth.

One would have assumed that the greatest missionary and theologian in the annals of the faith would surely have come from the ranks of the Twelve. Yet how intriguing is the fact that Paul never met Jesus personally during his public ministry, to our knowledge. It was only *after* his transit to the spiritual dimension that Jesus went out of his way to meet Paul, the apostle later claimed. But the spiritual symmetry of it all shows up clearly against the background of the first Pentecost. If this were a celebration of God inspiring the Church despite the physical absence of Jesus, how appropriate that the greatest convert should have come this route and gone on to change a world as the Christ-infused man he was. But this is far ahead of his own story.

Student Saul

Paul's original name, of course, was Saul, that of Israel's first king, and he had already made his fanatic debut in the pages of *Acts* as persecutor of the infant Church. Saul's childhood is very sketchy. He was born, not much later than Jesus himself, in Tarsus, the capital of Cilicia, a Roman province that wrapped itself around the northeastern corner of the Mediterranean. His family derived from the tribe of Benjamin and were Pharisees by persuasion, which meant that young Saul would get an excellent education in Hebrew law at home and in the synagogue. His later writings show that he was conversant in at least three languages—Hebrew, Aramaic, and Greek—and in two worlds: secular Greco-Roman civilization as well as Judaism.

Saul probably had a number of brothers and sisters, but only one sister is recorded (23:16), who is unnamed. He inherited Roman citizenship from his father, a high advantage in the ancient world, but why his family had this privilege is not known. Back in 171 B.C., in order to stimulate business, Jews were promised citizenship if they emigrated to Tarsus, and Saul's ancestors may have come with this group.

A youth spent in Tarsus had its own rewards. The city was an important cultural center where East met West, and it boasted a university second only to those of Athens and Alexandria. It was here that Mark Antony had first met Cleopatra a half-century earlier, when the Egyptian queen sailed up in her golden barge. It was here that the overland trade route to Rome stopped before traversing Asia Minor through the Taurus mountain pass, bestowing crucial commercial advantages on the city. Tarsus was a microcosm of the Mediterranean world.

Though a bright student who was destined for advanced religious study, Saul nevertheless had to learn a trade of some kind in accord with Jewish custom, which prescribed some sort of craft even for scholars. The famed Rabbi Hillel had also been a woodcutter, and Jesus of Nazareth a carpenter. For Saul it was tentmaking,[1] a skill he may have learned from his father. One of the prime products for which Tarsus and its province, Cilicia, were famed was a feltlike cloth woven from goat's hair called *cilicium*. Still used today by Bedouins for their tents, cilicium could have been woven and sewn by Saul into cloaks, awnings, or even sails, in addition to tents. His skills with this fabric would remain with him for life, rendering him economically independent.

Probably as a late-teenager, Saul, like so many promising youths of the Jewish Dispersion, sailed to Jerusalem to continue his studies. There he enrolled in the rabbinical school of the Pharisees, where, he later claimed, "I advanced in Judaism beyond many among my people of the same age, for I was far more zealous for the traditions of my fathers" (Gal. 1:14). We have seen how such zeal turned to fanaticism in the case of Stephen and the Christians, despite the liberal tolerance of his teacher, Gamaliel.

The Road to Damascus

And now, as a postgraduate anti-Christian zealot, Saul was on his way to Damascus with credentials from the high priest for the extradition of any heretic followers of Jesus he could find in that ancient Syrian metropolis, which boasted a sizable Jewish population. The distance from Jerusalem was about 170 miles over the caravan route northward, an eight- or nine-day trip for normal travelers, but presumably less for Saul and his eager band.

About noon on the last leg of their journey, on the southern approach to Damascus, Saul suddenly staggered in his steps and fell to the ground. Ordinary sunstroke, his men might have concluded, but for the uncanny sounds they were hearing too, apparently from nowhere. Saul, however, was also blinded by a blazing light from the sky, and, as he was to repeat the story many times afterward, he heard a voice addressing him, "Saul, Saul, why do you persecute me?"

"Who are you, Lord?" he stammered. "Lord" (Kyrie) here meant, not Jesus, but a person with mastery and authority, which the voice obviously possessed.

"I am Jesus of Nazareth whom you are persecuting."

The horror of such a response, considering Saul's record, might have unhinged a lesser mind. Even managing a reply was an act of bravery: "What . . . what shall I do, Lord?"

"Get up and go to Damascus; there you will be told everything that has been assigned to you to do" (22:10).

Throughout the momentous dialogue, Saul's eyes had been shut tight in shock. Now, shakily, he got to his feet and opened his eyelids. With a torrent of new anxiety he found that he was blind. His men had to lead him by the hand into Damascus.

For the next three days Saul of Tarsus endured the greatest turmoil of his life. He hovered close to despair in his pool of darkness, unable to eat or drink. But he could still think, and his agonizing reappraisal of Jesus of Nazareth must have torn into his very soul. No one likes to learn that he is in deadly error, but when such an error takes on supernatural dimension, the implications are staggering. Saul's only recourse was prayer.

In the meantime, an equally critical dialogue was taking place between the chief Christian in Damascus, a man named Ananias, and the One who had interrupted Saul's journey. In a vision Ananias was told to go to "the street called Straight, and inquire in the house of Judas for a man of Tarsus named Saul" and heal his blindness.

Poor Ananias must have flinched in terror at the very mention of Saul's name. The first Christians seem to have had their own underground

The ancient Jerusalem-Damascus road, still in use, at Deraya in Syria. Here, according to local tradition, Saul received his vision of Jesus.

communications network, since Ananias was very well informed of Saul's activities in Jerusalem and his ominous mission to Damascus. But, according to the dialogue in *Acts*, "the Lord said to him, 'Go, for he is an instrument whom I have chosen to bring my name before Gentiles and kings and before the people of Israel . . .'" (9:15).

Obediently, even bravely, Ananias threaded his way through the streets of the oldest still-inhabited city in the world, where he found Straight Street, then Judas' house, and—once inside—the blinded persecutor of Christians. "Brother Saul," he said, "the Lord Jesus, who appeared to you on your way here, has sent me so that you may regain your sight and be filled with the Holy Spirit."

Something like scales fell from Saul's eyes, and he regained his sight. Then, with ebullient joy, he asked for baptism and received it. *Conversion,*

An underground chapel in Damascus marks the presumed site
of Ananias' home. The painting over the altar shows Saul
receiving his sight from Ananias.

that wonderful Latin word that means a "turning around to the other
side," a "changing direction," a "whirling about," could not better char-
acterize Saul's experience. Peter had been transformed. Now, even more
dramatically, Saul was too. The marvel of Pentecost was continuing.

A few solid meals and Saul was back to normal. Some of his personality traits were not changed. His zeal and enthusiasm, for example,
persisted—only in the new direction. After a few days with the astonished
Christians of Damascus, he was his overactive, zealous self once again,
this time as a champion of Christianity, not its persecutor. Eagerly, he
visited the synagogues of Damascus to proclaim variations on the
message, "Jesus is the messianic Christ, the Son of God." Shock waves
rocked the Jewish community in Damascus: the man who was supposed
to quarantine the followers of Jesus had become a victim of the contagion.

Explanations

Ever since the most celebrated conversion in history took place, it has been debated by many. Ascribing Saul's transformation to the Christ vision or to inspiration by the Spirit strikes many critics as too exotic for belief, and they have suggested alternative explanations. Briefly, these may be grouped as follows.

Sunstroke: Saul, in this view, simply suffered some variety of heat exhaustion and lost all composure, even sanity, until his natural recovery, but the experience permanently warped him. The elements alone, according to this theory, made Saul a Christian.

Admittedly, the heat in the near-desert flatlands south of Damascus can be intense in the summertime, but sunstroke rarely, if ever, manifests the symptoms ascribed to Saul in this account, and recovery from it would hardly confer a drastic change of belief. In a familiar pun, Christians *do* claim a "Son-stroke" here.

Hallucination: This perception of sights and sounds that are not actually present would be more impressive if the phenomenon had involved only Saul. His comrades, however, partially shared the experience, and group hallucination is extremely unlikely.

Epilepsy: Saul suffered a *grand mal* seizure on the road to Damascus, which warped his personality ever afterward, according to other critics. The main problem with this theory, however, is its overuse. Epilepsy has become a catchall explanation for problems among too many ancient personalities, including Julius Caesar, and it ought to be gracefully retired. Moreover, nearly all epileptics return to the same condition of life and belief after their seizures, which could hardly apply in Saul's case.

Psychology: Certain important predisposing factors were long preparing Saul for eventual conversion, it is argued. He was perhaps having spiritual problems with Pharisaism—much as later on Luther would be troubled by medieval theology—and his fanatic attempts to eliminate the Early Church only mirror these theological misgivings. Then he was confronted with apologists, such as Stephen, who could debate convincingly from Scripture that Jesus *was* the Messiah. Stephen's martyrdom had a further impact on him, as did that of Jesus through reports he must have heard.

Psychology may have some bearing in fact. Saul, for example, could well have been among "those from Cilicia" bested in debate with Stephen

Traditional section of the Damascus wall from which Saul made his escape.

(6:9). However, something *must* have occurred on the Damascus Road that not only triggered a possible psychological preparation in the man, but also radically changed him. In the future Paul would tell and retell the story of his genuine confrontation with the living Jesus. So real was the experience in his life that he staked his entire claim to apostleship on this encounter. An apostle, by definition, had to be a witness of the risen Christ. Cheerfully, Paul could affirm that he was as much qualified by this requirement as any of the Twelve.

The Sites Today

A few miles south of Damascus on the Jerusalem road there is a small Arab village called Deraya. The place is singularly unimpressive, but the name itself is not, for *Deraya* means "The Vision" in Arabic. Most of the Syrian inhabitants are not sure why the village is called that, but Christians are. For it was there, according to the hoary tradition that provided the very name for the town, that Saul sustained his vision of Christ. A small Roman Catholic chapel in Deraya today memorializes that theophany.

In Damascus the "Street called Straight" is still identifiable and is still called *Darb el-Mustaqim* in Arabic, "The Straight Way," because it is the east-west *decumanus*, or axis, of the Roman city. At the eastern end of the street are the remains of a triple-arched gateway, erected by the emperor Hadrian, that mark the *decumanus*.

Modern visitors are shown what is presumed to be the house of Judas off this thoroughfare, although its authenticity is not above question. The house of Ananias is also pointed out, and in its undercroft is a chapel dedicated to his memory.

A section of the old Damascus wall is still exhibited—even the window where the ropes were played out to lower Paul in the basket when, later on, he had to escape from the city.[2] But this sort of precision is hardly necessary, and the entire site is doubtless not authentic.

However, the transition of Saul the Fanatic to Paul the Apostle was genuine indeed, and the course of civilization itself would reflect that transformation.

31

Paul's First Journey

The Holy Spirit said, "Set apart for me Barnabas and Saul
for the work to which I have called them." Then after
fasting and praying they laid their hands on them
and sent them off. ACTS 13:2–3

MUCH as there were silent or "hidden years" in the life of
Jesus—the time he spent growing up in Nazareth—so also
there were hidden years in the life of Paul—the time he spent growing
up as a Christian. Between his conversion at perhaps age twenty-five and
the start of his First Missionary Journey, about thirteen years elapsed. It
was a period of preparation for his great mission, an interim when he had
to rethink his entire theology in view of the confrontation on the Damascus
Road. The Jesus who had been the object of his contempt as a false prophet
was in reality the messianic Son of God, who had triumphed over death
at the first Easter. The harried Christians, whom he had sought to persecute out of existence as deluded errorists, had been right the entire time.
And, perhaps even more amazing to Saul, God had for some reason
specifically destined him, even before he was born, to be his apostle (Gal.
1:15). It would take years of study for so total a reordering of his thought.

The first three years of this period Saul seems to have led a monastic
sort of existence, probably at some oasis in the northern Arabian desert
near Damascus. He may, however, also have begun mission work among
the Nabataean Arabs during this interval. But at last he felt ready to make
another attempt at converting the Jews of Damascus.

Like a second Stephen, Saul returned to the city of his conversion
and took on all comers in debate, boldly demonstrating from Scripture

253

that Jesus was the promised Messiah. Under these circumstances it is not surprising that a plot against Saul's life was launched, which also involved the ethnarch of the Nabataean Arabs in Damascus, since Saul was thought to be under the ethnarch's jurisdiction from his study sojourn in the Arabian desert. The city gates of Damascus were placed under surveillance day and night to single out Saul for some dagger thrusts.

The Christians of Damascus, however, had their own rather effective surveillance system, for they learned of the plot and the stakeouts at the gates. Late one night, in possibly the most unorthodox exit staged by anyone in the Bible, they let Saul down over the city walls in a wicker basket. He then fled southward to Jerusalem.

There he met the two leading apostles, Peter and James, the brother of Jesus, who was emerging as head of the Jerusalem church (Gal. 1:18). Saul spent fifteen days with them, during which he must have convinced them of his apostolate, while they, in astonishment at his conversion, must have related their eyewitness accounts of Jesus.

Saul finally sailed back to Tarsus, where he spent the next ten years as an independent missionary in Cilicia and northern Syria (Gal. 1:21). It was a period of practical experience in preaching and teaching, an internship in which he had to learn to deal with people as well as with words. His first attempts in Damascus had been less than effective, owing possibly to his extravagant zeal. Now he was readying himself for better use as that "chosen instrument" whenever the Spirit should summon him.

Joseph Barnabas

Usually, of course, the Spirit worked through people. Shortly after the first Pentecost, when the Jerusalem Christians were building a common treasury, a Jew from Cyprus named Barnabas sold some property that belonged to him and delivered the proceeds to the apostles. A sturdy, imposing figure who had the confidence of the Jerusalem church, Barnabas had helped introduce Saul in the Holy City, allaying any fears the believers there might naturally have had about the former persecutor (9:26).

Then Barnabas was sent northward to what seemed the most promising seedbed for Christianity in the Near East, the Syrian capital of Antioch. The church was growing vigorously there, since the Gospel was being proclaimed to both Jews and Gentiles with astonishing results. It

The Roman gateway in the western wall of Tarsus, Saul's hometown, is sometimes called "Cleopatra's Gate." Mark Antony and Cleopatra first met at Tarsus.

was at Antioch, in fact, that the faith abandoned the bulky epithet "Followers of The Way" and took on the name by which it would be known ever afterward, "Christians" (11:19).

Barnabas quickly sensed the need for more church workers in Antioch. Taking the road that wound around the corner of the Mediterranean to Tarsus, only eighty miles away, he found his friend Saul and returned with him to Antioch. For the next year Barnabas and Saul formed a teaching-preaching team in the Syrian capital, until they were required for special services elsewhere.

Luke records their summons very simply. One day, probably in 47 A.D., the Spirit told the praying believers there, "Set apart for me Barnabas and Saul for the work to which I have called them" (13:2). That work turned out to be the first specially organized missionary expedition in church annals, an ideological invasion of the Greco-Roman world that aimed to announce Christianity in the very heart of paganism.

It was a threesome who ultimately embarked on ship from the port of Seleucia near Antioch. Barnabas had invited his cousin, John Mark, to join the expedition, the young man at whose house Peter had stood knocking on the door after his deliverance in Jerusalem.

Like charity, mission work begins at home, and—doubtless due to Barnabas' urging—they sailed first to the island of Cyprus. Presumably they started with the opening of the sailing season on or about March 10, for strong westerlies blow later in the spring and their voyage would not have been so direct. Landing at the eastern port of Salamis, they traversed Cyprus until they reached Paphos on the west coast, the provincial capital of the island.

Cyprus was one of Rome's senatorial provinces, and at this time it was governed by a proconsul named Sergius Paulus. The governor himself met the missionary trio and inquired about their mission. Saul seems to have taken the initiative in responding, giving so eloquent a proclamation that the Roman was much impressed. But Sergius Paulus, like most heads of state, also had opportunists and hangers-on at his headquarters, and one of them was a *magus* named Elymas, a practitioner of the same occult crafts associated with Simon Magus. Fearing lest his influence over the governor slip if he converted to Christianity, Elymas interrupted Saul to oppose him.

"You *son of the Devil!*" snapped Saul in some of the strongest language recorded from his lips. "Will you not stop making crooked the straight paths of the Lord?" What particularly nettled the apostle was not only an interruption of possibly his first major Gentile conversion, but the fact that Elymas was a renegade Jew who should not have been dabbling in magic. "And now listen—the hand of the Lord is against you," Saul continued, "and you will be blind for a while, unable to see the sun" (13:11).

Struck with blindness, Elymas had to be led away by others. It was the first recorded wonder from the hand of Saul, and it impressed Sergius Paulus so thoroughly that he believed the apostolic message—certainly a strategic conversion.

Although some have questioned whether or not the Roman governor actually became a convert, no one can dispute the man's existence. According

These ruins mark all that remain of ancient Seleucia, the port of
Antioch from which Saul and Barnabas set sail on the First
Missionary Journey.

to an inscription from Rome, an "L. Sergius Paullus" was formerly a
"Curator of the Banks and Beds of the Tiber," a river and flood control
commissioner, most probably prior to taking up his post in Cyprus.[1]

In reporting this incident Luke inserted his famous shift in nomen-
clature: "Saul, also known as Paul" (13:9). And from here on he was called
only Paul. "Paulus" was either a Roman cognomen added to his given
name, Saul, or, more likely, the similar-sounding name by which he
preferred to be known in the future because of its familiarity to Greeks
and Romans, the targets of his mission. Some scholars have suggested
that Saul renamed himself in honor of his first distinguished convert,
Sergius Paulus, but this seems merely coincidental.

257

Asia Minor

Their mission to Cyprus accomplished for the present, Paul, Barnabas, and Mark took ship from Paphos and sailed in a northwesterly direction to Perga on the coast of Asia Minor. There, however, the missionaries suffered some kind of personal crisis. Young Mark suddenly abandoned his colleagues and returned to Jerusalem—*why* is not stated in the New Testament.

Various suggestions have been offered involving Mark's physical health or his character—somehow, the callow youth was not able to put up with the hardships of missionary travel—but these seem less than convincing. One, hopefully fresh, surmise might be this. When the three had set out from Antioch, Barnabas appeared clearly in charge of their expedition, with Paul second in command. Yet by the time of their first landfall and, indeed, throughout the rest of the journey, Paul had plainly taken over leadership of their mission travels. John Mark, as Barnabas' cousin and friend, may have resented what he thought a usurpation of leadership by an "outsider" to the Christian cause from such "insiders" as themselves who had participated in the original Pentecost and the earliest activities of the church in Jerusalem. Whatever the cause of Mark's defection, apostles were obviously also human beings.

The first goal of Paul and Barnabas' thrust into Asia Minor was the city of Antioch in the Roman province of Galatia (not to be confused with the Syrian capital). It was no easy journey. Antioch lay about 100 miles to the north across the formidable Taurus Mountains and about 4,000 feet in altitude. It had a handsome setting in the lofty tablelands and lake district of southwestern Asia Minor, and it was also one of the most cosmopolitan communities Paul ever visited. The city boasted native Galatians, Phrygians, Greeks, Jews, and also Romans, for Antioch had recently hosted a large influx of veterans from the Roman army.

Of all these ethnic groups, however, Paul and Barnabas would first present the Good News to their own kind, a standard Pauline practice from now until the end of his mission in Rome. On the Sabbath they went into the synagogue at Antioch and sat down. They heard the standard two readings from the Law and the Prophets, and then the ruler of the synagogue extended them a cordial invitation: "Brothers, if you have any word of exhortation for the people, give it."

Paul stood up to deliver a sermonette that could not more effectively have linked Jesus to scriptural prophecy. Like the martyred Stephen, he skimmed some of the highlights of Israel's past, but when he reached King David he moved directly to David's messianic descendent. Jesus, Paul said, was prosecuted by Jerusalem authorities who "because they did not recognize him or understand the words of the prophets that are read every sabbath, they fulfilled those words by condemning him" (13:27). But rejection and death were followed by resurrection and new life for Jesus as well as for all believers, a prospect also available to the Jews of Antioch.

Paul's message raised a sensation in the synagogue, and he was invited back for the next Sabbath. A week later the word-of-mouth phenomenon had caused "almost the whole city" to turn out for the two missionaries. The multitudes, however, also included some representatives of Jewish orthodoxy who contradicted Paul's claims.

After what was doubtless a heated debate, Paul finally grasped what would become his cardinal alternative whenever confronted by Jewish rejection of the Christian message. Ominously, he warned:

> It was necessary that the word of God should be spoken first to you. Since you reject it, and judge yourselves to be unworthy of eternal life, we are now turning to the Gentiles. For so the Lord has commanded us, saying, "I have set you to be a light for the Gentiles, so that you may bring salvation to the ends of the earth." (13:46; Isa. 49:6)

There were more than enough Gentiles for a mission field in Antioch, with its crazy-quilt of different ethnic groups. It is just possible, in fact, that Paul and Barnabas had originally aimed for Antioch on the recommendation of Sergius Paulus, because archaeology has shown that the family of the governor of Cyprus had important roots in that city. With only paganism as their religious schooling, the Gentiles of Antioch gave a positive response to the Christian message, and a congregation was founded there.

Unhappily, however, increasing pressure from the synagogue finally led to outright expulsion of the two missionaries. But before leaving Antioch, they had the satisfaction of seeing their new converts "filled with joy and with the Holy Spirit" (13:52). The wonder of Pentecost was continuing.

Paul and Barnabas now headed eastward to Iconium (called Konya in modern Turkey), a city well located on a fertile fruit- and grain-producing plain. They pursued a mission pattern similar to what they had accomplished in Antioch, preaching first in the Jewish synagogue of the city. Their success here was again challenged by an orthodox Jewish reaction, which divided the city. Even though they soon had to yield to pressure and move on, the second church of Asia Minor had been founded, and it would thrive.

An Attempted Deification

Lystra lay twenty-five miles south-southwest of Iconium, and although a sister city to Antioch in boasting a colony of Roman army veterans, it was clearly more rural and less sophisticated, if the next extraordinary scene is any indication. After the two missionaries arrived in Lystra, Paul used a great sign to authenticate his great message. Fixing his gaze on one of his listeners, who had crippled feet and had never walked in his life, he shouted, "Stand upright on your feet!" In Luke's language, the cripple "sprang up and began to walk."

The phenomenon was too much for the crowd that had gathered. Abandoning the Greek in which they and Paul had been communicating, they shouted, in their native Lycaonian tongue, "The gods have come down to us in human form!" And such gods! Barnabas they hailed as Zeus, father of the gods and men; while Paul, the chief spokesman, they called Hermes, the god of communication.

For centuries the names have led scholars to conclude that Barnabas must have had the more imposing figure and countenance of the two, with Paul smaller but more agile. It is true that *paulus* is a Latin adjective that means "small" or "little," but it was also a common proper name in several of the great families of Rome, whose bearers were not necessarily small. More convincing are the earliest portraits of Paul in the Roman catacombs, which usually show him as a smallish figure with pointed, prying gray beard.

The acclaim at Lystra was more than the sort of flattery accorded King Agrippa that fateful morning in Caesarea. Those were only words. Here the bedazzled pagans went on to action. The local priest of Zeus was so sure that the chief Olympian deity had indeed arrived in Lystra, that he was processing happily up toward the gates of the temple with oxen and garlands to do public sacrifice! Lest we laugh at the naïveté of the Lystrans, it should be noted that it was in exactly this area of the world that the famous Greek myth of Baucis and Philemon had its setting. They were an aged couple who one day supposedly offered hospitality to *Zeus* and *Hermes* as the two gods wandered by in the *likeness of men*, for which the couple's miserable cottage was transformed into a splendid temple.[2] Would lightning strike twice in the same area?

Paul and Barnabas quickly put an end to such speculation. Tearing their garments at the sacrilege, Paul cried, "Why are you doing this? We are mortals just like you, and we bring you good news, that you should turn from these worthless things to the living God," whom he went on to describe (14:15).

Was it chagrin at their blunder that made the crowd lend ready ears to adversaries who had just made a special trip from Antioch and Iconium to denounce the apostles? An instant, drastic change of mood swept the multitude. The gods were now impostors and must be punished. Paul was dragged outside the city by a shrieking mob and stoned to death before his supporters could save him.

Or so the Lystrans thought. Actually, Paul was doubtless knocked unconscious by one of the stones and presumed to be dead. For when Barnabas and the new believers of Lystra gathered anxiously about him, Paul regained his senses and stood up, bruised, but not mortally injured. No thoughts of self-pity swirled in his mind, for he would have been the first to remember a man named Stephen, and how he was here receiving a slight taste of his own medicine.

The next day they left for Derbe, the last town on their itinerary, about a day's journey eastward. Here they preached without incident and "made many disciples," the first place in Galatia where they had not encountered opposition.

From Derbe it would have been simplest for Paul and Barnabas to continue eastward through the Taurus mountain pass and home to Antioch. But what was simplest was not always best for the Gospel. Since it was important to check on the progress of the new missions they had founded, the apostles went three times as far homeward in the opposite direction, bracing up the new believers in Lystra, Iconium, and Antioch, and appointing elders to guide them. This wise gesture led to permanent Christian churches in all these cities.

261

Finally, they returned southward to the Mediterranean coast and caught a ship bound for Syria. When Paul and Barnabas arrived in Antioch, they could deliver a very colorful missionaries' report, for God "had opened a door of faith for the Gentiles" indeed (14:27).

32

Quarrels and Controversy

Then certain individuals came down from Judea and were
teaching the brothers, "Unless you are circumcised
according to the custom of Moses, you cannot be saved."
And . . . Paul and Barnabas had no small dissension
and debate with them. . . . . ACTS 15:1–2

ACERTAIN nostalgia for early Christianity and its rapid growth
rate moves many believers today. At a time when modern
culture is becoming more secular than ever and so many more babies are
born than baptized, when church membership seems to be drooping and
even the Sunday school is in trouble, it is small wonder that Christians
are trying to revive church life by harking back to the verve and successes
of the Early Church.

The experiences of primitive Christianity, however, can easily be
overidealized; the first Pentecost was not followed by one prolonged glory
story. Besides the spectacular extension of the Church, *Acts* very honestly,
very realistically, also records the instances of smallness and inconsistency
among the apostles, the squabbles between the missionaries, the dishonesty and economic jealousies of some Early Church members, and, inevitably, the theological controversies that could rage in the Church, then as
now. All was hardly sweetness and light.

Shortly after the original Pentecost, for example, there was the sad
story of a couple named Ananias and Sapphira. In joining the apostolic
collective in Jerusalem, they had sold some of their property and had
pretended to give the entire proceeds from the sale to Peter, while actually

withholding some of the money. For this bit of dishonesty they were both struck dead.

Sunday school children reportedly have no trouble with this story, but many adults do, for it seems an obvious case of overpunishment. The harshness is best explained by the timing: this was just after Pentecost, during the critical birth process of the church, when divine entry into human affairs had to be taken with utter seriousness. As Peter put it, "You have not lied to men but to God" (5:4). The supernatural sign also authenticated the apostolic ministry, however severely. Still, so extremely punitive a miracle was not repeated in early Christianity, and one can only hope that the unfortunate couple somehow found ultimate salvation, since they surely seem to have been punished enough in this life.

Other problems in the Early Church were economic in nature, and some, such as the Hellenist widows' complaints in Jerusalem, have been cited. A sizable number of poor Jewish Christians in Palestine also seem to have been in continuing financial straits. The Jerusalem leaders mentioned their problem to Paul during one of his visits to the Holy City (Gal. 2:10), and on several occasions Paul and his associates delivered relief money to the elders there. Those with no love for socialism have suggested it was all due to the unwise collectivistic experiments of the Jerusalem Christians, but the periodic famines in the Near East may also have been a factor.

The Jerusalem Council

Far more significant issues, however, were now confronting the Church. Among the Jerusalem Christians was a group of very strict interpreters of Jewish law—"the circumcision party" noted earlier—Christian Pharisees who were also called Judaizers. A foretaste of their theology had surfaced when Peter returned from his mission to Cornelius and they asked him, "Why did you go to uncircumcised men and eat with them?"

Though Peter's reply satisfied them for a time, the narrow-minded legalists now dispatched representatives to Antioch, who insisted that the only way a Gentile could become a Christian was to become a Jew first: "Unless you are circumcised according to the custom of Moses, you cannot be saved" (15:1). Despite the coming of Christ, they taught, Old Testament Law still applied to Christians in its entirety.

Paul and Barnabas opposed this notion vigorously. In their journey through Asia Minor they had not required that their Gentile converts be circumcised or that they observe all of Jewish law, since salvation was not achievable through the Law but only through faith in Christ. Quite a debate raged in the Antioch church, since the Judaizers were calling Paul and Barnabas' entire mission enterprise into question.

The Christians of Antioch finally sent Paul, Barnabas, and Titus to Jerusalem to consult with the apostles on so basic an issue. Titus was one of Paul's Greek converts, most probably from Antioch, and he had *not* been circumcised. In other words, here was a walking, breathing test case on the theological question: Was Titus a true Christian as he was, or would he have to be circumcised?

The meeting in Jerusalem was the first church council in Christian history, and its importance was categorical for the future of the faith. But for the decision it made, Christianity might not have become a world religion. Highest authorities in the Church at this time were the apostles and elders who had gathered to consider the issue, with James the brother of Jesus, Peter, and John the leading three "pillars of the church."

Paul, who had been warmly received by the Jerusalem Christians, opened by giving the conclave a sample of the sort of gospel he had been preaching to the Gentiles, "in order to make sure that I was not running, or had not run, in vain," he put it poignantly (Gal. 2:2). If he had preached a wrong version of the faith, his fifteen years of study and missionizing would have been utterly wasted.

Paul's theology sat well with everyone but the Judaizers, who insisted adamantly, "It is necessary to circumcise the Gentiles, and to order them to keep the law of Moses."

A drone of discussion greeted that opinion, until Simon Peter stood up and fully seconded Paul's theology. The genial fisherman reminded the council of how God had elected the Gentiles also, as witness his own special mission to Cornelius. "Now therefore," he summed up, "why are you putting God to the test by placing on the neck of the disciples a yoke that neither our ancestors nor we have been able to bear?" (15:10).

During the ensuing silence Paul and Barnabas reviewed how extraordinarily God had blessed their efforts in Asia Minor. Would He have given them power to perform wonders there if they had been preaching a wrong gospel?

265

Panorama of Jerusalem today from the Mount of Olives.
In the foreground is the Kidron Valley. At left center stands
the Dome of the Rock, marking the site of the great Temple.

James now showed his leadership by bringing the council to a decision. He readily sided with Peter, Paul, and Barnabas. Arming himself with scriptural precedent, James announced,

> My brothers . . . I have reached the decision that we should not trouble those Gentiles who are turning to God, but we should write to them to abstain only from things polluted by idols and from fornication and from whatever has been strangled and from blood. (15:19)

Paul's more liberal message, then, was God's message; his preaching was authentic! Titus would not have to be circumcised, and Gentiles could convert directly to Christianity without going through a kind of Jewish halfway house. The fourfold restrictions—three dietary and one moral—were very mild tokens asked of the Gentiles so as not to offend their

To the left of this and in the background is the location of Golgotha, near the white tower.

fellow Jewish Christians. (In rabbinical tradition, the three sons of Noah, who were thought to be progenitors of both Jews and Gentiles, had had the same restrictions placed on them.)

But the Jerusalem Council had clearly opted for salvation by faith rather than salvation by law, a momentous turn for the future of Christian theology. As Paul would later write to the Galatians, ". . . We did not submit to them [the Judaizers] even for a moment, so that the truth of the gospel might always remain with you" (Gal. 2:5). Paul's victory was confirmed by a letter that the elders of the Jerusalem church wrote to the congregation in Antioch, and it was delivered by special emissaries. Paul had not run in vain. The gospel of God's free grace was Good News indeed.[1]

Squabbles in Antioch

Because of Paul's evident success with the Gentiles, an almost official division of labor had been agreed upon at the close of the Jerusalem conclave: James, Peter, and John would concentrate primarily on the Jewish Christians, whereas Paul and Barnabas would specialize in Gentile mission work (Gal. 2:9). This may help explain the unhappy scene that followed soon after the council ended.

The Judaizers of Jerusalem, despite their enormous setback, were still trying to advance their cause, and a party of them returned to Antioch. Peter happened to be paying a visit to the church in Antioch at about the same time, and at first he had had no scruples about dining with the Gentile converts there. When the Judaizers showed up, however, he surrendered his table fellowship with the Gentiles to forestall any criticism from the militantly orthodox. But Peter's inconsistency grew contagious, and soon even Barnabas and other Jewish Christians were also dining on a strictly kosher basis, leaving Gentile believers by themselves . . . and justifiably offended.

Possibly Peter felt that his mission, now mainly to the circumcised, dictated such conduct, but it remains a sad little gesture in an otherwise noble career, a throwback to the Simon Peter of pre-Pentecost days.

Paul quickly set Peter straight. "I opposed him to his face, because he stood self-condemned," Paul later wrote to the Galatians. "When I saw that they were not acting consistently with the truth of the gospel, I said to Cephas [Aramaic for Peter] before them all, 'If you, though a Jew, live like a Gentile and not like a Jew, how can you compel the Gentiles to live like Jews?'" (Gal. 2:11). The freedom of the gospel was at stake, and Paul would not let Peter risk it or return to legalism.

The scene of one of the two greatest apostles castigating the other in public is extraordinary, of course, and it used to bother some of the later Church fathers, like Jerome, who tried to explain away the episode. But this is not possible.[2]

Nor is it necessary. There is something distinctly refreshing about the realism and candor of the squabble in Antioch. Saints are sinners too, prone to failure and error, and their story is so much more believable when it is told in full. Most other biographies in the Greco-Roman world to that date are laced with fulsome flattery of their subjects, and therefore lose much credibility. The Bible, on the other hand, is the one religious book in ancient literature that admits that its heroes are sinners too, and then provides a candid look at the sins. So instead of glossing over such negatives, *Acts* and the letters of Paul, with bracing honesty, report them in detail.

Another purpose for including such scenes in the record may have been to comfort future generations of Christians. If, in the ruddy afterglow of the first Pentecost, the Early Church, informed and inflamed as it was by the Holy Spirit, could *still* become an arena of controversy between liberals and conservatives, parties and ethnic groups, then there is some small consolation for later generations of Christians, which have done—and are doing—the same thing.

However, there is also a lesson from the first Christians on how to *solve* such controversies. The decision at the Jerusalem Council involved several elements:

1. *A Face-to-Face Confrontation:* There was no whispering campaign, no rush to publish, no indirect attacks or misunderstandings, but a candid exchange between reasonable men, not extremists.

2. *Listening:* Possibly the most important verse in Luke's report on the conclave is 15:12: "The whole assembly kept silence, and listened. . . ." An honest effort was made by each side to hear the other side.

3. *A Scriptural Solution:* James based his decision on three prophets—Isaiah (45:21), Jeremiah (12:15), and Amos (9:11).

4. *Compromise:* While the word has both bad and good connotations, there is no question but that the resolution at Jerusalem, while not "compromising" (in the negative sense) a syllable of the gospel, still found a "compromise" solution (in the positive sense) between opposing viewpoints, for the sake of harmony in the Church.

Feuders-in-the-faith today might well look back to Christian origins for Christian solutions.

269

33

Paul's Second Journey

After some days Paul said to Barnabas,
"Come, let us return and visit the brothers in every
city where we proclaimed the word of the Lord,
and see how they are doing." ACTS 15:36

THE Jerusalem Council had not intended to solve all future problems in the Church. In fact, it was just after this conclave that two "shockers" transpired: the Paul-versus-Peter spat in Antioch, previously discussed, and now the Barnabas-versus-Paul quarrel on whether or not John Mark should come along on the Second Missionary Journey.

Barnabas agreed that it was time to revisit the new churches in Galatia, but he wanted his cousin to accompany them. Paul, however, "decided not to take with them one who had deserted them in Pamphylia, and had not accompanied them in the work" (15:38). Was Paul being unforgiving? Or just realistic? The kind of expeditions they were undertaking demanded total commitment and reliability.

Barnabas refused to back down, and it actually led to a split between the two apostles, which had doubtless been exacerbated by Barnabas' weakness in the face of Judaizers at Antioch. In any case, Barnabas now took Mark with him on a separate mission journey to Cyprus, while Paul chose a new partner, named Silas, who had helped deliver the letter of decision from the Jerusalem Council to the church in Antioch. But good can come of evil: the net result of the apostolic altercation was *two* missionary expeditions instead of one.

Paul and Silas started overland northward, probably first to Tarsus and then across the Taurus Mountains through the most famous pass of antiquity, the Cilician Gates. The Gates are a series of sharp defiles that notch the otherwise impregnable Taurus barrier for a distance of nearly ten miles. At one point the Gates taper down to a narrow, precipitous pass that resembles a dry gorge. Paul and Silas would undoubtedly have stopped at this spot to gather in its full significance. Here was the aorta of the ancient world through which pulsed the conquerors of the past during four thousand years of history. Hittite, Assyrian, Persian, Greek, and Roman armies had marched through that mountain gap. Xerxes, Cyrus, Xenophon, and Alexander the Great had all traversed the Cilician Gates for military conquest. Now a lonesome pair of missionaries were using the same pass for a spiritual conquest that would have far more permanent results.

Once on the higher Anatolian plateau, they turned westward to revisit the four Galatian cities that Paul had missionized some months earlier and deliver to them the decision of the Jerusalem Council. At Lystra he was so impressed with a young man named Timothy, who enjoyed an excellent reputation among the Christians of the area, that he invited him to accompany them as co-worker. With a Jewish mother and a Greek father, Timothy was a personal symbol of the universality of the faith, and he accepted.[1]

After moving on to Iconium and Antioch, the three fully intended to pass into the Roman province of Asia—roughly the western third of what is today Turkey. Instead, Paul, Silas, and Timothy found themselves heading northwestward toward the Dardanelles, "having been forbidden by the Holy Spirit to speak the word in Asia" (16:6). This passage has knitted many Christian brows, but it need not mean that God was playing favorites with the gospel. Rather, it was all a matter of timing: Paul would spend many months in Asia and its chief city, Ephesus, in the future, but for now, the continent of Europe was waiting for their message.

On reaching the Aegean coast at Troas, very near the site of ancient Troy at the mouth of the Dardanelles, Paul dreamed one night of a Macedonian who pleaded, "Come over to Macedonia and help us." The significance of the vision was unquestioned.

"Immediately," writes Luke, "we tried to cross over to Macedonia, being convinced that God had called us to proclaim the good news to them." Here, of course, is the celebrated "we" passage (16:10), in which Luke has shifted from the third person, leading to the conclusion that he had joined the missionary trio at Troas. What Luke was doing there,

The narrowest point of the Cilician Gates, the famous pass through the Taurus Mountains near Tarsus. Paul and Silas walked through here at the start of the Second Missionary Journey, as did a host of armies and conquerors ranging from Xerxes to Alexander.

where his home was, and other background details are indefinite, but that Greek Gentile physician, now a missionary and later an author, would make incalculable contributions to Christianity.

A New Continent

The four sailed to Macedonia via the island of Samothrace and landed at the port of Neapolis, Christianity's first step onto the continent of Europe. Their objective was an important city of the area, Philippi, which lay nine miles inland across a steep mountain ridge. From the top of this rise they could easily see Philippi lying at the spur of another hill and intercepting the Via Egnatia, the main Roman highway running from Europe to Asia. And just west of the city they viewed the broad plain on which, ninety-three years earlier, the armies of Antony and Octavian had defeated those of Brutus and Cassius in avenging Caesar's assassination.

The missionaries broke their usual pattern at Philippi. With apparently no synagogue in town, they waited until the Sabbath and then went outside the city walls to the banks of the Gangites River about a mile west of Philippi, where there was supposed to be a gathering place of some kind for worship, possibly a synagogue. Indeed, a group of pious women did meet there, among them a wealthy businesswoman named Lydia, who was either a Jewess or a "God-fearer." Lydia sold purple textiles. The Phoenician "patent" on dyeing fabrics in the simmering glands of the purple sea snail had now lapsed, and Asia Minor had also learned the secret of producing garments of royal purple that never faded. Lydia regularly imported these into Philippi and had a thriving business.

Paul's homily at the riverside chapel won her over to Christianity, and she asked for baptism. Lydia was Europe's first convert, and her household quickly joined her in the faith. When she prevailed upon the four missionaries to use her house as the base for their ministry at Philippi, they gladly accepted.

A very strange confrontation catapulted them into public attention in the city. One day as they were going to the riverside shrine, a slave girl who was a soothsayer pursued Paul and his colleagues, crying out, "These men are slaves of the Most High God, who proclaim to you a way of salvation!" Paul ignored the girl, but in the days following, each time the missionaries came upon her horizon, she shouted something similar. Her

Neapolis, where the missionaries landed in Macedonia, was
Christianity's "first step in Europe." Today the port is called
Kavalla.

claim was accurate enough, but coming from a gypsy sort who profited
from divination, it could hardly help the Christian cause in Philippi.

One day Paul lost his patience. He stopped and turned to her,
addressing the spirit inside the girl, "I order you in the name of Jesus
Christ to come out of her." Immediately, the girl returned to normal—joy
for her, but unhappiness for the shabby syndicate of her owners, who
were profiting from the girl's weird abilities. Seizing Paul and Silas, they
dragged them into the central *agora*, or marketplace, at Philippi and
indicted them before the city magistrates. "These men are disturbing our
city," said their spokesman with anti-Semitic slurs. "They are Jews who
are advocating customs that are not lawful for us as Romans to adopt or
observe" (16:20).

274

Romans? "Macedonian Greeks" might have been more accurate, but Philippi, like Antioch and Lystra, also had the status of a Roman colony, and its official title was Colonia Augusta Julia Philippensis. And since Jews were not supposed to make converts of Roman citizens, the girl's exploiters seized on this as a convenient charge against the missionaries.

But now the ever-present downtown crowds had joined in attacking Paul and Silas, and the city magistrates—without bothering to hear a defense from the pair, and against every standard of Hellenic justice—ordered the two stripped and beaten with rods. Luke and Timothy, evidently, were not with their colleagues when the girl was healed, and whether they arrived at the agora in time to see them beaten with "many blows" is not known.

Paul and Silas were thrown into the city prison, where the jailer consigned them to the inner keep and fastened their feet in stocks—a bit of security and a bit of torture, because stocks forced their legs apart in one cramped position. Rather than commiserate their condition, Paul and Silas prayed and sang cheerful hymns until midnight. Whatever catcalls may have come from the other prisoners at such a performance were soon hushed into a curious silence.

Suddenly, a severe earthquake shook the very foundations of the jail, tearing the prisoners' chains from their anchor sockets and flinging open the doors to their cells. Somehow, the jailer had been dozing through all the singing in his keep, but he could not sleep through an earthquake. No sight was more horrifying for a warden in ancient times than open doors and an empty prison. With death the usual punishment for such laxity, the befuddled jailer drew out his dagger and opted for suicide, since, in Greco-Roman law, his widow could then inherit his estate without penalty.

"Don't harm yourself, for we're all here!" Paul shouted from the murky depths of the dungeon.

"Torches!" the jailer cried, and when light was brought, he rushed inside his prison and found it just as Paul had said. Falling down before them, he cried, "Sirs, what must I do to be saved?" Some have found the jailer's question a little too pat, too abrupt for such a situation, as indeed it seems. Very likely, however, the man had already had some knowledge of the sort of message Paul and Silas were bringing to Philippi.

Ruins of the ancient agora or marketplace at Philippi, where
Paul and Silas were beaten.

Paul replied with what might be called the gospel-in-a-sentence: "Believe on the Lord Jesus, and you will be saved, you and your household" (16:31).

The jailer brought Paul and Silas out of prison and into his house, where he washed their wounds and fed them while Paul expounded on his original statement. Before the night was over, the elated jailer and his whole family had been baptized.

The next day the city magistrates, with uneasy consciences, sent some lictors over to release the missionaries. But Paul would have none of that. Bristling with injured innocence, he replied, "They have beaten us in public, uncondemned, men who are Roman citizens, and have thrown us into prison; and now are they going to discharge us in secret? Certainly not! Let them come and take us out themselves" (16:37).

Paul was not being difficult. He had his good name to clear in Philippi so that the Good News might be more credible. The city magistrates, however, trembled at the tidings; Paul had them on three counts of miscarrying justice, and the worst, certainly, was the fact that Roman citizens were *not* to be scourged or beaten. One can almost see the town fathers falling all over themselves as they personally arrived to apologize to Paul and Silas and give them V.I.P. treatment while escorting them out of prison.

Paul and his colleagues paid a final visit to the new congregation meeting at Lydia's house, and then departed after what must have been a tender good-bye. Of all the churches that he founded, Paul had a special bond with the believers at Philippi, and no congregation supported him with more genuine love, prayers, and gifts than the Philippians, as Paul's later letter to them would show. Possibly Luke had a hand in this, because he seems to have remained at Philippi for the next months to serve the new Christians there.

The Sites Today

Unlike Derbe and Lystra, which at present are nothing but barren mounds blanketed by the same carpet of buff-green scrub grass that covers the Turkish plateau, Philippi boasts some impressive ruins. Fortunately, there is no modern Philippi, which means that the excavations there show the very streets and building foundations of Paul's day. The

Entrance to ruins of the prison at Philippi. The sign across the gate reads, in translation from the Greek: "The traditional Prison of the Apostle Paul."

central agora or civic center where Paul and Silas were beaten is plainly visible, and borders the Via Egnatia, the arterial Roman highway that the missionaries used in traveling westward after leaving the city. And in the eastern sector of the ruins, at the base of a large rise, a sign in Greek hangs at the entrance to what looks like a cavern. It translates, "The traditional prison of the Apostle Paul." This site is reasonably authentic—it was the city jail—although it appears considerably smaller than would seem indicated by the account in Acts 16.

The next target city for Paul, Silas, and Timothy was Thessalonica. Even though he was called "the Apostle to the Gentiles," Paul began his ministry at Thessalonica in the synagogue, as he did wherever possible. With Christianity resting on a Jewish foundation and calling itself "the new Israel," this was the logical place to start. For three weeks he debated Scripture in the synagogue, showing how Jesus fitted the parameters of Old Testament prophecy. Some of the Jews were persuaded, including a hospitable sort named Jason, who threw open his home to the apostles. Certain prominent Greeks of Thessalonica also joined the fledgling congregation, although Paul and his companions had to do some tent-making in order to support themselves here (1 Thess. 2:9).

One day, when the missionaries were away, an angry crowd, fired up by opponents in the synagogue, stormed into Jason's house looking for Paul. Unable to find him, they grabbed Jason and several other believers instead, hauling them before the city magistrates with an indictment—which, incidentally, testified to the spread of the faith: "These people who have been turning the world upside down have come here also, and Jason has entertained them as guests. They are all acting contrary to the decrees of the emperor, saying that there is another king named Jesus" (17:6).

Pontius Pilate would have recognized the last charge, and it was disturbing enough for the civic leaders. But Jason and the other Christians posted a peace bond and were released. In order not to embarrass their host further, the missionaries slipped away by night and traveled on to Beroea. The church in Jason's house flourished, however, and Jason himself would later join Paul in Corinth (Rom. 16:21). He was another man marked by the gospel, and appropriately so, since Hellenized Jews generally chose the name Jason in Greek for their Semitic names, Joshua or Jesus.

Beroea lay about sixty miles to the west-southwest, and the synagogue there gave Paul a better hearing, for "those Jews were more "receptive than those in Thessalonica," according to *Acts*, "for they examined the scriptures every day to see whether these things were so" (17:11). Many in this Beroean Bible class came to the faith, but the apostolic visit was again cut short by anti-Christian agitators who now arrived from Thessalonica to stir up a riot. Paul was quickly smuggled out of Beroea and onto a ship bound for Athens, while Silas and Timothy "fronted" for him by staying a while longer in Beroea. The ruse worked.

Athens

Not only the chief city of Greece, then and now, Athens was also the cultural capital of the ancient world. Paul's visit there marks the first time that Christianity was announced in the heart of Mediterranean antiquity, and so the confrontation of the apostle and the Athenians is of enormous interest.

The historian finds this section of *Acts* particularly intriguing, and easily reacts to the text on a nearly verse-by-verse basis:

TEXT (ACTS 17)	COMMENTS
[16]While Paul was waiting for them [Silas and Timothy] in Athens, he was deeply distressed to see that the city was full of idols.	Yes, the chief one, Phidias' gold-and-ivory statue of Athena, stood inside the Parthenon, thirty feet high, surrounded by satellite statuary.
[17]So he argued in the synagogue with the Jews and the devout persons, and also in the marketplace every day with those who happened to be there.	Indeed, the *agora*, or marketplace, was the forum for this kind of exchange. It has been excavated.
[18]Also some Epicurean and Stoic philosophers debated with him. Some said, "What does this babbler want to say?" Others said, "He seems to be a proclaimer of foreign divinities." (This was because he was telling the good news about Jesus and the resurrection.)	Very likely, for these were the two chief philosophical schools of Hellenistic Athens, rather than the Platonists or Aristotelians.

The "babbler" would say enough to cause the erection, later, of a Greek Orthodox church over the very ruins of the *stoa poikile*, the "painted porch" where Stoicism was founded! |

¹⁹So they took him and brought him to the Areopagus and asked him, "May we know what this new teaching is that you are presenting?

²⁰"It sounds rather strange to us, so we would like to know what it means."

²¹Now all the Athenians and the foreigners living there would spend their time in nothing but telling or hearing something new. . . .

The Aeropagus is Greek for "Mars' Hill," a gray, rocky rise that still looms up northwest of the Athenian Acropolis.

The Greeks called foreigners *metics*, a very discerning touch here. In Athens' three-class society (citizens, metics, slaves) it was the foreigners who had vastly increased their numbers at this time. And Demosthenes, the great Athenian orator, tried to awaken his city to the dangers of Philip of Macedon by warning, "Are you content merely to run around asking one another, 'Is there any news today?'" (*I Philippic*, 10)²

Because of the natural way in which the text correlates with Greek history, an ancient historian would have to award Luke an A for accuracy.

When they brought Paul up to the Areopagus,³ the Athenians also provided him with one of the most spectacular preaching stations he would ever use, for Mars' Hill still stands immediately adjacent to the great Acropolis and that diadem of classical antiquity that crowns it, the Parthenon. The gigantic gray rock that is Mars' Hill also overlooks the agora, excavated to the northwest, where Paul first encountered the philosophers. Today it is difficult to decide which is more impressive: the view of the Acropolis–Mars' Hill area from Athens below, or the panorama of Athens from atop Mars' Hill.

Paul's address to the Athenians is fascinating, for it shows the best of his sermon technique. (In the many months of later association with Paul, Luke undoubtedly learned both the thrust and the details of the speech from Paul himself.) He opens by complimenting his audience: "Athenians, I see how extremely religious you are in every way." In a secular age this may not rank as complimentary, but it was intended as an accolade at the time. Paul always began his addresses before Greco-Romans with marks of respect and graciousness. No practitioner of the shock method, he!

Then he mentioned having seen one of their altars inscribed, "TO AN UNKNOWN GOD," and he used this observation as a brilliant opening illustration that snared their attention and led into his message. To the Athenians, who had hedged their spiritual bets by assigning an altar to placate any unknown deity, Paul now revealed his glorious *ho theos*—*The* God, the Creator, in the singular—who was a little more mature than the Athenians' deities, since God needed neither temple nor tending.

His comments in 17:26 about God creating "every race of men of one stock" (NEB) would have found a very responsive echo among his Stoic hearers, who taught something quite similar in their *Logos* concept of God. And his quotations from Epimenides and Aratus (v. 28) demonstrate that Paul of Tarsus was at home in Greek literature.

Paul also delivered a larger concept of God than is often preached or taught. The God he announced in Athens is the universal Creator, who is very interested in other nations besides Israel, who is pleased to have mankind grope after him in its various halting ways, and who is an immensely understanding and forgiving God:

> While God has overlooked the times of human ignorance, now he commands all people everywhere to repent, because he has fixed a day on which he will have the whole world judged in righteousness by a man whom he has appointed, and of this he has given assurance to all by raising him from the dead. (17:30)

The transition to Jesus and the heart of the gospel is natural and logical: Christ is not thrust abruptly into the ears of uncomprehending hearers. No sloganeering ("Are you saved, brother?") for Paul.

At the same time, of course, the man who was never ashamed of the gospel immediately affirmed one of its stumbling blocks, the resurrection of the dead, a ridiculous notion for any sophisticated Greeks. Yet the reaction among his hearers, perhaps to Paul's surprise, was negative and yet positive too. While some mocked, others said, "We will hear you again about this."

Among those who did were Dionysius, a member of the court that sat on the Areopagus, and a woman named Damaris. These were Paul's first Athenian converts. Whatever became of them is not known, but today's visitor to Athens is reminded of them with crushing impact. Even if Paul may have thought his mission to Athens less than successful, Mars' Hill and the Acropolis stand at the intersection of two streets in modern Athens named "Avenue of Dionysius the Areopagite" and "St. Paul's Street." And Paul's address is engraved on a bronze plaque embedded at the base of Mars' Hill today, a place where the words of even the great Pericles are absent.

Corinth

Paul left Athens via the Sacred Way and traveled westward along the Saronic Gulf to Corinth, the most commercial of the cities of ancient Greece. Like Troy (and, later, Panama), Corinth was perfectly situated at an isthmus to control all land traffic moving north and south, as well as all sea traffic moving east and west. Before the present Corinthian Canal was cut, ships were portaged across the narrows on rolling logs.

Corinth would also be central to Paul's mission in Greece, for he stayed there eighteen months. To support himself he returned to tent-making, and it was in this connection that he fell in with Aquila and Priscilla, a Jewish couple who worked the same trade. They had recently arrived from Rome, because the emperor Claudius had issued an edict in 49 A.D. expelling Jews from the city. Aquila and Priscilla not only converted to Christianity but became close associates of Paul for the rest of his life.

Again Paul launched his mission by debating the faith in the synagogue each Sabbath day, and soon Silas arrived with Timothy to help him. As elsewhere, some believed, including Crispus, the ruler of the synagogue, whom Paul baptized. But many did not, and once more the missionaries turned to the Gentiles.

A man named Titius Justus offered his home for Christian services in Corinth, and his premises served as Paul's headquarters for a growing mission effort over the next year and a half that saw an astonishing number of Corinthian converts. Paul himself was firmed up in his efforts here when, as Luke tells it, "One night the Lord said to Paul in a vision, 'Do not be afraid, but speak and do not be silent; for I am with you, and no one will lay a hand on you to harm you, for there are many in this city who are my people'" (18:9).

Perhaps understandably, the Jews of Corinth were nettled at these developments. First the ruler of their own synagogue converted to Christianity because of Paul, and then—with all the subtlety of a tidal wave—the Christians started holding services directly *next door* to their

The ruins of ancient Corinth, looking south along the Lechaion
Road toward the citadel, or Acrocorinth. The Jewish synagogue,
Paul's Christian headquarters, and the *macellum,* or meat
market, were all located along this street. At its southern end,
the Lechaion Road meets the agora.

synagogue! For here is where Justus' house happened to be located, near
the agora and along the Lechaion Road that led northward to the port.
A Greek inscription on a block of white marble has been discovered at
this spot, that translates, "Synagogue of the Hebrews." And now, with
the increasing number of conversions to what they deemed a heretical
sect next door to them, the Jews of Corinth apprehended Paul and brought
him before the tribunal.

Here, however, no mere city magistrate awaited them. Sitting on the
marble platform in the center of the agora at Corinth was no less than the
Roman governor of all Greece, L. Junius Gallio, officially titled "proconsul
of Achaea." When Rome absorbed Greece, it made Corinth its provincial
capital, and so the governor's headquarters were in this city.

The prosecution opened its case against Paul under the general theme, "This man is persuading people to worship God in ways that are contrary to the law." Unquestionably, the ominous parallel was not lost on Paul: here, for the second time, a leading Christian was facing a Roman governor with the power of life and death over him. Would Gallio go Pilate's route, and he Christ's? Unlike Jesus, however, Paul would have much to say in his own defense. He opened his mouth to speak, but Gallio interrupted him.

"If it were a matter of crime or serious villainy," the governor announced, frowning at the prosecution, "I would be justified in accepting the complaint of you Jews; but since it is a matter of questions about words and names and your own law, see to it yourselves; I do not wish to be a judge of these matters" (18:14). Then he threw the case out of court and cleared the area. Paul's prosecutor now received some buffeting from anti-Semites in the crowd, and although Gallio saw it, he ignored it.

So ended the first "test case," in a sense, of organized Christianity. Had Gallio decided otherwise, Paul's career would have been curtailed or terminated. A swarm of happy Christians clustered about Paul. They realized that as a Roman citizen he was not judicable under Jewish law in Corinth—it too was a Roman colony—so the apostle was free. Neither Paul nor Gallio could know it at the time, but about fifteen years after this scene, both of them would stand before the tribunal of another judge in Rome: the emperor Nero.

Anyone interested in Roman history is electrified by the name of Lucius Junius Gallio. He may have only a "bit part" in the *Book of Acts*, but he is a major figure in Roman imperial history. Gallio, who hailed from Spain, was uncle of the poet Lucan and brother of Annaeus Seneca, the great Stoic philosopher who also tutored the later emperor Nero and would thereby virtually govern Rome in a short time. (The difference in names is due to Gallio's adoption by a wealthy friend of the Annaeus family, also named Junius Gallio.) According to one of Seneca's letters, the climate in Greece had made Gallio ill, possibly due to malaria, and he was likely glad to return to Rome.

Gallio's term as governor in Greece can be dated, due to the exciting discovery of four stone fragments at Delphi, fifty miles northwest of Corinth, on which a rescript from the emperor Claudius to the city of Delphi, datable to 51–52 A.D., is inscribed. Just before the fragments are obliterated comes the significant line:

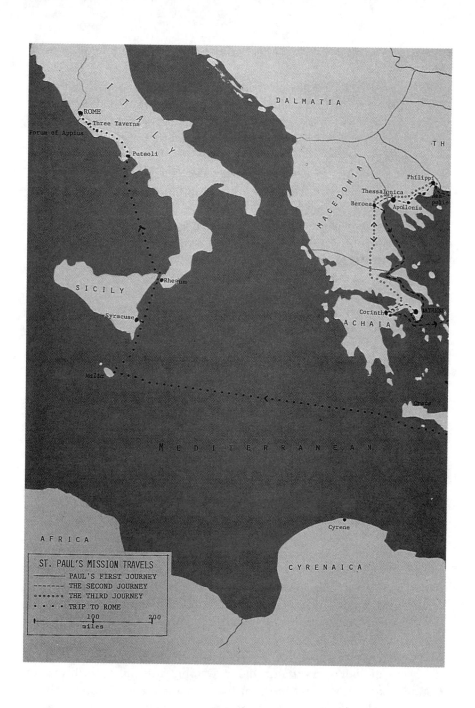

286

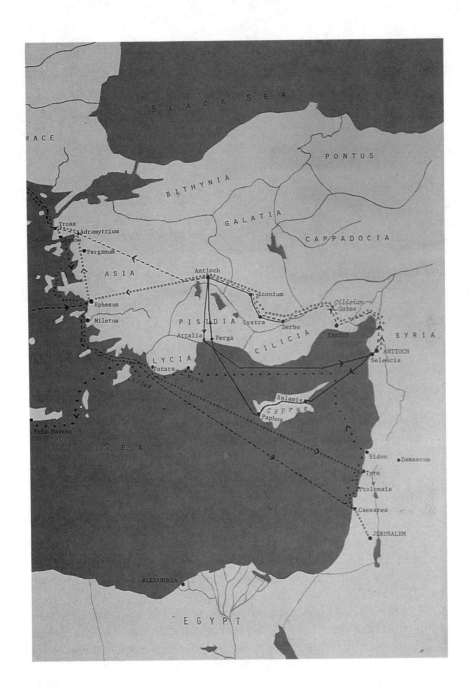

The *bema*, or tribunal, in the agora of ancient Corinth, where
Paul stood before the Roman proconsul, L. Junius Gallio.

[Concerning] the present stories, and those quarrels of the citizens of
which [a report has been made by Lucius] Junius Gallio, my friend, and
[pro]consul [of Achaea]. . . .

This inscription has become an anchor for Pauline chronology. Because
Roman proconsuls held office for only one year, or, less frequently, for
two, the time of this confrontation at Corinth must have been in or about
51–52 A.D.

Gallio may have been "friend" of Claudius, but upon the emperor's
death two years later, when Gallio had returned to the Senate in Rome,
he coined the witty remark that if Claudius had indeed been deified after
his death, he must have been "hooked up to heaven."[4] (Hooks were used
to drag the bodies of criminals down to the Tiber.) Gallio's opinion of the
next emperor, Nero, was even worse. Though for a while he served as
announcer at some of Nero's spectacles, Gallio was ultimately involved

288

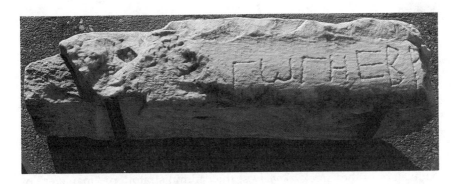

Marble slab discovered at Corinth with Greek lettering "[SYN]AGOG HEBR[AION]," "Synagogue of the Hebrews."

A limestone plaza near the theater of Corinth bears the inscription, in Latin: "ERASTVS·PRO·AED / S·P·STRAVIT," "In his aedileship, Erastus laid this pavement at his own expense."

with his brother in a conspiracy against the emperor and, like Seneca, was forced to commit suicide.

As does history, the stones, then, corroborate Luke also. No archaeological site in the world better reflects Paul's ministry than Corinth. Besides the marble block from the synagogue, excavations along the southern edge of the agora have uncovered the large marble-faced *bema*, or tribunal, before which Paul stood. Aside from the Roman governor, Paul could not have missed gazing at the Acrocorinth, a massive rock formation that soars over the city from the south, while Gallio, in facing northward

289

toward the crowd, could have rested his eyes from time to time on a background slashed with the cool turquoise of the Gulf of Corinth.

No less than the "city manager" at Corinth—Erastus—was converted (Rom. 16:23), and undoubtedly the stones cry out his name too. A plaza near the theater at Corinth is paved with limestone blocks, one of which is inscribed, in translated Latin, "Erastus, during his aedileship, laid this pavement at his own expense." The Latin *aedile* is easily the equivalent of the Greek *oikonomos*, the "administrator" or "manager" of the city. Even the *macellum*, or "meat market," Paul refers to in 1 Corinthians 10:25 is mentioned in an inscription, and it, too, seems to have stood near the church and synagogue on the Lechaion Road.[5]

During his eighteen months in Corinth, Paul worried particularly about the new Christians in Thessalonica. But when Timothy returned from a pastoral visit there with happy news about their faith and growth, Paul wrote them a commendatory letter that also answered several questions that had been bothering them about the second coming of Christ. This letter, later known as *1 Thessalonians*, is the very earliest writing in what would one day be called the New Testament.

But just as some today are using the *Book of Revelation* in mistakenly overliteral ways to predict the imminent return of Christ, so some of the Thessalonians had misused Paul's letter to preach that the Second Advent was in the immediate future or had already come. The apostle soon dispatched another letter northward—*2 Thessalonians*—to correct this view and counsel moderation. It seems to have had the desired effect.

By now almost three years had elapsed on the second missionary expedition, and it was high time to return to the East. Aquila and Priscilla accompanied Paul on a voyage from Cenchreae, Corinth's eastern port, as far as Ephesus, where Paul taught briefly, promising to visit the city again. Then he sailed to Caesarea and home to Antioch. It was the close of his most spectacular foray for the faith in the Mediterranean world. The seed was well planted in Europe.

34

Paul's Third Journey

> While Apollos was in Corinth, Paul passed through the
> interior regions and came to Ephesus, where he found
> some disciples. ACTS 19:1

BECAUSE Paul's activities play so predominant a role in the second half of the *Acts* account, one may well wonder what was happening meanwhile to Peter or John or Philip and the other disciples. Though many speculations have been offered, the plain fact is that no one knows with much certainty, since the surviving sources are largely silent. Unquestionably, however, the apostles were carrying on a mission effort parallel to Paul's in various directions radiating away from Jerusalem. The disciple Thomas, for example, once the risen Jesus had dispelled his doubts, preached the Good News as far eastward as Parthia and India, according to Church traditions.[1] Others evangelized elsewhere.

Still others became missionaries in oblique ways. One of these was Apollos of Alexandria, who was neither one of the Twelve nor of the Seventy (Luke 10:1). Apollos was a learned and eloquent Jew who converted to Christianity, but without a complete knowledge of the faith. Nothing daunted, Apollos arrived at Ephesus and started speaking boldly about Jesus in the synagogue there. Listening to him in the congregation were none other than Paul's tentmaking co-workers, Aquila and Priscilla, who invited Apollos to their home and corrected his doctrinal defect on baptism, since Apollos "knew only the baptism of John" (18:25).

A quick learner, Apollos was soon a fully qualified Christian missionary. Armed with letters of recommendation from the Christians of Ephesus, he now traveled to Corinth and powerfully "watered" what Paul had

291

"planted" there (1 Cor. 3:6). Because of his specialty in relating Jesus to Hebrew Scripture, Apollos may very well have authored the *Letter to the Hebrews*, as Martin Luther surmised. Apollos, at any rate, symbolizes the dozens, perhaps hundreds, of other emissaries for the faith in various parts of the Near East and the Mediterranean.

Meanwhile, after resting several months, Paul undertook yet a third mission expedition, once again taking the road northwestward from Antioch, through the Cilician Gates, and onward to the churches he had founded in Galatia. This was now the third time he had visited Derbe, Lystra, Iconium, and Antioch in the "interior regions" of Asia Minor, which showed their importance to Paul. Perhaps it was for this reason that the diehard Judaizers made a last, determined effort to undermine his message in these churches shortly after he left them. When Paul learned of it, he promptly wrote his most impassioned *Letter to the Galatians*.[2] After the briefest introduction, it begins:

> I am astonished that you are so quickly deserting the one who called you in the grace of Christ and are turning to a different gospel—not that there is another gospel, but there are some who are confusing you and want to pervert the gospel of Christ. But even if we or an angel from heaven should proclaim to you a gospel contrary to what we proclaimed to you, let that one be accursed! . . . (Gal. 1:6)

Following this scolding, however, Paul continued with a magnificent document that has well been called the "Magna Carta of Christian Liberty," a noble affirmation of the doctrine of justification by faith alone.

Ephesus

In his previous journey Paul had veered northwestward to the Dardanelles, but this time he turned toward Ephesus in the southwest, the leading metropolis in the Roman province of Asia. Located three miles from the Aegean, though connected to it by the Cayster River, Ephesus was a rich commercial center like Corinth, yet it also sheltered the wildest collection of pagan priests, exorcists, magicians, religious prostitutes, cultists, and charlatans in the Roman Empire. Since the great marble Temple of Artemis was the pride of Ephesus and one of the fabled Seven Wonders of the Ancient World, the city annually played host to hordes of pagan pilgrims from all over the East during the festival of Artemis in

March–April. These facts were not lost on Paul of Tarsus, and his mission strategy seems clear: win for Christ in Ephesus and he could win anywhere. Ultimately, he would spend three years here, his longest sojourn in a target city thus far.

For the first three months Paul was permitted to preach his message in the synagogue, until opposition made him withdraw his converts and move over to the "hall of Tyrannus," where he would hold forth on a daily basis for the rest of his Ephesian ministry. Ancient sources do not identify this Tyrannus, but he seems to have been a Greek teacher or philosopher who owned the hall and rented it to Paul for a nominal fee. Why nominal? Because the early Western manuscript of the Greek text of *Acts* adds the telling phrase that Paul taught in the hall of Tyrannus "from the fifth hour to the tenth," that is, from 11 A.M. till 4 P.M., the hottest part of the day when, presumably, Tyrannus' students had long since left the hall.

While the variant additions of the Western text are not usually favored, this one has much to commend it. The schedule would permit Paul to earn his living as a tentmaker in the mornings (20:34) and still be able to preach to other citizenry and craftsmen in the afternoons when they had abandoned their own labors in the heat of the day.

His audience, in any case, must have been a large, interested ethnic conglomerate of Jews and Gentiles, Asiatics and Greeks. One early group that Paul instructed more fully consisted of twelve followers of Apollos, who now received proper baptism and the gifts of the Spirit, including *glossolalia*—speaking in tongues—and prophecy. Paul himself demonstrated similar gifts in an extraordinary ministry of healing and exorcism at Ephesus, which led to a humorous story.

Ephesus was such a center for ancient magic that books on the occult arts were often styled "Ephesian writings." It was only natural, therefore, that cousins-by-profession of Simon Magus or Elymas of Cyprus should be concentrated here. Among such were seven sons of a priest named Sceva, all itinerant Jewish exorcists who were so impressed by Paul's healings in the name of Jesus that they decided to invoke that name too, merely as a magic charm and without any belief in Christ. This, in essence, remains the great difference between religion and magic: in the former, personality and faith are involved; in the latter, only forces and formulas. Gathering around a victim of demon possession in his own house, the seven sons of Sceva began their solemn exorcism, "I adjure you by the Jesus whom Paul proclaims—"

293

"Jesus I know," the evil spirit interrupted, "and Paul I know. But *who are you?*" Instantly, the demoniac leaped on all seven, tore their clothes off, and gave them a terrible pommeling before they were able to flee the premises, bruised and naked (19:11ff.).

One can only hope that Paul visited the powerful maniac shortly afterward to cure him, so that moderns can release their pent-up laughter at this story without seeming to make fun of the possessed. Paul appears to have cured him in fact, because this incident was all over the streets of Ephesus before the day was out, and a hush of reverence for Paul's God started to blanket the pagan metropolis.

Many practitioners of the mystical arts abruptly changed professions, gathering their magic textbooks and paraphernalia and burning them in the agora. Among them were some red-faced Christian converts who had secretly been pursuing a parallel interest in the occult. Before the bonfire had turned to embers, materials worth 50,000 silver drachmas (probably about $25,000) had been destroyed.

Speaking in Tongues

Paul ached to visit the new church at Corinth once again, but the opportunities in Ephesus were so obvious that he had to delay his trip there while sending Timothy on ahead of him. Shortly afterward he received disturbing reports about the Corinthians, as well as a long letter from them posing many questions about the faith. The church in Corinth, it seems, had neatly quartered itself into a Paul Faction, an Apollos, a Peter, and a Christ Faction. As if this were not enough, the Christians there were reeling under a variety of problems. One supposed convert was living in incest, others in open immorality, and still others were feuding in the pagan courts. Their letter also raised questions about food sacrificed to idols, the role of women in the church, and the nature of glossolalia and charismatic gifts.

Paul answered such queries in his incomparable documents, later called 1 and 2 *Corinthians*. In a book on the first Christian Pentecost, however, it may be well to emphasize what the apostle had to say about glossolalia, for speaking in tongues is an important hallmark of the current neo-Pentecostal or charismatic movement.

294

The two most prominent instances of glossolalia in the New Testament, precedent-setting as they certainly became, are the Day of Pentecost (Acts 2) and the practice of the Corinthian church (1 Cor. 12–14). Clearly, two *differing* forms of glossolalia occurred on these occasions. At Pentecost three correlated phenomena appeared: a rush of wind, tongues of fire, and speaking in recognizable foreign languages, not irrational or ecstatic utterances. At the Corinthian church, however, not one of the three Pentecostal phenomena transpired. Instead, the glossolalia that occurred there was of the irrational utterance variety.

To be sure, attempts have been made to equate the two instances, one school insisting that it was foreign languages on both occasions, another claiming it was irrational utterances both times, but these attempts have been unsuccessful. It seems obvious, however, that practitioners of glossolalia across the centuries since then—and currently—have followed the Corinthian form: unintelligible speech, *not* the experience of Pentecost.

A vivid picture of the practice at Corinth shows up in chapters 12 and 14 of Paul's first letter to the Christians there. Those who claimed the gift of tongues would stand up during services and pour out a flood of unintelligible syllables, ecstatic prose presumably inspired by the Spirit. When the glossolalia had ended, someone with the gift of interpreting tongues would translate them, if possible.

Many religious historians deem the phenomenon a carryover into the Corinthian church from pagan backgrounds, especially the Greco-Roman mystery cults, in which such religious ecstasies and glossolalia were common. In this view, Paul tolerated the phenomenon at Corinth in his vast adaptability to be "all things to all men" that none be lost.

However, Paul goes into much detail in dealing with glossolalia, and no one today should debate the practice without first reading 1 Corinthians 12 and 14. The apostle does establish common ground with practitioners of tongues by claiming to have the gift himself, but he uses it only on a personal (Paul-to-God) basis, not publicly in the church, where it is patently unedifying because it is unintelligible (14:18).

The practice, to Paul, is certainly the least of the Spirit's gifts, offering opportunities for pride and ostentation and offense to others. He would rather speak five logical words than utter ten thousand words in a tongue! (14:19) If everyone in the church practiced glossolalia, outsiders would consider Christians a pack of madmen (14:23). Accordingly, if tongues *had* to be used, not more than two or three were to speak, in order, and then

295

were to wait for an interpretation in each case. If no interpreter were present, silence was to prevail (14:28).

To any fair-minded reader these chapters show Paul's attitude toward glossolalia as decidedly negative on balance. Reading between his otherwise diplomatic lines, the message is clear: he would be a happy apostle if the Corinthians simply dropped the practice on any public basis, although he did not put it that baldly for fear of offending any new convert.[3]

Gifts of Healing

Among the other spiritual gifts listed by Paul are "healing . . . the working of miracles" (1 Cor. 12:9). The current charismatic movement stresses these as well as glossolalia, insisting that the Spirit's miraculous gifts to the apostolic church *do* continue today much as they did then.

All Christians agree that the Spirit continues to bestow his gifts on the Church, but they do not agree that these must be precisely the same gifts accorded the first Christians. Are there *no* differences between the miracles of Jesus and the apostles and the "miracles" claimed today? There certainly are, as the following table illustrates:

MIRACLES CLAIMED IN THE NEW TESTAMENT	. . . AND TODAY
People were raised from the dead.	The dead are *not* raised. (Claims of actual resurrections in Indonesia and elsewhere have been proved patently false.)
Jesus changed water into wine, walked on water, stilled tempests, and the like.	Such supernatural control over the elements of nature is not duplicated.
Miracles attempted by Jesus succeeded in each case, as also by the apostles in *Acts*.	Miracles attempted today do *not* succeed in so many, many instances.
Biblical miracles were attended by great restraint. Often they were performed *only* to authenticate the gospel message.	"Miracles" are lavished indiscriminately to whole audiences by many practitioners without any restraint.

296

The feeling of guilt was first *re-moved* by Jesus in most of his signs ("Your sins are forgiven"), spiritual before physical healing.	A feeling of guilt is frequently *instilled* by some current practitioners of healing. When their healing fails, the victim is often accused of not having enough faith.
Biblical miracles had permanent, positive effect.	"Miracles" claimed today sometimes result in aggravating the condition: diabetics lapsing into comas when taken off insulin, and the like.

More contrasts could be noted. This is certainly not to say that miracles *cannot* happen today. In Christian theology God never binds himself, and believers should be the very last to try restricting the Almighty. If someone has truly experienced healing, let him or her be grateful for it. But, beyond any debate, whoever insists that today's "miracles" are fully equal to those reported in the Gospels and the *Book of Acts* is actually *diminishing the latter.*

The New Testament signs were necessary to authenticate the message of Jesus and the disciples and to assist the spread of Christianity. But when, after the apostolic age, the faith was broadly established in the Mediterranean world, the great wonders seem to have ceased on any regular basis. God, evidently, did not feel obliged to keep supplying believers with supernatural proof after supernatural proof, necessary as these were in the first century to help launch the faith.

A Theater Riot

Meanwhile, one of the most dramatic scenes in all of Paul's travels was unfolding at Ephesus. A silversmith named Demetrius was making his fortune by manufacturing statuettes of the goddess Artemis and miniature silver models of her temple in Ephesus—much like the tourist trinkets still available at that Turkish site today. But business had been falling off in a strangely direct proportion to Paul's mission successes. The relationship was not lost on Demetrius.

Calling a meeting of all craftsmen and jobbers in the Ephesian metalworking guild, Demetrius delivered an emotional harangue, warning that Paul had tainted both Ephesus and most of the province of Asia with the perfectly awful opinion that "gods made with hands are not gods"

Artemis (Diana) of Ephesus as the multibreasted fertility goddess of Asia Minor. This marble statue stands in the museum at Ephesus in Turkey.

(19:26). (A better slogan Paul could not have devised!) Demetrius continued, "And there is danger not only that this trade of ours may come into disrepute but also that the temple of the great goddess Artemis will be scorned, and she will be deprived of her majesty that brought all Asia and the world to worship her" (19:27).

Their profits threatened, the angry craftsmen started shouting, "Great is Artemis of the Ephesians!" Pouring into the street, they kindled a demonstration by yelling at all the citizens, "To the theater!" A general confusion ensued, in which many of the townspeople rushed over to their massive 24,000-seat theater carved into the side of a mountain looming up from Ephesus.

Two of Paul's companions in travel, Macedonians named Gaius and Aristarchus, were discovered by the silversmiths and dragged into the theater also. When Paul learned of it, he wanted to go there too, but the Christians of Ephesus wisely prevented that, as did a timely message from some of his friends among the *Asiarchs* of the city, who warned him not to venture outside. The Asiarchs were Roman officials whose duty it was to advance the emperor's cult and supervise his festivals in the provinces. Doubtless they were friendly to Paul, because he had finally broken Artemis' religious monopoly in Ephesus, something they had been trying to do for years.

Over at the theater a full-dress riot was brewing. The Ephesian Jews prompted one of their number, Alexander, to stand up in the orchestra and make it clear to the crowd that Paul did not represent them. Alexander raised his hands for silence. Then someone yelled that Alexander was a Jew, and bedlam broke out. Most of the theater started chanting, "Great is Artemis of the Ephesians!"

The craftsmen were nearly as suspicious of Jews as they were of Christians, for Jews, too, taught that "gods made with hands are not gods," and they were known to disrupt pagan shrines.

"GREAT IS ARTEMIS OF THE EPHESIANS!" The shouts, now as synchronized and rhythmic as a cheering section at an athletic event, went on for no less than two hours. "Great" she was indeed, that versatile deity of Ephesus. Originally a local fertility goddess like the Phoenician Astarte, she was claimed by the Greeks as Artemis and by the Romans as Diana, though all surviving statues in the area show her cluttered with many breasts as the fecundity figure she originally was, rather than as the more refined Diana who was twin sister to Apollo and moon goddess in Greco-Roman mythology.

The highest magistrate available in Ephesus during the riot was the city clerk, who soon arrived and quickly quieted the crowd. "Citizens of Ephesus," he cried, "everyone *knows* that our city is temple keeper of the great Artemis, and of the sacred stone that fell from the sky [probably a meteorite that fell in Galatia, sacred to Cybele]. Since these facts are beyond debate, you should be quiet and do nothing rash against these innocent men!" Continuing, in Luke's words:

> If therefore Demetrius and the artisans with him have a complaint against anyone, the courts are open, and there are proconsuls; let them bring charges there against one another. If there is anything further you want to know, it must be settled in the regular assembly. For we are in

The Arcadian Way at ancient Ephesus looking eastward toward
the great theater, carved into the side of the mountain
overlooking the city.

danger of being charged with rioting today, since there is no cause that
we can give to justify this commotion. (19:38)

With that he dismissed the crowds. Too tired and too hoarse to
challenge him further, the throng dispersed.

Moderns can sit in the very seats so vacated, for the great theater at
Ephesus has finally been fully excavated, a magnificent structure in three
vast tiers of semicircular marble seats on which the audience faced westward to view the waterfront. Perhaps the most beautiful boulevard of
antiquity, the Arcadian Way, connected the theater with the port of Ephesus, and its pavement still shows cruciform grafitti cut by some early
Christians there. No one can sit in any of the 24,000 empty seats today
and fail to hear a speaker plainly in the orchestra below—and perhaps
also the faint echo of a crowd chanting, "Great is Artemis of the Ephesians!"

A Last Visit to Greece

Soon after the riot, Paul took his leave of the believers in Ephesus and traveled to Greece via Macedonia. Quite naturally he had to see if conditions had improved in Corinth, and he stayed there for three months during the winter of 56 A.D. He had also been tending a pet project over the previous months. To symbolize the unity of Jewish and Gentile Christians and to show to the believers in Palestine the concern their Gentile brothers felt for them, Paul was collecting contributions from all the Gentile churches on his itinerary for the needy Jerusalem Christians. Such gifts might also put to rest any suspicions the church there might have had about his ministry.

At Corinth he also wrote his longest and greatest epistle, the powerful *Letter to the Romans*, in which he discussed law and gospel more fully than he had ever done previously. He also told the Christians in Rome of his plans for a future visit to the western Mediterranean world, including Rome and even Spain.

But now it was time to take his collection to Jerusalem. A sea voyage would have been quickest, but when a plot against him was discovered— possibly involving sabotage of the ship—Paul shifted his plans and returned overland instead. This also gave him the opportunity of revisiting the new churches in Beroea, Thessalonica, and Philippi, accompanied by what was now a total of eight co-workers, including Luke, who seems to have rejoined the missionary band at Philippi and would stay at Paul's side from this point on (20:4).

They spent a week along the Dardanelles in Troas, and on the night before their departure Paul still had so much to tell the Christians there that he actually talked on until midnight. They were meeting in an upper room, where many burning oil lamps warmed the atmosphere and made at least one member of the congregation very sleepy, a young man named Eutychus. Even if his name meant "fortunate" in Greek, Eutychus was not so lucky. Falling asleep, he dropped out of the third-story window where he had been sitting, onto the ground below. Though the youth was "picked up dead" by the crowd, Paul bent over him and said, "Don't be alarmed, for his life is in him." And so it was, for he soon revived. Whether this was a case of concussion or resurrection is not clear in the *Acts* text. But the happy congregation now broke out the food, after which Paul and the flock conversed until daybreak (20:7ff.).

View from the top of the 24,000-seat theater at Ephesus, where the silversmiths' riot against St. Paul occurred (Acts 19). At upper right is the Arcadian Way. The harbor has now silted into dry land.

The missionary band then set sail southward along the coast of Asia Minor to the port of Miletus. There Paul sent word to the elders of the church at Ephesus to come meet him for a final good-bye—final because Paul now had premonitions that this would be his last journey to that area: "The Holy Spirit testifies to me in every city that imprisonment and persecutions are waiting for me. . . . None of you . . . will ever see my face again" (20:23f.).

His manner, however, was not lugubrious. He rather gave the Ephesian elders a bracing little course in church administration: "Keep watch over yourselves and over all the flock, of which the Holy Spirit has made you overseers, to shepherd the church of God that he obtained with the blood of his own Son" (20:28). After a final prayer together, and weeping embraces, they saw Paul off to his ship.

Sailing across the eastern Mediterranean on Paul's first visit to Phoenicia, they landed at the port of Tyre, where a Christian congregation was already thriving. That group had heard enough about the apostle to love him and also to warn him of difficulties he could expect in Jerusalem. Paul dismissed the warning, because he wanted to take his collection to the Holy City by Pentecost if possible. Thence they sailed to Caesarea, where they spent some time at the home of the same Philip who had opened a mission thrust to Samaria. Two great apostles had been reunited. The church's outreach had come full circle.

35

Jeopardy in Jerusalem

"What are you doing, weeping and breaking my heart?
For I am ready not only to be bound but even to die in
Jerusalem for the name of the Lord Jesus." ACTS 21:13

THUS Paul addressed his friends in the house of Philip. A prophet named Agabus had arrived at Caesarea and had performed a symbolic act on Paul. Taking the apostle's belt, he had bound his hands and feet, warning, "This is the way the Jews in Jerusalem will bind the man who owns this belt and will hand him over to the Gentiles."

Paul, however, would not be deterred. When the missionaries reached Jerusalem, they visited James and the elders of the church, delivering to them the Gentile collection. It was there, rather than in Antioch, that Paul reported on his third expedition, and the leaders of the Jerusalem church were thrilled by his account. They also told Paul of "many thousands" of Jewish Christian converts in Palestine.

In that group, however, there was a problem. Some of its more legalistic members, the Judaizers, were still carrying on their campaign against Paul, this time charging that in his mission work the apostle was telling not only Gentiles but also Jews to "forsake Moses" and refrain from circumcising their children. The charge was untrue—the church leaders knew that—so they proposed that Paul publicly observe Hebrew law by paying for the Temple sacrifices of four Jewish Christians who had taken a Nazarite vow (Num. 6) and then purify himself with them.

Diplomatically, Paul agreed. He surely had better things to do, but he went through the week-long ritual at the Temple and had nearly

304

finished it when disaster struck. A group of Jewish pilgrims from Ephesus suddenly recognized Paul in the Temple precincts and grabbed him.

"Men of Israel, help!" they shouted, and then identified Paul as a teacher who attacked the Jews, the Law, and the Temple everywhere he could. "More than that," they added ominously, "he has actually brought Greeks into the Temple and has defiled this holy place" (21:28). The last was a lethal charge. Marking off an inner enclosure in the Temple were thirteen *stele*—stone slabs—that bore the following inscription in Hebrew and Greek:

> Let no Gentile enter within the balustrade and enclosure surrounding the sanctuary. Whoever is caught will be personally responsible for his consequent death.

Two of these notices have been discovered; one is still intact. Later on, the Roman conqueror Titus would attest to the power of these signs when he told some Jerusalemites, "Have we not given you permission to put to death any who pass beyond [these notices], even if he were a Roman?"[1]

Here, then, was one Roman Jew from Tarsus whom the enraged crowd that had gathered would dispose of in short order. Paul was dragged out of the Temple and was well on his way to getting stoned to death while he doubtless protested that it was all a dreadful mistake. Previously, his accusers had seen him in Jerusalem with an Ephesian Gentile, one Trophimus, yet Trophimus had *not* accompanied Paul inside the Temple as they had supposed. But try to argue with a mob.

Fortunately for Paul, the Roman cohort of Jerusalem was stationed in the Tower Antonia, which overlooked the entire Temple precinct from its northwestern corner. The uproar brought the Roman tribune and his troops running out of the Antonia and over to Paul, whom they arrested and chained. Because the throng now pressed in on every side, yelling, "*Away with him!*" Paul actually had to be carried up the steps in front of the fortress.

Just before they moved inside the gate, Paul spoke to the tribune in Greek. This surprised the commander, since he had assumed Paul was a troublemaking pseudoprophet from Egypt who had previously led 4,000 men out of the desert to attack Jerusalem. (Josephus also reports the episode, though, with less restraint than Luke: he sets the number of

For a presumed violation of the warning on this slab, Paul was arrested in Jerusalem. One of thirteen such signs surrounding the inner Temple area, it threatened death to any Gentile who walked into the sacred precincts. The Greek term for "death," *thanaton*, is the last word on this inscription, which is now at the Archaeological Museum in Istanbul.

rebels at an improbably high 30,000.[2]) Paul quickly set the tribune straight and then begged permission to address the crowd. Permission was granted.

Using the staircase at the Antonia as his pulpit, Paul delivered his message with passionate honesty, beginning with his background at Tarsus and his education under Gamaliel, and continuing in detail with his conversion experience on the Damascus Road. He next reported a theophany while praying at the Jerusalem Temple, in which Jesus had warned him to flee the city and testify instead to the Gentiles.

The last was too much for the crowd. They stopped listening and started yelling, *"Away with such a fellow from the earth!"* *"He shouldn't go on living!"* Some were throwing handfuls of dust into the air, while others waved their cloaks in what was now an out-and-out riot.

The tribune immediately ordered Paul inside the Antonia and had him stripped for scourging. With so much shouting by the crowd, the man must have been guilty of something, and a little lashing would wring a confession out of him. Coolly, Paul waited until they had tied him up with thongs before he asked a question with all the innocence of a Roman battering-ram: "Is it legal for you to flog a Roman citizen who is uncondemned?"

Astonished and embarrassed, the tribune corroborated the claim of citizenship with Paul before he stated, "I bought my citizenship for a large sum." His Greek name, Claudius Lysias, showed that purchase has been necessary.

"But I was *born* a citizen," Paul could reply proudly. Instantly, he was untied (21:27ff.).

Before the Sanhedrin

Lysias still had to have an explanation for the riot, so he convened a meeting of the Jewish Sanhedrin the next morning and brought Paul before it, not to try him, but to discover the basis of the furor. The hearing got off to a very bad start. Paul began, "Brothers, up to this day I have lived my life with a clear conscience before God."

"Strike him on the mouth!" someone shouted from the marble benches.

"God will strike *you*, you whitewashed wall!" cried Paul, glaring in fury at the figure. "Are you sitting there to judge me according to the law, and yet in violation of the law you order me to be struck?"

Some bystanders now identified Paul's antagonist. "Do you dare to insult God's *high priest?*" they asked.

Paul lowered his voice and replied, "I did not realize, brothers, that he was high priest; for it is written, 'You shall not speak evil of a leader of your people'" (23:1–5).

High priest at the time was Ananias Ben-Nebedeus, and his unwarranted, arbitrary conduct here correlates well with the cruel streak in his character known from purely Jewish sources. Ananias would later be hunted down and killed by Jewish rebels when they found him hiding in an aqueduct at the start of their war with Rome.[3]

As with other speeches in Acts, Luke has not necessarily provided complete transcripts, and Paul probably went on with a lengthy defense that was likely terminated by dangerous murmuring or shouting in the Sanhedrin. For now he rather cleverly extricated himself by crying, "Brothers, I am a Pharisee, a son of Pharisees. I am on trial concerning the hope of the resurrection of the dead."

This statement immediately set the chamber to quarreling, because the majority in the Sanhedrin consisted of Sadducees, who rejected any resurrection, or angel or spirit, whereas the Pharisees upheld them all and would now serve as at least temporary allies of Paul while the two parties squared off in theological combat. Soon the debate reached the physical level, and the tribune ordered Paul removed for safety (23:1–10).

The episode is refreshing. It shows Paul as a very human sort, who was not above using tricks and ploys to get himself out of a scrape if necessary. A larger-than-life saint of God might well have taken a passive, resigned stance before the Sanhedrin. Not Paul.

During his next day or two at the Antonia fortress, things went well for Paul, who was more under detention than imprisonment. He also experienced another reassuring theophany, which predicted, "You must bear witness also in Rome" (23:11). But then his young nephew visited him with some alarming news. Paul thought only a moment before telling the lad to carry this information to Lysias.

It was nothing less than a plot on Paul's life. The tribune would be asked to send Paul back to the Sanhedrin for further questioning. "But don't yield to them," the youth begged Lysias, "for more than forty of their men are lying in ambush for him. They have bound themselves by an oath neither to eat nor drink until they kill him."

The tribune's brow wrinkled as he replied to Paul's nephew, "Tell no one that you've informed me of this." Summoning two centurions, the tribune ordered them to prepare a guard for about 9 P.M. that night to conduct Paul safely to Felix, the provincial governor in Caesarea. Two hundred soldiers would be needed, again as many spearmen, and seventy cavalry. The size of such a guard is astonishing, although if Paul had been discovered within the city and a riot had broken out, all 470 men would have been kept busy enough protecting their prisoner—and themselves.

Everything worked as planned. Paul was given a mount to ride, and when they reached the Plain of Sharon safely, only the seventy horsemen continued with him to Caesarea. The rest of the guard returned to Jerusalem.

Upon arrival at Caesarea the guard brought Paul before Felix and handed the governor a letter from Lysias, detailing the circumstances of Paul's arrest. The letter went on, accurately enough:

> I found that he was accused concerning questions of their law, but was charged with nothing deserving death or imprisonment. When I was informed that there would be a plot against the man, I sent him to you at once, ordering his accusers also to state before you what they have against him (23:29).

During the five days that intervened between Paul's arrival and that of his accusers, the apostle was kept under guard in Herod's palace at Caesarea, where Pontius Pilate had lived and Herod Agrippa had spent his last days.

Antonius Felix

Like Gallio (Paul's judge in Corinth), Felix (his judge in Caesarea) is very well known in Roman sources. His rise to power as procurator of Judea—for so the governors were now titled—was from the very bottom of Roman society. Felix and his brother Pallas had been slaves who had somehow won their freedom and were later both appointed to high posts by Claudius. Pallas, in carrying a secret message to Capri, had once averted disaster for the emperor Tiberius by alerting him to a conspiracy against him. Serving subsequently as Claudius' finance minister, Pallas became one of the richest and most powerful men in all the Empire, and it was doubtless due to his influence that his brother Felix was appointed as governor of Judea in 52 A.D.

For his part, Felix had been marrying repeatedly, but well. In all, he wed three women of royalty: one wife is unknown, another was a grand-daughter of Antony and Cleopatra, and his current spouse was a beautiful Jewess named Drusilla, a daughter of Herod Agrippa I. With his powerful connections in Rome, however, Felix felt he could conduct a government of extortion, cruelty, and oppression in Palestine with impunity, as even the Roman Tacitus admits in pointing to Felix as a prime cause of the great Jewish rebellion against Rome in 66 A.D.

Such was the man who sat on his tribunal before Paul and his accusers, who had now arrived from Jerusalem. They included the high priest himself and some of the members of the Sanhedrin. When Felix called for the accusation, a spokesman for the prosecution, one Tertullus, arose and flattered the governor with a flowery, saccharine introduction that was laughably false, though true to Roman court procedure. Then Tertullus lodged his formal indictment of Paul:

> We have, in fact, found this man a pestilent fellow, an agitator among all the Jews throughout the world, and a ringleader of the sect of the Nazarenes. He even tried to profane the Temple, and so we seized him. By examining him yourself you will be able to learn from him concerning everything of which we accuse him. (24:5)

The Sanhedrists seconded his charges against Paul, supplying whatever evidence they could.

Next, Felix called for the defense. With a far less flattering introduction, Paul took on all three charges and disposed of them as follows:

1. *A pestilent agitator?* In Jerusalem, "they did not find me disputing anyone or stirring up a crowd, either in the Temple or in the synagogues, or in the city."

2. *A ringleader of the Nazarenes?* In effect, yes, but so what? As Paul put it, "According to the Way, which they call a sect, I worship the God of our fathers, believing everything laid down by the law or written in the prophets, having a hope in God which these themselves accept, that there will be a resurrection of both the righteous and the unrighteous." Thus Paul's thesis here and everywhere: Christianity was the fulfillment of Judaism.

3. *Profaner of the Temple?* This, of course, would be the easiest charge to disprove, and doubtless Paul had, or would soon get, a deposition from Trophimus that he had *not* set foot in the sacred precincts. Paul affirmed that he was merely on a charitable mission to Jerusalem and was observing the Temple rites when he was attacked by some pilgrims from Ephesus who "ought to be here before you to make an accusation, if they have anything against me" (24:10ff).

Paul, who knew his Roman law, was eminently correct on the last point.

Having heard the evidence, Felix pondered the case. Since he "was rather well informed about the Way," as Luke states, he probably realized that the religious dimension of the quarrel was beyond his jurisdiction.

But if he simply released Paul, he would further antagonize the Jewish authorities, who likely were building a brief against him for maladministration. On the other hand, he could not sentence Paul for any political or criminal act. Nor could he abandon him to the Sanhedrin, because he was a Roman citizen.

And so—no decision. Felix merely stalled, telling the prosecution that he would decide the case in the future. Meanwhile, he left Paul under loose confinement with some liberties, including unrestricted access to friends. But there was something about the apostle that intrigued the governor, and he sent for him repeatedly in months to come. Once, he had Paul speak in the presence of his wife, Drusilla, too. Knowing Felix's true character, his response is almost humorous: when Paul held forth on "justice, self-control and the coming judgment, Felix became frightened and said, 'Go away for the present' . . . " (24:25). If truth were told, Felix wanted nothing more than a big bribe to release his prisoner, which was quite in character for the governor.

For the next two years Paul was in confinement at Caesarea due to this impasse. Felix kept him incarcerated because "he wanted to grant the Jews a favor."[4] But the time was not lost. Paul was busy with his letters to the churches.

It was also during these months that Luke most likely visited Jerusalem to learn from the elders there all the many facts about Jesus that the gifted Greek would later work into the Gospel bearing his name. He must also have had special interviews with Mary, the mother of Jesus, who was presumably staying with John at Jerusalem. This would explain Luke's crucial portrayal of the Christmas story, details that only Mary would know.

Appeal to Caesar

About 58 A.D. Felix was recalled by the emperor Nero, and a delegation of Jews lost no time in sailing to Rome to indict the ex-governor for maladministration. Felix's brother Pallas, however, had enough influence with Nero, even in retirement, to have the charges quashed. After this, Felix and his wife drop out of history, and only their son and daughter-in-law are cited, a luckless couple who died during the famous eruption of Mt. Vesuvius in 79 A.D.

Ruins of a jetty at ancient Caesarea, the Mediterranean port and Roman capital of Palestine, where Paul was imprisoned for two years.

The new governor sent to Palestine was Porcius Festus, certainly an improvement on Felix. Quite diplomatically, Festus spent his first days at the religious, not political, capital of Judea—Jerusalem. When the priests mentioned Paul's case to Festus, he invited them to return with him to Caesarea and renew their charges.

They accepted the suggestion, and Paul soon had a second formal hearing. It was much like the first, except that the prosecution seemed to have even less evidence after the two-year lapse. Besides, the high priest Ananias was deposed about this time, so the charges against Paul were tenuous at best. Had Festus been firmly in office for some months, he would doubtless have released Paul. But he was a neophyte, quite anxious to please his new subjects and still treat Paul fairly. He thought he had the perfect solution in an ingenuous suggestion for Paul: "Are you willing to go up to Jerusalem and stand trial on these charges before me there?" (25:9, NEB).

"Twenty-four months in confinement for *this?*" Paul must have thought, struggling to keep his temper under control. His next statement would change his life irrevocably, and he uttered it with passion:

> I am standing before Caesar's tribunal, where I ought to be tried; to the Jews I have done no wrong, as you know very well. If then I am a wrongdoer, and have committed anything for which I deserve to die, I do not seek to escape death. But if there is nothing in their charges against me, no one can give me up to them. *I appeal to Caesar.* (25:10, RSV)

It was his right as a Roman citizen. Festus immediately turned to confer with his advisers. After some shoulder-shrugging and head-nodding from them, Festus faced the prisoner with his decision: "You have appealed to Caesar, to Caesar you *will go.*" Then he cleared the court.

In the next days Festus had more of a problem than Paul, who suddenly found his long-planned trip to Rome underwritten by the state. The Caesar (emperor) at this time was Nero, who, though he already had several crimes to his credit, was not yet the lurid ruler that history would come to know so well. Nero was still a youth, and it was his tutor, Seneca, Gallio's brother, who virtually ran the government for him the first five years. Seneca did so noble a job that the later emperor Trajan regarded that quinquennium as the best government Rome ever had.[5] Paul's appeal, then, was an extremely shrewd way to surmount the local miscarriage of justice.

When Paul appealed to Caesar from the tribunal of Festus, it
was to the Roman emperor Nero, who ruled from 54 to 68 A.D.
This bust of Nero stands today in the Capitoline Museum at
Rome. He was emperor during the great fire of Rome in 64 A.D.,
and was also the first persecutor of the Christians.

One thing Festus dared not do, however, was to send Paul on to Rome without a bill of definite charges against him, and he had been unable to determine such charges. He raised this problem before the son and daughter of the dead King Agrippa—Herod Agrippa II and his sister Bernice—who had just arrived in Caesarea to pay a visit of welcome to the new governor. Agrippa II was only seventeen when his father died and was deemed too young to succeed him. In the meantime, he had become ruler over lands northeast of Palestine with the near-medical names of Trachonitis and Batanaea, as well as parts of Galilee. His attractive sister Bernice was one of the extraordinary Herodian princesses. Married three times, she was undoubtedly carrying on an incestuous relationship with her brother Agrippa II, and she would eventually become the mistress of no less than Titus, the future Roman emperor.[6]

Interested in hearing Paul speak, this unlikely couple entered the audience hall at their father's one-time palace with great pomp and ceremony for the scheduled interview. When the prisoner was brought in, Festus announced the legal history of Paul's case, including his appeal. Then he added, almost poignantly, "But I have nothing definite to write to our sovereign [Nero] about him. Therefore I have brought him . . . before you, King Agrippa, so that, after we have examined him, I may have something to write" (25:26).

Paul offered an impassioned defense, reporting again his conversion experience and subsequent ministry, culminating in the words:

> To this day I have had help from God, and so I stand here, testifying to both small and great, saying nothing but what the prophets and Moses said would take place: that the Messiah must suffer, and that, by being the first to rise from the dead, he would proclaim light both to our people and to the Gentiles. (26:22)

"Paul, you are *mad!*" Festus interrupted. "Your great learning is driving you insane!"

Paul may even have laughed as he brushed off the suggestion. Continuing his focus on Agrippa, he pointed out that the king could corroborate some of his claims, for matters involving Jesus were "not done in a corner." Finally, Paul put it to him point blank: "King Agrippa, do you believe the prophets? I know that you believe—"

Agrippa smiled and said, "Are you so quickly persuading me to become a Christian?"

"Whether quickly or not," said Paul, "I pray to God that not only you, but also all who are listening to me today, might become such as I am—except for these chains!" (26:28).

Agripa II stood up and ended the hearing. When he had retired with Festus and Bernice, he said, "This man is doing nothing to deserve death or imprisonment. If he had not appealed to Caesar, he could have been set free" (26:31).

Somehow, Luke learned of this crucial statement. Doubtless he and Paul would make good use of it as something of a deposition in the subsequent hearing before Nero.

36

Rome and Nero

When it was decided that we were to sail for Italy, they
transferred Paul and some other prisoners to a centurion of
the Augustan Cohort, named Julius. ACTS 27:1

A SHIP bound for the Aegean had put in at the port of Caesarea,
and since it was not a military vessel, Aristarchus of Thessalonica and faithful Luke were allowed to sail along with Paul. Apparently
the centurion and his detail of guards had come to know Paul during his
months in prison, for when the ship sailed off on an overnight run
northward to Sidon, Julius allowed him to go ashore and visit the Christians in that Phoenician port.

From Sidon they had planned a direct northwesterly voyage toward
the Aegean, but stiff winds from that heading made them sail around the
north of Cyprus instead, and only then to the port of Myra in southwestern Asia Minor. There Julius found a huge Alexandrian grain ship
bound for Italy and transferred his party aboard it.

The largest ships afloat on the Mediterranean, such merchantmen
worked the famed Egypt-to-Italy grain shuttle, which sailed during the
summer months in a counterclockwise rotation. Leaving the Bay of Naples
and heading southeastward to Sicily with pottery, metalware, and passengers, these ships caught the northwesterly winds beyond the Straits and
ran before them directly to Alexandria in a brisk voyage of two weeks or
less. Unloading cargo in Egypt, they took on tons of wheat there and new
passengers, returning to Italy against the winds via a circuitous route
that saw them tack past Palestine, Asia Minor, and Greece.

It was on this leg of the shuttle that Paul and 275 other passengers set sail from Myra. A powerful but contrary wind was no help at all. They fairly crept along the south coast of Asia Minor and past Rhodes into the rougher waters of the Aegean. Now no longer shielded by land, they decided to sail under the lee of Crete for shelter from the northwesterlies. Rounding the eastern cape of that island, they coasted along with difficulty until dropping anchor at a small bay called Fair Havens in the south central coast of Crete.

They had gone far enough for that sailing season, Paul concluded, because so much time had been lost to contrary winds. "Sirs," he told the captain and staff, "I can see that our voyage [farther] is going to be disastrous and bring great loss to ship and cargo, and to our own lives also" (27:10, NIV). Paul knew the Mediterranean and its habits from his boyhood on the sea near Tarsus, as well as from experience: "Three times I was shipwrecked," he wrote (2 Cor. 11:25). His advice was accurate. Since "the Fast had already gone by" (27:9)—i.e., the Day of Atonement in early October—they were now in the danger interim on the Mediterranean beyond what the Romans called *secura navigatio* and near the period of winter's *mare clausum*, or "closed sea," from November 10 through March 10.

The owner of the ship happened to be a passenger also, and he discussed Paul's opinion with the captain and with Julius, the centurion. They chose to gamble on a last coasting run to a better wintering port on Crete named Phoenix, forty miles farther west, since Fair Havens was little more than a roadstead. A gentle, reliable south wind started blowing, so they weighed anchor and sailed westward with it, close inshore and very carefully. One can almost see Julius jovially tweaking Paul's gray beard on foredeck, suggesting that he stick to preaching after this and leave the navigation to them.

A Mediterranean Storm

Upon rounding Cape Matala, they were suddenly struck by a vicious *Euroclydon*, a violent wind from the east-northeast that area mariners would later call a *Levanter*. After futile attempts to face into the wind, the crew gave way to it and were driven southwestward across dangerously frothing swells. Just possibly, the two Greek Christians aboard, Luke and

Aristarchus, looked backward at Crete's 7,000-foot Mt. Ida, which seemed to be rolling the gale down on them, and they may have wondered wryly if this were the last blast from the pagan gods, since Zeus had supposedly grown up on Mt. Ida! Any levity, though, was abruptly swallowed in the ensuing emergency.

Drifting twenty-four miles to the south, the voyagers ran under the lee of Cauda, a small island that cut their wind enough to let them hoist up and secure the huge waterlogged lifeboat they had been towing. They also used the relatively calmer waters to reinforce the ship, dropping hawsers crosswise under the hull in U-shaped fashion and then tightening both ends of the cables at center deck.

Once they left the protection of Cauda, the northeaster could have driven them down onto the Syrtes—dangerous shoals off the North African coast. So they lowered their gear, lashing down on deck the sails and rigging except for some small storm sail to keep rudder control for a westerly course as the ship was driven before the wind. The next day, however, they lost all shelter from Crete and found themselves in the center of a seething Mediterranean tempest, which howled with relentless fury. The pitching and rolling tore pieces of the cargo loose, and they were banging from one side of the hull to the other. Quickly, the crew pitched the loose freight overboard. The next day, since the battered merchantman was taking on some water, they threw overboard even the ship's furniture and whatever tackle could be spared to lighten the vessel.

For more than ten days the storm screamed on, and without sun by day or stars by night, they had no bearings to fix their location. Eventually, the nauseated, terrified passengers lost all hope of surviving, and—even more horrifying—so did the captain and crew.

At that worst moment Paul gathered them together and said (with a predictable opener):

> You should have taken my advice, gentlemen, not to sail from Crete; then you would have avoided this damage and loss. But now I urge you not to lose heart; not a single life will be lost, only the ship. For last night there stood by me an angel of the God whose I am and whom I worship. "Do not be afraid, Paul," he said; "it is ordained that you shall appear before the Emperor; and, be assured, God has granted you the lives of all who are sailing with you." So keep up your courage; I trust in God that it will turn out as I have been told; though we have to be cast ashore on some island. (27:21, NEB)

319

On the fourteenth night of the storm, the sailors suspected that land was near, probably from the roar of nearby surf. They took a sounding and found twenty fathoms of depth. Then, several moments later, they measured fifteen fathoms. Rushing to the stern, they threw out four anchors to hold the ship off any rocks ahead. When the anchors finally caught on the seabottom, it marked the first time since Crete that captain and crew had the ship under general control.

Squinting in the darkness, they saw either surf or points of lamplight in the distance. It *was* land! Word raced along the deck, and soon the crew were lowering the great lifeboat to escape ship. Paul caught them at it.

"We're laying out anchors from the bow," one of the seamen explained, though Paul knew it was a lie. Calling Julius, Paul said, "Unless these men stay in the ship, you cannot be saved." Now with implicit faith in Paul's judgment, the centurion had his men cut away the ropes of the lifeboat.

Near dawn Paul addressed passengers and crew, urging them to eat something, as he himself promptly did, giving thanks to God. They followed his example, heartened at the proximate landfall. Then they lightened the ship still more, throwing the remaining wheat cargo into the sea.

When day broke, they saw a bay with a beach dead ahead. Hoisting their foresail and cutting away the anchors, they scudded before the wind until their bow rammed into a shoal at the head of the bay and stuck fast. When the pounding surf started breaking up the stern, the Roman guards drew out their swords to kill the prisoners, lest any swim off and escape. Julius, however, vetoed this customary procedure and instead told all who could swim to plunge into the water and make for shore, while others should float in on planks and debris from the ship. Venturing overboard as ordered, they were pulled out of the swirling surf and onto the beach by friendly natives. Only then did they learn that they had landed on Malta, the smallish island below Sicily.

Malta

That all 276 people on shipboard should have been saved in such a fashion may seem incredible, but a visit to that landfall today on the northern shore of Malta suggests that "St. Paul's Shoal" within "St. Paul's

St. Paul's Shoal and St. Paul's Bay on the north shore of the
island of Malta. A statue of the apostle stands atop the island at
left center today, commemorating the famous shipwreck.

Bay" are sites not only correctly named, but so near surrounding shores
that loss of life from drowning could indeed have been prevented, especially with friendly Maltese wading out to assist them.

Other islanders were busy building a bonfire on the beach to warm
the survivors, since a cold drizzle had started. Paul helped out by gathering a bundle of sticks and throwing them on the fire, when suddenly
he felt a painful stinging in his hand. Fastened to it was an ugly viper,
driven out of the fagots by the heat! Immediately, he shook the snake off
his hand and into the flames.

Anyone else might have done the same, but would soon have suffered
painful swelling, loss of consciousness, and then death, like Cleopatra of
Egypt, who was bitten by the same species of asp viper. The Maltese
assumed that Paul must have been a murderous criminal, marked by the

gods for death despite his escape from shipwreck. But when Paul carried on with impunity, the credulous islanders changed their minds and deemed him a god!

Several miles south of the bonfire lay the estate of Publius, chief magistrate of Malta, who hosted Paul and his companions for their first three days on the island. Publius' father lay ill with dysentery and fever, but when Paul laid his hands on him, he was cured. Word of the healing spread quickly across Malta, and Paul had a busy ministry during the three months they wintered on the island.

In late February or early March of 58 or 59 A.D.—Pauline chronology is still not absolute—the survivors set sail on the *Dioscuri*, another great Alexandrian grain ship that had wintered in Malta. It was named for the Twin Brothers, the gods Castor and Pollux, who were adorning its prow as wooden figureheads. This time their brief voyage was simple and traceable, as they put in at Syracuse on Sicily and then at Rhegium at the toe of the Italian boot. There they waited for a reliable south wind to carry them through the Straits of Messina without foundering on the rock and whirlpool there—Homer's fabled Scylla and Charybdis. When a spring breeze developed, they easily ran with it through the Straits and up to the Bay of Naples.

Gliding past Capri toward evening, they may well have seen the breast-shaped hulk of Mt. Vesuvius lording it over the eastern shore of the bay. In just a score of years it would rumble into life and bury the towns of Herculaneum and Pompeii, nestled near its base, in a cataclysm of mud, lava, and fiery ash. Now the *Dioscuri* reached its destination, the commercial port of Puteoli on the north shore of the Bay of Naples. Today it is called Pozzuoli, and ruins of the market hall there show one of the first buildings Paul would have seen after landing, since it faces the waterfront.

If the year of Paul's arrival were 59, and if his ship set sail from Malta on March 10—maritime insurance could have been vitiated by any earlier voyage during the wintertime *mare clausum*—then one of the most bizarre coincidences in ancient history could well have occurred, which has thus far escaped scholarly notice. The run from Malta to Puteoli, with stops at the various ports of call cited in Acts 28:12ff., probably took about nine or ten days, making the estimated date for Paul's arrival at the Bay of Naples the evening of March 20. Something else was happening several miles west of Paul's ship that very night. The emperor Nero had just given

The port of Puteoli, where Paul and his party landed at the Bay of Naples. The city is called Pozzuoli today.

his mother a banquet at Baiae, his villa on the western rim of the bay, and then seen her off at his dock for a short cruise across the bay to the villa where she was staying. Unfortunately, her boat was nothing less than a collapsible cabin cruiser, rigged by Nero and his associates so that its ceiling would cave in and crush her to death. If that failed, levers were to open the hull and sink the ship.

As it happened, neither device worked properly. Metal bars in the ceiling missed her, and hinges on the trapdoor in the hull had been mounted on the *wrong side*, opening *outward* against the water pressure! Nero's mother saved herself by diving off the ship and swimming in the bay until she was rescued by some oyster fishermen, who brought her safely back to her villa on shore. By dawn, however, a detail of Nero's marines stormed into the villa and clubbed her to death anyway, as she lay in her bed.[1]

One of the first structures Paul would have seen upon
disembarking at Puteoli was the *macellum*, or covered market,
the ruins of which survive from the first century A.D. At center
is the circular base of a temple to Serapis.

Paul obviously could not know of the mortal events taking place just
west of his ship while it was sailing toward Puteoli, and of course this
coincidence is neither proved nor provable. But it does point out, ominously
enough, the sort of Caesar Paul had appealed to!

Christians were already established at Puteoli—Paul's fame had
preceded him there—and the missionaries were invited to stay with them
for a time. In an extraordinary concession Julius allowed Paul a week in
Puteoli, unquestionably a favor in return for Paul's crucial services on the
voyage. It may be from this early congregation that the faith expanded
around the Bay of Naples, because there were Christians in nearby Herculaneum shortly afterward. One of the houses in that resort town, today
liberated from its lava burial by Mt. Vesuvius, shows the clear outlines of
a metal cross that had been set in the wall over a charred *prie-dieu* in an

324

upstairs room. The cross evidently is just as old a Christian symbol as the fish.

The final leg of Paul's journey was beautiful in the early Italian spring. Soon their highway merged with the Appian Way, the famous artery that led them northward to Rome. At the forty-third milestone was a place called Forum of Appius. Both here and ten miles farther on at a village named Three Taverns, Paul, Luke, and Aristarchus were happily surprised to find a delegation from the Christians of Rome. The church there had been alerted to Paul's arrival, and possibly many of the people named in Romans 16 were clustering along the sides of the Appian Way in a grand welcoming committee. What enormously cheered the travelers must have astonished Julius.

Imperial Rome

At last they reached the great capital of the Mediterranean world, Paul's planned destination for years. Julius conducted his group northward past the Circus Maximus and the Forum, stopping finally at the Castra Praetoria on the northeastern fringe of Rome. Here he reported to the commandant of the camp of the Praetorian Guard,[2] delivering his prisoners and the documents of indictment on them. He may well have had a few generous things to say about Paul to the commandant, for Luke adds that after registering, "Paul was allowed to live by himself, with the soldier who was guarding him," doubtless nearby in northeastern Rome (28:16).

Only three days elapsed between the close of Paul's momentous journey and his resumption of mission work. Barely settled, he invited the local Jewish leaders to his rented abode and candidly introduced himself, his faith, and his mission.

"We have received no letters from Judea about you," the Jewish leaders replied, "and none of the brothers coming here has reported or spoken anything evil about you. But . . . with regard to this sect we know that everywhere it is spoken against" (28:21). Open-mindedly, however, the leaders of the Roman synagogues agreed with Paul on a day when they would bring their members in to hear him.

At the appointed time, they came to his lodging in large numbers. In perhaps his ultimate effort to Christianize Jewry, Paul lectured all day

A primitive Christian oratory in the upper room of the so-called
"House of the Bicentenary" at Herculaneum. A whitish
stuccoed panel shows the imprint of a large cross, probably
metallic, that had been removed or possibly used as a stamping
device. Before it are the remains of a small wooden altar,
charred by lava from the eruption of Mt. Vesuvius in 79 A.D.

The Appian Way near Rome, with ruins of patrician tombs alongside the highway and the moon overhead.

on Jesus as fulfillment of the Law and the Prophets, but with the same familiar results. With some exceptions, the Jews were not convinced, and Paul told them wistfully, "Let it be known to you then that this salvation of God has been sent to the Gentiles; they will listen" (28:28).

Luke closes this scene—and, alas, the *Book of Acts*—with the following intriguing verse:

> He [Paul] lived there two whole years at his own expense and welcomed all who came to him, proclaiming the kingdom of God and teaching about the Lord Jesus Christ with all boldness and without hindrance. (28:30)

What happened then, Luke? What was Paul's fate? Peter's? Yours? What about the great fire of Rome just three years after you break off your account? And Nero's horrible persecution of the Christians? And—

No serious reader of the New Testament has failed to fire these queries at the "beloved physician," and his less-than-satisfactory conclusion has been explained in various ways. Some have conjectured that Luke wrote an as-yet-undiscovered 2 *Acts*, and many biblical scholars dream of finding an ancient scroll that would begin, "This *third* treatise, O Theophilus. . . ." (That gentleman, of course, was the man to whom Luke had addressed both his Gospel and the *Acts*. Theophilus may have been an unknown Roman official, or possibly any "friend of God," as his Greek name translates.)

A *Second Acts*, however, is unlikely. Aside from the dozen other explanations for what may have happened, another reading of the concluding verse shows that it is not only quite ahead of its time literarily ("Leave 'em wondering"), but is, in fact, honest and satisfactory after all: Luke's great purpose was merely to show how the gospel had spread from Jerusalem to Rome. And he did that.

Paul's Last Years

Other sources shed some light on Paul's fate—his own writings, for example. During his detention in Rome, he most likely wrote his famed "prison epistles": *Philippians, Colossians, Ephesians,* and *Philemon*.[3] Passages in these letters attest to the astonishing success of his mission in the imperial capital, despite his confinement. To the church at Philippi he wrote: "I want you to know, brothers, that what has happened to me has actually helped to spread the gospel, so that it has become known throughout the whole Praetorian Guard and to everyone else that my imprisonment is for Christ" (1:12). There was even a Christian group growing in the palace itself, for Paul closes with "All the saints greet you, especially those of the emperor's household" (4:22). Such claims to the growth of the faith could hardly be inflated, because in only four years that "vast multitude" of Roman Christians would be persecuted, according to the pagan author Tacitus. In this same revealing letter Paul seems confident of visiting Philippi in the near future (2:24), and he may indeed have done so.

Surveying all the evidence and clues available from the sources, the following seems to have been Paul's legal fate. The long delay of his hearing before Nero—two years—was likely due primarily to the fact that the emperor was not even in Rome for eighteen months after the murder of his mother. Nero feared that the Roman populace would stone him for matricide, so he wandered through southern Italy instead of returning to Rome. When he finally did return, there must have been a large backlog in the docket of the imperial court.

The court also had to wait until Paul's accusers had arrived from Judea, because the documents indicting him—if they had actually survived the shipwreck at Malta!—would have been in a very messy condition in both form and content. Festus had been worried about the problem of sending along with Paul a *clear* statement of charges against him, and the hearing before Agrippa and Bernice had hardly achieved that. In fairness to the prosecution, then, witnesses from Judea may have been invited to come testify against Paul in Rome. That they did not bother to do so, at least for two years, is quite understandable. Paul's was no longer a *cause célèbre*. His chief prosecutor, the high priest Ananias, had been deposed, and Ananias' successor may not have been interested in the case. Those who *were* interested, among the Sanhedrists, must have realized that their charges were flimsy, particularly on the alleged defilement of the Temple. While flimsy charges could be pressed at home, it would have been dangerous to press them in the capital of the Empire, where such legal conduct was penalized.

Paul's opponents in Palestine, then, could achieve much more by doing nothing at all, for this would leave their man not "turning in the breeze" but in a peculiar limbo legally. Incredibly, Roman law did not really cover a situation in which a person's accusers failed to appear to support their indictment, since Roman *accusatores*, or their representatives, regularly seem to have made their appearance.

Nevertheless, there is little doubt that Paul finally did face Nero himself for trial, because Acts 27:24 clearly presupposes this. What probably happened, accordingly, is that one of Paul's more powerful Roman friends pressed the case for him, and Paul eventually had his day in court. Working from the documents of indictment (again, *if* they survived), some Jewish or Roman prosecutor would have raised the three original charges first lodged against Paul at Caesarea by Tertullus. Allowing another party to renew an accusation in the absence of the original accusers was permitted under Roman law at this time (*Digestae* xlviii, 16, x, 2).

For his part, Paul would have offered a by-now predictable defense, including the episode on the Damascus Road, which might have made the superstitious Nero a bit uncomfortable. And although Nero had

329

Model of Nero's Vatican hippodrome, site of the first Christian persecution. The obelisk on the *spina* stands today at the center of the colonnade in front of St. Peter's basilica at the Vatican (see photograph on page 336).

eliminated his mother and his list of crimes was growing, he had not yet reached the stage of dissipation and cruelty associated with his later reign. Accordingly, with Paul's eloquence on the one hand and the less-than-impressive charges on the other, Nero may indeed have acquitted the apostle—particularly if, as seems likely, the philosopher Seneca and respected senators were serving as imperial assessors in helping to decide the case. At this point, too, the Roman state had not yet declared Christianity illegal.

Although some important scholars disagree, there is strong, though not conclusive, evidence that Paul actually *was* acquitted after his first trial at Rome and that he subsequently visited both Spain in the West and his beloved mission churches in the East. The pastoral epistles, *1* and *2 Timothy* and *Titus*, cannot be fitted satisfactorily into the three missionary journeys,

The road on which Paul most probably traveled to his
martyrdom led from the Ostian Gate (today called the Gate of
San Paolo) at the southwestern corner of Rome, past the
pyramid tomb of Gaius Cestius (d. 12 B.C.), and out on the
Ostian Way at the lower part of the photograph. This model,
like the previous, is part of the vast scaled reconstruction of
ancient Rome in the Museo della Civilitá Romana at Rome.

331

and they tell of Paul's later activities in the Aegean world, although the authenticity of the pastorals is much debated. Clement of Rome, however, in his *Epistle to the Corinthians* of 96 A.D., asserts that Paul "reached the limits of the West" before he died, which, for a Roman author, would imply Spain or Portugal. Romans 15:28 shows that Paul had surely planned a trip to Spain via Rome, and a second-century document, the *Canon Muratorii*, speaks of "Paul's journey when he set out from Rome for Spain" (xxxviii).

If he did visit Spain, Paul would next have returned eastward to confirm the believers in a "fourth missionary journey" to the Aegean. *Titus* refers to Paul's work on the island of Crete, and the other pastorals have him back in Greece and then Asia Minor. There, for some reason, he was arrested a second time and sent to face Nero once again. A postscript found in some later manuscripts of *2 Timothy* states that that epistle was "written from Rome, when Paul was brought before Nero the second time."

Now, about 66–67 A.D., Paul would have been in mortal danger when he stood before the emperor, whatever the indictments that had brought him there: Two years earlier, Nero, in deflecting from himself the public outcry that he had set Rome ablaze, blamed the Christians for arson, as noted, and tortured them to death. Being a Christian now carried the death penalty, so Nero or his justices could hardly acquit this strange and troublesome *leader* of the Christians.

This time Paul had no illusions about being freed, as *2 Timothy* shows so poignantly. When his last day had come, the apostle was presumably accompanied in his final journey across Rome to the Ostian Gate by a grieving group of friends who had survived the cruel first wave of persecution. Several miles beyond the Gate, on the road to the port of Ostia, stood the chopping block. While the sword was being prepared by the executioner (Roman citizens were not crucified), Paul doubtless made a last statement. His words were probably similar to what he had written earlier to his young co-worker, Timothy:

> The time of my departure has come. I have fought the good fight, I have finished the race, I have kept the faith. From now on there is reserved for me the crown of righteousness, which the Lord, the righteous judge, will give me on that day, and not only to me but also to all who have longed for his appearing. (2 Tim. 4:6)

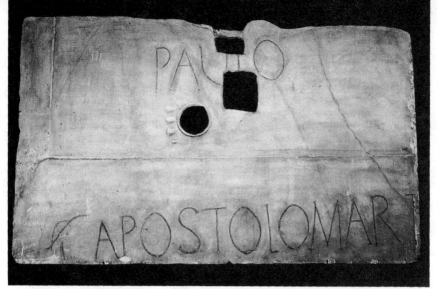

A whitish marble slab from the time of Constantine covers the presumed sepulcher of Paul in the basilica of St. Paul's Outside-the-Walls at Rome. The inscription in red—"To Paul, Apostle and Martyr"—shows fourth-century lettering style. The slab measures 1.27 by 2.12 meters, and is 4.5 meters above the sarcophagus. The round aperture at the center is the most ancient of the perforations, and was used to lower and replace an incense burner at the annual Feast of St. Paul. The rectangular openings above it were made later to permit the faithful to lower objects into the tomb area, which they regarded with veneration afterward.

The blade dropped, the apostle died—the greatest missionary, the greatest theologian in the history of Christianity, and the one who had universalized its message.

Sustained by the resurrection hope that was the culmination of all his preaching, Paul's friends buried him nearby, along the Ostian Way. The much-traveled apostle would have appreciated that gesture—burial alongside a highway. Today the road connects Rome with her international airport at Ostia.

The early church fathers—Clement, Tertullian, Origen, and others—all agree that Paul was finally executed by the Roman government, and no tradition disputes that he met his end along the Ostian Way just outside of Rome. The magnificent basilica of St. Paul's Outside-the-Walls now stands over the presumed place where he was buried. It is erected over earlier memorial structures dating back to the time of Constantine. Under the high altar of the basilica is a slab on which the lettering "PAVLO

APOSTOLO MART" indicates an early Christian memorial "To Paul, Apostle and Martyr."

Peter's Last Years

This, of course, is only Paul's story, and parts of it were being replicated elsewhere in the Mediterranean by the other apostles. In most earliest Church histories the focus is inevitably on Paul because of his centrality in the *Acts* account, and one wishes that similar sources were extant on the early Christian efforts elsewhere.

Only sketchy information survives on the later years of Simon Peter, "prince of the apostles." His last mention in *Acts* shows him defending Paul at the Jerusalem Council (15:7), but reflections of his activity appear in Antioch, Corinth, and eventually Rome. The provenance of the persecution documents 1 and 2 *Peter* is Rome, not literally "Babylon" (1, 5:13), which is the cryptic name for Rome in apocalyptic literature. Indeed, earliest Church tradition as well as archaeology point to Peter's presence in Rome at the close of his ministry and his martyrdom there, probably before Paul's. Clement's letter to Corinth strongly links the martyrdoms of Peter and Paul with those of the Roman Christians enduring the Neronian persecution,[4] and a short time later, in 107 A.D., Ignatius of Antioch's letter to Rome contains the telling phrase, "Not like Peter and Paul do I give you [Roman Christians] commands" (iv, 3).

In the next century there are numerous references to the martyrdoms of Peter and Paul in Rome, and one of these is particularly interesting. The church historian Eusebius cites a second-century presbyter, Gaius of Rome, who stated: "I can point out the monuments [or trophies] of the apostles: for if you will go to the Vatican hill or to the Ostian Way, you will find the monuments of those [Peter and Paul] who founded the church."[5] The monuments marked the traditional sites of their martyrdoms and likely their places of burial as well, since Gaius was countering a claim from Asia of apostolic *tombs* in that province. Constantine later erected the basilicas of St. Peter and St. Paul respectively at these locations, where the newer so-named structures that replaced them stand today.

That Peter was martyred in Rome is supported by a great majority of modern scholars, even though they still argue over the time, place, and nature of that martyrdom. From various indications it seems to have been in connection with Nero's persecution, and there is no dispute over where that series of tortures was inflicted. Because the vast Circus Maximus had been scorched in the great fire of Rome (and the Colosseum had not yet been built), Nero staged his spectacle across the Tiber in the Vatican Valley, where he had gardens and a private hippodrome for racing his horses. It was here that the grisly scene was played out, as recorded, not by a Christian hagiographer, but by a pagan author, Cornelius Tacitus:

> A farce was made of their deaths. Dressed in the skins of wild animals, they [the Christians] were torn to death by dogs; or they were fastened to crosses, and when daylight ended, were burned to serve as torches by night. Nero had provided his gardens for the spectacle. (*Annals* xv, 44)

The emperor Caligula had imported a lofty obelisk from Egypt and had set it up in the *spina*, or central barrier, of his hippodrome across the Tiber, which Nero had inherited and enlarged. If this obelisk had eyes, it would have witnessed the lurid persecution just described, and probably the crucifixion of Peter also.[6] If it had a tongue, the obelisk could tell us about it, because today it stands at the center of the great circular colonnade in front of St. Peter's basilica at Rome.

The Other Apostles

While Paul and Peter dominate early Christian history, other apostles also carried on important ministries. Unfortunately, details on their efforts are scanty.

Mark, happily, was reconciled again with Paul in Rome (Col. 4:10), where, according to the Church fathers, he also served as Peter's secretary, and under Peter's influence composed the earliest Gospel, which bears his name. Tradition also has Mark the founder of the Christian church in Alexandria, Egypt.

James, half-brother of Jesus and first bishop of the Jerusalem church, is credited with authoring the New Testament letter bearing his name, but in 62 A.D. he met a fate similar to Stephen's. Josephus tells the story. Festus, Paul's last judge at Caesarea, had died in office, and before Nero could send a successor to Palestine, the high priest in Jerusalem, Ananus, took it upon himself to indict James before the Sanhedrin, which condemned

The 84-foot obelisk that witnessed Nero's first great persecution of the Christians. The emperor Caligula had brought it to Rome from Heliopolis in Egypt, and set it up in the hippodrome at the Ager Vaticanus, where it graced the *spina* of that racecourse under Nero. Later, the obelisk was crowned with a cross and transferred in 1586 to its present location at the center of the semicircular colonnade in front of St. Peter's basilica at the Vatican.

336

the apostle and several others to death by stoning. It should be noted that these executions took place in the *absence* of the new Roman governor, who was later so angry at such arrogation of power by Ananus that he was dismissed from office. This item, from a non-Christian source,[7] should be recalled by some misguided scholars today who would seek to deprive the Sanhedrin of all responsibility for opposing Jesus and the early Christians and transfer it to the Romans instead.

John, "the beloved disciple," carried his ministry to Ephesus, according to early Christian tradition, where he also acted as dutiful foster son to Mary, the mother of Jesus, a role assigned to him at Calvary. To avoid persecution by the emperor Domitian, John for a time took refuge on the tiny Aegean isle of Patmos, where tradition has him composing the *Book of Revelation*, after which he returned to Ephesus. Here, presumably, he wrote the Fourth Gospel and the letters bearing his name, although critical scholars have proposed other authors, also for *Revelation*.

The other apostles fanned out elsewhere, according to various traditions.[8] Barnabas missionized the islands; Peter's brother Andrew went to the north shore of the Black Sea—Scythia then, Russia today; Thaddaeus preached in Syria and Armenia; Bartholomew and Thomas in Persia and India. Luke—upon finishing his Church history and the Gospel named for him—possibly labored in Bithynia. Matthew, his coevangelist, also completed his Gospel and then carried the Good News to both Jews and Gentiles before enduring probable persecution and death. Silas, Paul's companion on the second journey, filled a similar role with Peter and then served as missionary to northern Asia Minor. Church traditions also have Timothy ministering to western Asia Minor from Ephesus, while Titus preached in Crete and Dalmatia, today's Yugoslavia.

All the apostles endured daunting hardships for the faith, many suffering martyrdom. Not one of them could see the ultimate triumph of Christianity—except through the eyes of faith and the inspiration of the same Spirit who had arrived on that extraordinary Pentecost and had never withdrawn. Though at the time the Christian cause seemed persecuted, burned, crucified, beheaded, and even eaten out of existence by the greatest power in the world, a greater power was at work that would see Christianity conquer Rome a little more than two centuries later, and "the ends of the earth" after that, in Jesus' own prediction.

It was Christ, not Caesar, who captured the future.

Notes

Part I – *The First Christmas*

1. THE POLITICS: A CAESAR'S CENSUS

1. **ROMAN CENSUS EDICT IN EGYPT**: This decree, from 104 A.D., begins, "Gaius Vibius Maximus, prefect of Egypt, says: The house-to-house census having started, it is essential that all persons who for any reason whatsoever are absent from their homes be summoned to return to their own hearths, in order that they may perform the customary business of registration. . . ." See A. H. M. Jones, ed., *A History of Rome Through the Fifth Century* (New York: Harper & Row, 1970), II, 256f.

2. **CENSUS DECLARATION FROM BACCHIAS, EGYPT**: See J. G. Winter, ed., *Papyri in the University of Michigan Collection*, III (Ann Arbor: Univ. of Michigan Press, 1936), 185–187.

3. **AUGUSTUS**: The harangue against the bachelors is recorded by Dio Cassius, *Roman History* (hereafter merely "Dio Cassius") 1vi, 1–10. The "Acts of Augustus," recording his censuses, are *Res Gestae Divi Augusti* 8. For the emperor's career, see Suetonius, *Augustus;* Dio Cassius, 1i–1vi; Velleius Paterculus, *Compendium* ii, 84–124.

4. **JOSEPH BEN-IACOB**, etc.: These reconstructions of their names mean "Joseph, son of Jacob" and "Mary, daughter of Joachim." For the identities of these fathers, see notes to chapters 10 and 11.

2. THE LAND: PALESTINE THE PARADOX

1. **MOHAMMED'S TRIP TO JERUSALEM**: *Sura* xvii, 1ff. in the Koran.

2. **DEAD SEA AREA**: The Hebrews called it the Salt Sea; the Greeks, the Asphalt Lake. See Strabo, *Geographica* xvi, 2, 42. The destruction of Sodom and Gomorrah is related in Genesis 19.

3. THE COURTSHIP: A GALILEAN COUPLE

1. **DEATH PENALTY FOR ADULTERY WITH BETROTHED:** According to Deuteronomy 22:23, "If there is a young woman, a virgin already engaged to be married, and a man meets her in the town and lies with her, you shall bring both of them to the gate of that town and stone them to death. . . ."

2. **MARRIAGE CUSTOMS:** References to engagement and marriage in biblical times are scattered widely across the Old and New Testaments. Extracanonical sources are I Maccabees 9:39; Tobit, *passim*.

4. THE TIME: AN UNDATABLE DATE

1. **DEATH OF HEROD:** The chronology is discussed by Jack Finegan, *Handbook of Biblical Chronology* (Princeton, 1964), 230ff. See also W. E. Filmer, "The Chronology of the Reign of Herod the Great," *The Journal of Theological Studies* (hereafter *JTS*), XVII (October 1966), 283–98. An excellent response to Filmer is P. M. Bernegger, "Affirmation of Herod's Death in 4 B.C.," *JTS*, XXXIV (1983), 526–531; and Harold W. Hoehner, "The Date of the Death of Herod the Great" in J. Vardaman and E. M. Yamauchi, eds., *Chronos, Kairos, Christos* (Winona Lake, IN: Eisenbrauns, 1989), 101–111.

2. **CHRONOLOGY OF JESUS' LIFE:** See Finegan, *Biblical Chronology*, 215ff.; Paul L. Maier, "Sejanus, Pilate, and the Date of the Crucifixion," *Church History*, XXXVII (March 1968), 1–11; and Maier, "The Date of the Nativity and the Chronology of Jesus' Life" in Vardaman, *Chronos*, 113–130.

3. **QUIRINIUS:** Tacitus, *Annals* ii, 30; iii, 22, 23, 48; Suetonius, *Tiberius* xlix; Dio Cassius liv, 48; Josephus, *Antiquities* 17:355; 18:1, 26; 20:102. For Quirinius and the census, see also *Corpus inscriptionum Latinarum*, III, Suppl. 6687; Lily R. Taylor, "Quirinius and the Census of Judaea," *The American Journal of Philology*, 54 (1933), 120–33; Finegan, *Biblical Chronology*, 234–38; and A. N. Sherwin-White, *Roman Society and Roman Law in the New Testament* (Oxford: Clarendon, 1963), 162–71. The last calls a provincial census of Judea during the reign of Herod the Great "an impossibility "(p. 163), but Herod, as client-king, might easily have cooperated with Augustus' well-known proclivities for censuses in the provinces. See Tacitus, *Annals* vi, 41.

4. **SHEEP IN THE FIELDS MOST OF THE YEAR:** The *Mishnah* has differing views on the length of time sheep spent in the wilderness, but *Bezah*, 40a, suggests that they remained in the open both in the hot days and in the rainy season, i.e., all year round. See also *Shekalim*, vii, 4, and Alfred Edersheim, *The Life and Times of Jesus the Messiah* (Eerdmans, 1936), I, 186f.—The statement of Stephen A. Haboush is from his letter to the author, January 23, 1971.

5. THE PLACE: A BETHLEHEM GROTTO

1. **WAS JESUS BORN IN BETHLEHEM?** Scholars who doubt this include R.E. Brown, *The Birth of the Messiah* (Garden City: Doubleday, 1977); and M. Grant, *Jesus: An Historian's Review of the Gospels* (New York: Scribner's, 1977).

2. **DAVID AND BETHLEHEM:** I Samuel 17:12ff.; 20:6, 28; 16:1–13. The messianic ruler also was expected to hail from Bethlehem, according to Micah 5:2.

3. **JESUS BORN IN A CAVE:** Justin Martyr, *Dialogus* lxxviii. Justin's reference to a cave as the site is also supported in the *Protevangelium of James* xviii, 1ff.

6. THE GUESTS: LOCAL SHEPHERDS, DISTANT MAGI

1. **FLOCKS DESTINED FOR THE TEMPLE?** Several Old Testament references suggest that the Messiah was expected to be revealed from *Migdal Eder*, "the tower of the flock," near the place where Jacob had buried his wife Rachel (Gen. 35:19–21; Mic. 4:8). Tradition identifies *Migdal-eder* with the shepherd's village of Beit Sahur, near Bethlehem, and the *Mishnah* suggests that flocks pastured there were destined for Temple sacrifice. See *Shekalim*, vii, 4, and Edersheim, *Jesus the Messiah*, I, 186f.

2. **THE MAGI:** For a full discussion of their origin, see Edwin M. Yamauchi, "The Episode of the Magi," in Vardaman, *Chronos*, 15–39.

3. **BAR-KOKHBA:** Led the Jewish revolt against Rome during the reign of the emperor Hadrian, but was killed by the Romans in 135 A.D. See Dio Cassius lxix, 12–14; Eusebius, *Ecclesiastical History* iv, 6.

4. **SUETONIUS ON RULERS FROM JUDEA:** *Vespasianus* iv.

7. THE ASTRONOMY: AN EXTRAORDINARY STAR

1. **SATURN AS STAR OF ISRAEL:** Amos 5:26, in which *Sakkuth* and *Kaiwan* are both names for the Babylonian Saturn. See also Tacitus, *Histories* 5, 4.

2. **THE STAR OF BETHLEHEM:** For a summary of current scientific explanations, see Finegan, *Biblical Chronology*, 238–48; W. Burke-Gaffney, "Kepler and the Star of Bethlehem," *Journal of the Royal Astronomical Society of Canada*, XXXI (December 1937), 417–25; and Roy K. Marshall, *The Star of Bethlehem* (Univ. of North Carolina: Morehead Planetarium, 1963). The best monograph arguing for planetary conjunction as explanation for the star is Konradin Ferrari d'Occhieppo, *Der Stern der Weisen* (Wien: Verlag Herold, 1969). This astronomer also suggests that zodiacal light might have appeared between Jupiter-Saturn and Bethlehem. See also his "The Star of the Magi and Babylonian Astronomy," in Vardaman, *Chronos*, 41–53.

3. THE WILLIAMS CATALOG: John Williams, *Observations of Comets from B.C. 611 to A.D. 1640 Extracted from the Chinese Annals* (London: Strangways and Walden, 1871).

8. THE MONSTER: HEROD THE KING

1. HEROD: Josephus, *Antiquities* 14:158–17:199; *Jewish War* (hereafter *War*) 1:203– 1:669; Matthew 2.

2. "HEROD'S PIG": Macrobius, *Saturnalia* ii, 4.

9. THE JOURNEYS: UP TO JERUSALEM, DOWN TO EGYPT

1. THE ROBBER STORY: *Arabic Gospel of the Infancy*, xxiii. This and other apocryphal writings about Joseph, Mary, and the child Jesus are most conveniently available in text or outline form in Montague R. James, *The Apocryphal New Testament* (Oxford: Clarendon, 1924).

2. MARY AND THE PALM TREE: The *Gospel of Pseudo-Matthew* 20f.

3. ARCHELAUS KILLS 3,000: Josephus, *Antiquities* 17:213ff.

10. THE FOSTER FATHER: JOSEPH THE CARPENTER

1. THE FATHER OF JOSEPH: Given as Jacob, son of Matthan, in Matthew's genealogy (1:15f.), but as Heli, son of Matthat, in Luke's account (3:23f.). The two genealogies are different up to David, after which they are identical back to Abraham. Various attempts to account for this divergence suggest that one is the legal, the other the natural descent of Joseph, or that Matthew gives the descent through Joseph's line, while Luke records it through Mary's.

2. DESTRUCTION OF SEPPHORIS: Josephus, *Antiquities* 17:289.

3. JESUS EXTENDS JOSEPH'S BEAMS: *Gospel of Thomas* (Greek A) xiii.

4. JOSEPH DIES AT 111: *History of Joseph the Carpenter* x, xviiiff.

5. SISTERS OF JESUS: They are named as Anna (or "Lysia") and Lydia in *History of Joseph the Carpenter* ii.

11. THE MOTHER: MARY THE VIRGIN

1. THE FATHER OF MARY: Given as Joachim in Christian tradition (*Protevangelium of James* i, 1ff.). The name Heli (see previous note on the father of Joseph) is the diminutive of Eliachim, which is an alternate form of Joachim. Therefore, some scholars consider Luke's genealogy that of Mary herself and the name of her father in the *Protevangelium* substantiated. However, no definite name for Mary's father or mother is given in the New Testament.

2. "LIKE A DOVE": *Protevangelium* viii, 1.

3. ANNUNCIATION AT THE WELL IN NAZARETH: "And she [Mary] took a pitcher and went forth to fill it with water. And behold, a voice said, 'Hail, thou that art highly favored, the Lord is with thee . . . '" (*Protevangelium* xi, l). But this apocryphon has the angel complete the Annunciation back in her home as she wove the Temple veil.

4. APOCRYPHAL VERSIONS OF MARY'S DEATH: Coptic and Syriac texts, as well as Greek and Latin narratives grouped under the title, "The Passing of Mary," especially the *Transitus Sanctae Mariae*.

12. THE CHILD: JESUS OF NAZARETH

1. TEMPLE VISIT AT AGE TWELVE: Luke 2:41–52.

2. JESUS AND THE FISH: *Gospel of Thomas* (Latin) i.

3. JESUS AND THE BIRDS: *Gospel of Thomas* (Greek A) ii.

4. JESUS IN SCHOOL: *Arabic Gospel of the Infancy* xlviii–xlix.

5. JESUS SUPPOSEDLY CURSES A CHILD: *Gospel of Thomas* (Greek A), iv–v. The other childhood stories derive from this and other apocryphal infancy narratives.

6. JESUS' LINGUISTIC ABILITIES: Luke 4:17ff.; John 8:6–8. Mark 7:26ff. tells of the meeting with the Syrophoenician woman. The Latin terms in his recorded speech include *modius* (Matt. 5:15); *quadrans* (Matt. 5:26); *legio* (Matt. 26:53).

7. PLOWS MADE BY JESUS: Justin Martyr, *Dialogus* lxxxviii.

8. BRONZE STATUE OF JESUS: Eusebius, *Ecclesiastical History* vii, 18.

Part II – *The First Easter*

13. MINISTRY: TEACHING AND HEALING

1. BULTMANN QUOTE: From R. Bultmann, *Jesus* (Berlin, 1926), translated by L. P. Smith and E. H. Lantero as *Jesus and the Word* (New York: Scribner's, 1958), 8.

2. CHARLESWORTH QUOTE: From James H. Charlesworth, *Jesus Within Judaism* (New York: Doubleday, 1988), 168–169.

3. SYNAGOGUE AT CAPERNAUM: The later structure of white limestone is dated in the fourth century A.D. by some archaeologists, but the first-century synagogue of Jesus' time, built of black basalt, has been discovered underneath it. See James F. Strange and Hershel Shanks, "Synagogue Where Jesus Preached Found at

Capernaum," *Biblical Archaeology Review* (hereafter *BAR*), 9 (November–December 1983), 24–31.

4. PETER'S HOUSE: See James F. Strange and Hershel Shanks, "Has the House Where Jesus Stayed in Capernaum Been Found?" *BAR*, 8 (November–December 1982), 26–37; and Charlesworth, *Jesus Within Judaism*, 109–115.

5. THE GALILEE BOAT: For a well-illustrated account of its discovery, see Shelley Wachsmann, "The Galilee Boat—2,000-Year-Old Hull Recovered Intact," *BAR*, 14 (September–October 1988), 18–33.

14. FRIENDS: UP TO JERUSALEM

1. GENERAL SOURCES FOR THE PASSION AND EASTER ACCOUNTS: Matt. 21–28, Mark 11–16, Luke 19–24, John 11–21, and Acts 1. The lesser-known episodes, references, and problems are documented in the following notes.

2. THE DISCIPLES: Lists of their names in Matt. 10:2–4; Mark 3:16–19; Luke 6:14–16; and John 1:40ff. suggest that Bartholomew may be identified with Nathanael, Thaddaeus with Judas (son of James), and Simon the Canaanean with Simon the Zealot.

3. THE DINNER AT BETHANY: Matt. 26:6ff. and Mark 14:3ff. place the supper at the house of Simon the leper, while John 12:1ff. has it at the home of Mary, Martha, and Lazarus. Simon may have been husband to Mary or Martha, or he may have been their father.

15. ENEMIES: INTRIGUE AND CONSPIRACY

1. PLOTS AGAINST JESUS: Instances before Holy Week include Matt. 12:14; Mark 3:6; Luke 4:29, 6:11, 11:53, 13:31; John 7:1, 7:25–45, 8:39ff., 8:59, 10:31ff., 11:46ff., 12:10.

2. THE ARREST NOTICE: But for the caption and the last sentence, this proclamation is verbatim from the tradition on "Yeshu Hannozri" in *Sanhedrin* 43a of the Babylonian Talmud, trans. by Jacob Shachter (London: Soncino Press, 1935), Nezikin V, 281. The last sentence derives from what is probably the NT version of this proclamation in John 11:57.

3. TEMPLE CLEANSING AT THE HANUYOT: Major excavations at the southern edge of the Temple mount were undertaken by Benjamin Mazar. See his "Excavations Near Temple Mount Reveal Splendors of Herodian Jerusalem," *BAR* 6 (July–August 1980), 44–59; and G. Cornfeld, ed., *The Historical Jesus* (New York: Macmillan, 1982), 120–123.

16. BETRAYAL: A LAST SUPPER

1. JUDAS ISCARIOT: Still another opinion claims that Iscariot is Aramaic for "liar" or "hypocrite," and was added to Judas' name afterward. The fact that Simon Iscariot was his father, however, militates against this view.

2. THE CHRONOLOGY OF HOLY WEEK: The dates April 2, 33 A.D. for Maundy Thursday, April 3 for Good Friday, and April 5 for the first Easter are determined as follows. The most precisely given "anchor date" in the NT is Luke 3:1–2, which states that John the Baptist began his public ministry "in the fifteenth year of the reign of Tiberius Caesar," i.e., 28–29 A.D. Adding a half to one full year for John's independent ministry and three and one-half for Jesus' would seem to require 32–33 A.D. as the year of the crucifixion. (The frequent explanation that Tiberius shared a co-regency with Augustus from 12 A.D. so that the fifteenth year of Tiberius could fall as early as 26 runs counter to all practice in the Roman sources, and is used only to salvage a thirty-year age for Jesus at the start of his ministry (Luke 3:23), whereas, with birth in 5 B.C., he was at least 33 in fact. But Luke says *about* 30," which would allow for such a range.) The specific date for Good Friday—April 3, 33 A.D.—is derived from the Jewish calendar. Exod. 12:6 states that the Passover lambs were slain on Nisan 14, and this date fell on a Friday only on April 7, 30 A.D., and April 3, 33 A.D., within the range of probability. The later date is preferable for reasons cited previously and others. For further discussion, see Finegan, *Biblical Chronology*, 259ff., and Paul L. Maier, "Sejanus, Pilate, and the Date of the Crucifixion," *Church History*, XXXVII (March 1968), 1–11.

17. ARREST: IN THE GARDEN

1. THE PASSOVER MOON: The Hebrew calendar was lunar, and the chief spring and fall festivals, the Passover and the Ingathering, commenced at full moon. Since Easter followed Friday, Nisan 14—the Passover date in the Jewish calendar that year—the Christian custom arose of celebrating Easter on the first Sunday after the first full moon occurring on or after the vernal equinox. Easter, thus, can fall anytime between March 22 and April 25.

18. HEARINGS: ANNAS AND CAIAPHAS

1. ANNAS: Aside from the NT, references to Annas or Ananus appear also in Josephus, *Antiquities* 18:26, 34, 95; 20:197–98; *War* 2:240; and in *Pesachim* 57a of the Babylonian Talmud, the "Woe to the family of Annas" malediction.

2. CAIAPHAS: Aside from the NT, references to Caiaphas appear also in Josephus, *Antiquities* 18:35, 95.

3. TWO PROSECUTION WITNESSES NECESSARY: Deut. 19:15.

4. JUDICIAL PROCEDURE OF THE SANHEDRIN: See the Mishnah tractate *Sanhedrin* iv, 1 to v, 5.

19. JUDGE: PONTIUS PILATE

1. THE PILATE INSCRIPTION: Antonio Frova, "L'Iscrizione di Ponzio Pilato a Cesarea," *Rendiconti Istituto Lombardo*, 95 (1961), 419–34. Although Pilate's proper title, prefect, has been known ever since 1961, the number of Bible dictionaries and general encyclopedias published since then that perpetuate the mistaken term, procurator, is an embarrassment to serious scholarship.

2. THE AFFAIR OF THE STANDARDS: Josephus, *Antiquities* 18:55–59; *War* 2:169–174. See also Carl H. Kraeling, "The Episode of the Roman Standards at Jerusalem," *Harvard Theological Review*, XXXV (October 1942), 263–89.

3. THE AQUEDUCT RIOT: Josephus, *Antiquities* 18:62; *War* 2:175–177.

4. THE GOLDEN SHIELDS: Philo, *De Legatione ad Gaium* xxxviii, 299–305. See also Paul L. Maier, "The Episode of the Golden Roman Shields at Jerusalem," *Harvard Theological Review*, 62 (January 1969), 109–21

5. GESSIUS FLORUS: Josephus, *Antiquities* 20:252ff.; *War* 2:277.

6. PILATE'S FATE: The Samaritan episode is reported in Josephus, *Antiquities* 18:87–89. Origen, *Contra Celsum* ii, 34, tacitly admits that Pilate suffered no penalty. See also Paul L. Maier, "The Fate of Pontius Pilate," *Hermes*, 99 (1971), 362–71. Portions of this and the next chapter appeared also in my article on Pilate in *Mankind*, II (February 1970), 26ff., and my book *Pontius Pilate* (New York: Doubleday, 1968).

20. JUDGMENT: A ROMAN TRIAL

1. THE CHARGE OF SORCERY: *Acta Pilati* i; *Sanhedrin* 43a, the Babylonian Talmud.

2. "CAESAR'S FRIENDS": Suetonius, *Tiberius* xlvi; John 19:12. Cp. also Ernst Bammel, "Philos tou Kaisaros," *Theologische Literaturzeitung*, 77 (April 1952), 206ff.

3. RECENT CRITICISM OF NT ACCOUNTS OF THE TRIAL: S. G. F. Brandon, *Jesus and the Zealots* (New York: Scribner's, 1968); and *The Trial of Jesus of Nazareth* (New York: Stein and Day, 1968); Joel Carmichael, *The Death of Jesus* (New York: Macmillan, 1962); Haim Cohn, *The Trial and Death of Jesus* (New York: Harper & Row, 1971); Gerard S. Sloyan, *Jesus on Trial* (Philadelphia: Fortress, 1973); and others. Some important thoughts in these studies go back to Robert Eisler, *The Messiah Jesus and John the Baptist* (New York: Dial, 1931).

4. RABBINICAL TRADITIONS ON JESUS AND ANNAS: *Sanhedrin* 43a and *Pesachim* 57a of the Babylonian Talmud. Various versions in the original and in translation of the *Toledoth Jeshu* are available in Samuel Krauss, *Das Leben Jesu Nach Jüdischen Quellen* (Berlin: S. Calvary, 1902).

5. THE STONING OF JAMES: Josephus, *Antiquities* 20:200. Ananus, the son of the NT Annas, was the high priest responsible for prosecuting James before the Sanhedrin in the absence of the Roman governor Albinus, who had not yet arrived in Judea.

6. JEWS AND THE TRIAL OF JESUS: For a solution to this tangled problem, see Paul L. Maier, "Who Killed Jesus?" *Christianity Today*, 34 (April 9, 1990), 16–19.

21. EXECUTION: AT SKULL PLACE

1. BONES OF THE CRUCIFIED VICTIM: N. Haas, "Anthropological Observations on the Skeletal Remains from Giv'at ha-Mivtar," *Israel Exploration Journal*, XX (1970), 38–59; and V. Tzaferis, "Crucifixion—The Archaeological Evidence," *BAR*, 11 (January–February 1985), 44–53.

2. QUARRY SOUTH OF HOLY SEPULCHER: Kathleen M. Kenyon, *Jerusalem—Excavating 3000 years of History* (New York: McGraw-Hill, 1967), 146ff.

3. AUTHENTICITY OF THE SITE: For a well-illustrated study, see Dan Bahat, "Does the Holy Sepulchre Church Mark the Burial of Jesus?" *BAR*, 12 (May–June 1986), 26–45. Bahat concludes that the Constantinian rotunda predating the present structure "very likely" was built over the true site of Jesus' burial (p. 37). His study was based on the findings of archaeologist V. C. Corbo of the Studium Biblicum Franciscanum in Jerusalem.

22. THE UNANTICIPATED: EASTER DAWN

1. "WHICH TWENTY MEN COULD SCARCELY ROLL": At Matt. 27:60, Codex Bezae adds, "And when he was laid there, he put against the tomb a stone which twenty men could scarcely roll." The Sahidic Ms. has this addendum also.

2. "THE SPICES": The hundred pounds cited in John 19:39 were each about twelve of our ounces.

3. THE GRAVE CLOTHS: The first to call attention to the Greek in John 20:6–7 indicating that Jesus "withdrew from the grave clothes without disturbing their arrangement" is Henry Latham, *The Risen Master* (London: G. Bell, 1904).—That the much publicized "Shroud of Turin" is *not* the burial cloth of Jesus was demonstrated by three carbon-14 tests conducted in 1988 at Arizona, Zurich, and Oxford, which placed the fabric between 1260 and 1380 A.D., plus or minus a hundred years.

23. EXPLANATIONS: DOUBTS AND SKEPTICISM

1. "LETTUCE" THEORY: Tertullian, *De spectaculis* xxx.

2. CELSUS AND "SWOON" THEORY: Origen, *Contra Celsum* ii, 56. For Celsus and the hallucination theory, see Origen, *Contra Celsum* ii, 55.

3. SLAVONIC JOSEPHUS: The reference to "thirty Romans but a thousand Jews" is vii, 4–8, in R. Dunkerley, *Beyond the Gospels* (Penguin, 1957).

4. THE IDENTITY OF THE GUARD AT JOSEPH'S SEPULCHER: This is by no means definite. Was it Jewish or Roman? The Greek of Matt. 27:65 cities Pilate's statement simply as: "You have a guard," though this could also be translated, "You may have a guard." Yet the first interpretation seems preferable, since the watch reported the empty tomb directly to the chief priests rather than to Pilate (Matt. 28:11), which the Temple police would certainly have done. Roman auxiliaries would have reported to Pilate and only to him. Tertullian, *Apologeticus* xxi, 20, also speaks of a Jewish military guard at the tomb.

5. SURVIVAL AFTER CRUCIFIXION: Josephus, *Vita* 75.

6. STRAUSS CITATION: David F. Strauss, *The Life of Jesus for the People*, I (London: Williams & Norgate, 1879), 412.

7. MISCELLANEOUS OBJECTIONS TO THE EASTER ACCOUNTS: Aside from the problem of the variations, discussed in the text, there is the thorny issue of Jesus' own prediction that he would rise on the third day hardly being accommodated by his being in the grave only about thirty-six hours, according to the NT. Yet there is no reason to tear up Holy Week and convert Good Friday into Good Wednesday, as some biblical literalists and cultists have suggested. By inclusive reckoning, in Jewish practice, part of a day was counted as a whole day, and the three remaining hours of Friday afternoon following Jesus' death, plus Saturday, and the first twelve hours of Sunday (which began at 6 P.M. Saturday) would indeed add up to "the third day." Admittedly, this would make only a "rough fit" for Matt. 12:40 ("For as Jonah was three days and three nights in the belly of the whale, so will the Son of man be three days and three nights in the heart of the earth"). But this merely underscores the authenticity of the source material and the lack of any editorial tampering. Surely Jesus' comment must not be subjected to ultra-literalism, for neither was he buried anywhere near the "heart of the earth."

24. THE EVIDENCE: AN EMPTY TOMB

1. APOSTOLIC PROCLAMATION IN JERUSALEM: Acts 2–8.

2. JOSEPHUS ON JESUS: *Antiquities* 18:63–64. See also Schlomo Pines, *An Arabic Version of the Testimonium Flavianum and its Implications* (Jerusalem: Israel Academy of Sciences and Humanities, 1971); and Paul L. Maier, ed., *Josephus—The Essential Writings* (Grand Rapids: Kregel, 1988), 264–265.

3. JUSTIN: Justin Martyr, *Dialogus* cviii.

4. JUDA THE GARDENER: This account from the *Toledoth Jeshu* appears in the Wagenseil text, the Strassburg Ms., and especially the Vindobona Ms. See Krauss, *Das Leben Jesu*, xiv–xv.

5. PILATE'S ACTA: Justin Martyr, *Apologia* i, 35, 48.

6. ROMAN EDICT ON GRAVE ROBBERY: F. Cumont, "Un Rescrit Imperial sur la Violation de Sèpulture," *Revue historique*, clxiii (1930), 241–66; and F. de Zulueta, "Violation of Sepulture in Palestine at the Beginning of the Christian Era," *Journal of Roman Studies*, xxii (1932), 184–97.

Part III – *The First Christians*

25. TO APOSTLES: THE COMMISSION

1. AUGUSTUS: Suetonius, *Augustus* xcix. The emperor's *very* last statement, just after the quotation in the text, was: "Forty young men are carrying me off," an indication that his wits were wandering, though just possibly it was a reference to the Praetorian honor guard at his funeral.

2. LUKE: Paul calls him "the beloved physician" in Col. 4:14. That he was a Gentile seems strongly indicated in Col. 4:10ff., where Luke is grouped outside those "of the circumcision."

26. TO JERUSALEM: THE DAY OF PENTECOST

1. PENTECOST: This festival, among the Jews, did not commemorate the giving of the Law, as some would have it, until after 200 A.D., when it became also a feast of revelation. The date suggested for the first Christian Pentecost, May 25, 33 A.D., is based on the presumption of April 5 of that year for the first Easter. See notes to chapter 16.

2. SITE OF THE UPPER ROOM: Euthychius of Alexandria reports that the Jewish-Christians returned to Jerusalem in the fourth year of the emperor Vespasian (i.e., 73 A.D.), and built their church on Mt. Zion (J. P. Migne, ed., *Patrologia Latina* [Paris, 1844ff.], CXI, 985). The church marked the site of the Upper Room and was extant at Hadrian's visit, according to Epiphanius of Jerusalem, as cited in Donato Baldi, *Enchiridion Locorum Sanctorum* (Jerusalem: Franciscan Press, 1982), 96. For a handsome analysis of the tangled archaeology at this site, see Bargil Pixner, "Church of the Apostles Found on Mt. Zion," *BAR*, 16 (May–June 1990), 16–35.

3. JOSEPHUS: His statistic on the population of Jerusalem during the high festivals is 3,000,000 for the Passover of 65 A.D. (*War* 2:280). At least he is consistent with himself, because later he reports 256,500 paschal lambs slaughtered at a subsequent Passover. At twelve people per lamb, this would come to 3,078,000 people (*War* 6:422–425). Nearly all scholars reduce such figures to several hundred thousand.

4. TACITUS: His famous reference to the Christian persecutions under Nero is *Annals* xv, 44. Attempts have been made to discredit this passage as a Christian interpolation, but they have failed, and most scholars regard the passage as authentic.

27. TO JEWS: THE OPPOSITION

1. GAMALIEL: Judaic references to him are the tractates *Gittin* 4, 2; *Rosh Hashanah* 2, 5; and *Sotah* 9, 15 which states, "When Rabban Gamaliel the Elder died, the glory of the law ceased and purity and abstinence died." The reference to Theudas' insurrection as taking place before that of Judas in Luke's version of Gamaliel's speech (Acts 5:36ff.) conflicts with evidence from Josephus, *Antiquities* 20:97–98, which places the revolt of Judas in 6 A.D. and Theudas' after 44 A.D. Possibly there was an earlier Theudas, although this is unlikely.

28. TO SAMARIA: THE DISPERSION

1. GITTA: This is suggested as a site for Philip's activities because it is one of the few towns in hilly Samaria to which one would go *down* (Act 8:5) from the Jerusalem plateau. Justin Martyr also associates Gitta with the activities of Simon Magus in *Apologia* i, 26, 56.

2. SIMON MAGUS: Eusebius, *Ecclesiastical History* ii, 13, 1–8; Justin Martyr, *Apologia* i, 26, 56; Irenaeus, *Adversus Haereses* i, 23, 1–2.

29. TO GENTILES: PETER THE ROCK

1. THE ITALIAN COHORT: For the identity and full name of the *Cohors II Italica*, see "Cohors" in Georg Wissowa, ed., *Paulys Real-Encyclopädie der classischen Altertums-wissenschaft* (Stuttgart: Metzlersche Verlag, 1953ff.), VII, 304ff. (This massive reference work also has articles on most of the proper names cited in the text.) There is some debate on whether the Italian Cohort could have been in Judea prior to Vespasian, but also scholarly support for the implication in *Acts* that it must have been in Caesarea by this time.

2. HEROD AGRIPPA I: References outside the NT include Josephus, *Antiquities* 18 and 19. This is also the sole source of information on Agrippa and the interregnum at Rome following the death of Caligula. Josephus makes no mention of the embassy from Tyre and Sidon reported in *Acts*. The two citations in the text regarding the strange death of Agrippa are Louis H. Feldman's translation of Josephus, *Antiquities* 19:343ff. in the *Loeb Classical Library*. Used by permission.

3. THE THEATER AT CAESAREA: Some scholars hold that Agrippa made his appearance at one of the as-yet-unexcavated amphitheaters at Caesarea. Josephus, however, identifies the place as *to theatron*, not as *amphitheatron*, in *Antiquities* 19:343ff. Since 44 A.D. would have been the wrong year for the quinquennial

games at Caesarea, this spectacle was probably in honor of Claudius' birthday and was probably on a smaller scale. See F. F. Bruce, *New Testament History* (Doubleday, 1971), 263.

30. TO SYRIA: SAUL THE FANATIC

1. TENTMAKING: An alternate interpretation of the Greek *skenopoios* (18:3) is "leatherworker," according to the first Latin translation of this passage as well as several Early Church fathers. Because Paul's home province was famous for *cilicium*, however, "tentmaker" would seem preferable, as it is the more literal translation.

2. ESCAPE FROM DAMASCUS: Though *Acts* does not mention the Nabataean involvement against Saul, nor indeed his three-year sojourn in the Arabian desert, Paul himself cites the latter in Gal. 1:17–18 and the former in 2 Cor. 11:32ff., which demonstrates that his basket escape took place after his *second* visit to Damascus, following the visit to Arabia. The Aretas cited is Aretas IV of Petra, whose daughter had married, and had been jilted by, Herod Antipas (Josephus, *Antiquities* 18:116–119).

31. TO ASIA MINOR: PAUL'S FIRST JOURNEY

1. SERGIUS PAULUS: "L. Sergius Paullus" is listed as the third of five *"curator[es riparum] et alv[ei Tiberis]"* under Claudius in *CIL* VI, 31545. Another inscription discovered at Soloi in northern Cyprus mentions a *"Paulos [. . . anth]upatos,"* though whether this refers to Sergius Paulus is disputed (*IGR* III, 930).

2. BAUCIS AND PHILEMON: Ovid, *Metamorphoses* vii, 611ff.

32. TO CHRISTIANS: QUARRELS AND CONTROVERSY

1. THE JERUSALEM COUNCIL: The apostolic conclave of Acts 15 is most probably the same as that recorded by Paul in Galatians 2. Despite differences in reportage, the theological issue in both versions is idential. Titus, as one of the delegates, is cited only in Gal. 2:1.

2. PAUL VS. PETER SQUABBLE: This also caused bitter disagreement between Jerome, who deemed the controversy only play-acting or minor hypocrisy, and Augustine, who thought it both crucial and genuine. See Augustine, *Letter to Jerome*, No. 28 (c. 395 A.D.); and No. 40 (397 A.D.).

33. TO GREECE: PAUL'S SECOND JOURNEY

1. TIMOTHY: His circumcision (Acts 16:1ff.) was not inconsistent, in that he was considered a Jew because his mother was Jewish.

2. ACTS 17 TEXT AND COMMENTARY: Some of this material first appeared in Paul L. Maier, "Acts 17," *The Lutheran Witness*, 93 (June 16, 1974), 8–9. Used by permission.

3. THE AREOPAGUS: An alternate site for Paul's address is the *Stoa Basileios* in the Athenian agora, where the *Court* of Areopagus sometimes met. Whether *Acts* intends "Areopagus" as Mars' Hill or as court is not clear, although most scholars incline to the former.

4. L. JUNIUS GALLIO: His "hook" remark is attested by Dio Cassius lx, 35. See also lxii, 25; Pliny, *Natural History* xxxi, 62; Seneca, *Epistulae Morales* civ, l; Tacitus, *Annals* xv, 73. The Delphi inscription is published in Dittenberger, ed., *Sylloge Inscriptionum Graecorum*, 3d ed., 801 D.

5. CORINTH: The excavations there are reported in American School of Classical Studies at Athens, *Ancient Corinth, A Guide to the Excavations* (6th ed., 1954); H. J. Cadbury, "Erastus of Corinth," *Journal of Biblical Literature* (hereafter *JBL*) L (1931), 42ff.; and "The *Macellum* of Corinth," *JBL*, LIII (1934), 34ff. See also Victor P. Furnish, "Corinth in Paul's Time—What Can Archaeology Tell Us?" *BAR*, 15 (May–June 1988), 14–27.

34. TO THE AEGEAN: PAUL'S THIRD JOURNEY

1. THOMAS: Eusebius, *Ecclesiastical History* iii, 1.

2. GALATIANS: Paul's letter to them is difficult to date. Some scholars place it just after his return from the First Missionary Journey, making it not 1 *Thessalonians*, the earliest of his epistles. But in view of the report in Gal. 2 on what is undoubtedly the Jerusalem Council, a majority of scholars date the letter at the close of the Second or during the Third Missionary Journey, since its content is so similar to that of *Romans* and of the Corinthian epistles. As to the other problem involving Galatia as a geographical term, the so-called North Galatian hypothesis, which claims that Paul visited northern Asia Minor and the Celtic tribes there, seems very unlikely, because the apostle would have had to communicate with them in Celtic, not Greek.

3. GLOSSOLALIA: Parts of this discussion first appeared in Paul L. Maier, "Tongues Have Been Here Before," *Christian Herald*, 98 (October 1975), 16–22. Used by permission.

35. TO MAGISTRATES: JEOPARDY IN JERUSALEM

1. TEMPLE STELE: Josephus, *Antiquities* 15:418; *War* 5:193–194. Titus' statement about the warnings is cited in Josephus, *War* 6:124–126.

2. EGYPTIAN PSEUDO-PROPHET: Josephus, *War* 2:261–263.

3. ANANIAS BEN-NEBEDEUS: Josephus, *Antiquities* 20:103, 131, 205f.; *War* 2:409ff. The Babylonian Talmud also charges him with gluttony in *Pesahim* 57a. Cp. *Kerithoth* 28b.

4. FELIX: Tacitus, *Annals* xii, 54; *Histories* v, 9; Josephus, *Antiquities* 20:137ff.; *War* 2:247ff.; Suetonius, *Claudius* xxviii. The son of Felix is not named, but his death in the eruption of Vesuvius is reported in *Antiquities* 20:144.

5. TRAJAN ON NERO: Aurelius Victor, *De Caesaribus* 5:2.

6. AGRIPPA II AND BERNICE: Josephus, *Antiquities* 18–20; *War* 2 *et passim*; Suetonius, *Titus* vii; Dio Cassius lxvi, 15.

36. TO ITALY: ROME AND NERO

1. NERO'S PLOT: The emperor had used the Festival of Minerva, celebrated March 19 to 23, as a pretext for inviting his mother, Agrippina the Younger, down to Baiae for a banquet of reconciliation, since they had become estranged, suspecting each other of plots. The collapsible cabin cruiser ride seems to have taken place on the second night of the festival, or March 20. Cp. Suetonius, *Nero* xxviii; Tacitus, *Annals* xiv, 3–5; Dio Cassius lxi, 12–13.

2. THE PRAETORIAN COMMANDANT: The Western version of the Greek text in Acts 28:16 has an interesting variation: "When we came to Rome, the centurion handed the prisoners over to the commandant of the camp [*to stratopedarcho*], and Paul was ordered to remain by himself with the soldiers who were guarding him." In commenting on this variant, Theodor Mommsen equated the Greek term with the Latin *princeps peregrinorum*, the chief of a special logistics supply corps who lived in a camp on the Caelian. See T. Mommsen and A. Harnack, "Zu Apostelgesch. 28,16," *Sitzungsberichte der Kön. Preussischen Akademie der Wissenschaften zu Berlin* (1895), 491ff. But A. N. Sherwin-White, *Roman Society*, 108ff., more aptly suggests *princeps castrorum*, "commandant of the camp" (of the Praetorians), as the best translation for *stratopedarchos*.

3. THE PRISON EPISTLES: Whether they were written from Ephesus, Caesarea, or Rome is still debated, but a growing scholarly consensus leans strongly to the last, particularly because an Ephesian imprisonment is questionable, and Phil. 1:12ff. and 4:22 point almost conclusively to Rome.

4. CLEMENT: 1 Clement v, 1–7; cp. Strabo, *Geographica* ii, 1. Clement's linking the martyrdoms of Peter and Paul with the Roman Christians is 1 Clement v and vi.

5. EUSEBIUS AND GAIUS: *Ecclesiastical History* ii, 25.

6. PETER'S CRUCIFIXION: The apocryphal *Acts of Peter*, dated about 200 A.D., contains the moving legend that Peter was leaving Rome to escape Nero's persecution when he met Jesus along the Appian Way. "*Domine, quo vadis?*" asked Peter ("Lord, where are you going?"). Jesus replied, "I go to Rome, to be crucified again"—at which Peter, shamed one last time by Jesus, turned back toward Rome to endure martyrdom. However, one thing about the legend certainly is *not* true: Peter and Jesus would never have been speaking Latin to each other, but Aramaic.

Similarly, the legend that Peter was crucified by Nero head-downward because he did not deem himself worthy to suffer exactly as Jesus did is possible, but seems an embellishment. It was Origen, as quoted by Eusebius, *Ecclesiastical History* iii, 1, who first commented on the head-downward position of the apostle. No early Roman tradition reports Peter as crucified this way, even if such a position was not unknown. See Seneca, *ad Marciam* xx.

7. DEATH OF JAMES: Josephus, *Antiquities* 20:200.

8. OTHER APOSTOLIC MINISTRIES: Eusebius, *Ecclesiastical History* iii, 1.

Index

355

PHOTO CREDITS

All photographs in this book are by Paul L. Maier, except for the following:

Page 5: Courtesy of the Department of Rare Books and Special Collections, The University of Michigan Library.

Page 7: Courtesy of the Trustees of the British Museum.

Pages 12, 26–27, 30, 36–37, 92: Israel Gov't Tourist Office

Pages 18–19: Israel Information Service

Pages 34, 38: Swissair

Pages 46–47: Religious News Service

Pages 63, 142: *The Interpreter's Dictionary of the Bible.* © 1962, Abingdon Press.

Page 71: The Matson Photo Service

Page 74: NASA

Page 80: Palestine Exporation Fund

Pages 104, 112: Garo Nalbandian

Pages 110, 132, 140, 184: Israel Gov't Press Office

Page 201: Trans World Airlines

Color section following page 174:

Aerial photo of Israel, Jordan, and the Negev: Courtesy of NASA

Aerial view of Bethlehem: D. Rubinger, Israel Ministry of Tourism

Christmas Eve, from the Church of the Nativity: A. Lieberman, Israel Gov't Tourist Office, Chicago

Aerial view of Capernaum along the Sea of Galilee: Garo Nalbandian

Hull of first-century boat: Garo Nalbandian